DYNIX

THE OXFORD HISTORY
OF ENGLISH ART

Edited by T. S. R. BOASE

THE OXFORD HISTORY OF ENGLISH ART

Edited by T. S. R. BOASE

President of Magdalen College, Oxford

Plan of Volumes

ANGEL OF THE PASSION, PERCY TOMB, BEVERLEY MINSTER

ANGEL OF THE PASSION, PERCY TOMB, BEVERLEY MINSTER

ENGLISH ART

1307–1461

JOAN EVANS

OXFORD
AT THE CLARENDON PRESS
1949

Oxford University Press, Amen House, London E.C. 4

GLASGOW NEW YORK TORONTO MELBOURNE WELLINGTON
BOMBAY CALCUTTA MADRAS CAPE TOWN

Geoffrey Cumberlege, Publisher to the University

PRINTED IN GREAT BRITAIN
AT THE UNIVERSITY PRESS, OXFORD
BY CHARLES BATEY, PRINTER TO THE UNIVERSITY

ENGLISH ART

1307–1461

JOAN EVANS

OXFORD

AT THE CLARENDON PRESS

1949

Oxford University Press, Amen House, London E.C. 4

GLASGOW NEW YORK TORONTO MELBOURNE WELLINGTON
BOMBAY CALCUTTA MADRAS CAPE TOWN

Geoffrey Cumberlege, Publisher to the University

PRINTED IN GREAT BRITAIN
AT THE UNIVERSITY PRESS, OXFORD
BY CHARLES BATEY, PRINTER TO THE UNIVERSITY

EDITOR'S PREFACE

THE aim of the *Oxford History of English Art* is to set out chronologically the development of the visual arts as part of the general history of England. It is a scheme that, on this scale, has not hitherto been attempted, and in several periods the subject-matter presents problems as yet very partially explored. Art history, a clumsy but useful term, does not hold in this country the position that has been given to *Kunstgeschichte* on the Continent, and an academic discipline that in Europe and America is fully recognized has here few professorial chairs or university departments assigned to it. Our tradition of connoisseurship, the detailed study of works of art and objects of antiquity in order to decide their date and provenance, is, it is true, well established. Nineteenth-century enthusiasm for Gothic architecture produced notable handbooks on medieval structural methods and classifications of medieval ornament, while avoiding discussions of continental influences and explanations of changes in treatment. This resolute objectivity has been the complete antithesis of the exuberance of *Stilkritik*. We still suspect the wider speculations by which analysis of styles provides not only a precise instrument of attribution but also an indication of phases of emotional temperament. Yet our knowledge of the past is incomplete without some investigation of the use men made of visual images and the reasons that guided them in their selection of particular forms.

A work of art is primarily an object that gives aesthetic satisfaction: it is also a piece of historical evidence. The two functions need not exactly coincide, for some feeble piece made for easy popular consumption, some rough woodcut or over-sentimental print, may in some contexts be more historically significant than a great masterpiece produced for some élite circle. Visual formulas have often been tellingly used for propaganda purposes. But the vitality which endows such formulas, even when crudely handled, with an enduring power to please comes from earlier and memorable uses made of them by artists of genius. The lower reaches of

†

visual history must be considered but it is the masterpieces which can give, through some quality that remains indefinable, an aesthetic experience sufficient to mould the visual imagination and to leave its permanent mark. The prevailing cult of economic history directs attention to the everyday life of the normal man: art history deals primarily with the rare moments when genius creates the appropriate forms and symbols to express the thoughts and sensitivities of the milieu from which the artist comes.

The evidence of the arts can serve various purposes for the interpretation of the past. There are the simple documentary cases, long used in the illustration of history books, of the scenes of contemporary life with their details of dress and utensils, the portraits, the buildings designed to serve a particular way of life. More indirectly stated, there are the survival in time and distribution in space of forms and images. Visual motives have undergone strange dispersions. Pagan formulas have been adapted to Christian usage; the frenzied maenad has become the Magdalen under the Cross; the Master of the Animals travelling Westwards has served for Daniel in the lions' den; the gestures and attitudes of Michael-angelo's ceiling were borrowed to idealize the London society that sat to Reynolds; the ancient deities reappear in new guises but keep some of their half-understood attributes about them. It is a world of undertones, where traditional associations reveal the mental complex of a period more fully than the directer statement of the written word. Romanesque art imagined, carved, and painted non-natural beings, curving and twisting under the dictates of ornamental pattern, presided over by rigid figures of deities and saints, gazing over the heads of the congregation, hieratic and remote. The intensity lies in the brilliant, involved inventiveness of the design, not in the discerning skill with which humanity is portrayed. The Gothic artists brought a new humanism; the Virgin turns to look on the Child, even to nurse Him at her breast; new subjects are found such as the Pietà: on the cathedral façades the figures have their own defined space within a niche, not elongated on a column or compressed into a spandrel. Pattern reasserts itself in later Gothic art; then the constant dialectic between abstract ornament and naturalistic forms continues as the Renaissance gives way to the fantasies of Mannerism and the curving violence of Baroque. Security and confidence are favourable to humanist art; disturbance and anxiety find their release in more strained and agitated forms.

It is this sphere of suggestion that is the background of art history. In the foreground is the study of the works themselves: their technique; the purposes which they served and the patrons whom they pleased; the subjects chosen for illustration; the new needs which determined the plans of buildings; the structural discoveries which rendered new types of buildings possible. Architecture, the setting which men create for their own purposes, has a particular historical meaning of its own in its reactions to change of all kinds, reform of the liturgy, military innovations, redistribution of wealth; and in this series architecture is the framework in which the other arts are set.

The first great period of English art is that of Northumbria in the late seventh century, when in carving and illumination a school was formed out of the fusion of classical and barbaric motives which excelled in accomplishment any contemporary work on the Continent. From the expansion of this style came one of the main influences on the Carolingian renaissance, from which in turn England re-learned much for her tenth-century revival, after the first period of Scandinavian invasion and destruction was over. The so-called Winchester School will always be one of the great triumphs of English artistic genius. The Normans, apart from their new and massive conception of architecture, brought with them arts that were mainly French variations on themes that had been earlier current on this side of the Channel. In the twelfth century it is hard to speak of English art, for a common style was practised throughout north-west Europe, and England's contribution to the full development of Romanesque art, magnificent as it is, particularly in miniature painting, ceases to be markedly distinctive. In the thirteenth century there is still a European style, but now definitely under French dominance, and the Gothic of Wells soon gave way before the Court style of Westminster, with its dependence on Paris. It is not until the mid-fourteenth century that with the Perpendicular style a branch of the arts becomes again emphatically English. The strangest phase of English art history lies in the sixteenth century. Under the patronage of Henry VII and Wolsey, the Renaissance came to England, and a major continental artist, Holbein, settled in this country. But with the Reformation and the dissolution of the monasteries the impetus died away. Elizabethan art is curiously archaic in its flat, decorative patterns and strangely isolated from continental movements. Three great artists, Inigo Jones, Van Dyck, and Christopher Wren, brought England once more to the level of European achievement, though each in his own way adapted continental Baroque to the more rigid and restrained tastes of seventeenth-century English patrons. Neither Renaissance nor Baroque art was ever fully acclimatized, and the Georgian architecture of the eighteenth century, so singularly appropriate to the parklands in which it was set, while owing much to continental example, is a genuinely English style. In painting it was for portraiture that England provided a ready demand: subject paintings were occasionally attempted, but with little success apart from the moral anecdotes of Hogarth, which open a long period of English supremacy in caricature and link up with our marked medieval partiality for the grotesque. Landscape painting developed but slowly, and it was almost by accident that the water-colourists of the late eighteenth and early nineteenth centuries produced the great series of sketches which is perhaps the most fascinating of English visual achievements. Constable and Turner are now by European consent recognized as mighty figures, the precursors of impressionism. To their contemporaries the paintings of Wilkie and Landseer or the buildings of the Gothic revival seemed more immediately interesting. The Pre-Raphaelites, with their literary and moral approach to painting, were a last characteristically English movement, before the beginning of a new French domination.

Such in the briefest of outlines is the plot of this series. The rich variety of the detail, where now one, now another, branch of the arts becomes the main interest, will be revealed in the particular volumes. The defined field is England, but a study of English art requires consideration of borrowings from Scotland and Ireland, and of the expansion of English art into these neighbouring countries. The division of the volumes is related to periods of general history, and of necessity does not always coincide with the beginning or the close of some artistic movement. At times uncertainties of dates may leave a particular work in dispute between two periods, and the Chichester reliefs might be claimed both for Vol. ii and Vol. iii or the Westminster retable for Vol. iv and Vol. v. Dr. Evans, beginning in 1307, has, for instance, left carved wooden effigies and the late apocalypses to the preceding volume, whereas the Eleanor crosses are dealt with as the beginning of the Decorated style.

In any account of the arts, the illustrations have an essential part, but no documentation can hope to be complete. These volumes fortunately deal with familiar works of comparatively easy accessibility. The plates have been chosen to provide examples of the different branches of the arts discussed and of the main stylistic variations in the period. The photography of works of art, so as to give not only clarity of detail but also something of the aesthetic pleasure conveyed by the original, is in itself a high skill. English photography has been marked by that directness of statement which characterizes all our art researches, and there has been here, as compared with the Continent, less experiment with the interpretative powers of the camera. Satisfactory photographs are not always easily secured, and there is as yet no systematic corpus of photographs of English art. The National Buildings Record for architecture, the Courtauld Institute of Art for illumination and sculpture, and the Witt Library for painting are doing much to supply this want, and the Oxford History could not have been undertaken without their assistance. In particular, the co-operation of the Courtauld Institute, which has accepted special photographic commitments for this series, is of great importance both in the researches entailed for the various volumes and in the presentation of the final result.

The history of the past is inexhaustible: new facts come to light as we write it, traced in some document, dug up from the ground, found by chance in some junk-shop. Each generation has its own view of historical significance. English art has been studied selectively, and this survey of it reveals many points at which there is still much to be discovered; at others it is summarizing a long tradition of antiquarian learning and the more recent writings of contemporary scholars. It will achieve its aim if it leaves the subject in a more consistent form, better related to our history as a whole, the ground better prepared for the researches of the future.

T. S. R. BOASE

MAGDALEN COLLEGE
    OXFORD
      1949

NOTE

I AM greatly indebted to those who have helped me to write this book by the giving of encouragement, information, and illustrations. Among them I should like to name my Editor, the President of Magdalen; Dr. Margaret Whinney, who has kindly read the book in manuscript; the Warden of All Souls, Mr. C. F. Bell, Sir Alfred Clapham, Mrs. Martin Clark, Mrs. Clifford, Monsieur Paul Deschamps, Comte Blaise de Montesquiou-Fezensac, Mr. Maurice Hastings, Mr. T. D. Kendrick, Mr. H. D. Molesworth, Mr. Croft Murray, Mr. C. W. Dyson Perrins, Miss M. E. Seaton, Mr. J. Wardrop, and Professor Geoffrey Webb, who have helped me on points of detail; and Mr. W. J. Clark, Mr. F. H. Crossley, Mr. Arthur Gardner, Mr. R. P. Howgrave-Graham, Dr. Shirley Jones, Mr. J. B. Morrell, and the Directors of the Art Institute of Chicago, the New York Public Library, and the Pierpont Morgan Library, who have given me photographs.

My thanks are due to the staffs of the National Buildings Record, the British Museum Library, the London Library, and the Conway Library of the Courtauld Institute. I am particularly indebted to the Librarian, Dr. Deane, and the library staff of the Society of Antiquaries for their courteous and unfailing help at a time when want of heat and light made any service onerous.

J. E.

WOTTON–UNDER–EDGE

CONTENTS

LIST OF PLATES

THE ANGEL OF THE PASSION, PERCY TOMB, BEVERLEY MINSTER. Middle of the 14th century.
> Phot. courtesy of R. P. Howgrave-Graham, Esq., F.S.A. Frontispiece.

AT END

1. THE ELEANOR CROSS, GEDDINGTON, NORTHANTS, 1294.
> Phot. courtesy of Courtauld Institute of Art.

2. THE ELEANOR CROSS, HARDINGSTONE, NORTHAMPTON, 1291. Designed by John of Battle, the figures by William of Ireland.
> Phot. courtesy of Courtauld Institute of Art.

3. MONUMENT OF EDMUND CROUCHBACK, EARL OF LANCASTER, *d.* 1296. WESTMINSTER ABBEY. *Phot. Royal Commission on Historical Monuments. Crown copyright reserved. Reproduced with the permission of the Controller of H.M. Stationery Office.*

4. IVORY DIPTYCH, *c.* 1300. [8½ inches high.] Salting Bequest.
> *Victoria and Albert Museum. Crown copyright.*

5. PAGE FROM THE PSALTER OF ROBERT DE LISLE, *c.* 1295. THE RESURRECTION; THE MARIES AT THE TOMB; *Noli me Tangere*; AND THE SUPPER AT EMMAEUS. B.M. Arundel MS. 83 fol. 133.
> Phot. courtesy of the Trustees of the British Museum.

6. DETAIL OF THE WINDMILL PSALTER, *c.* 1300, Pierpont Morgan Library, New York, MS. 19 fol. 2.
> Phot. courtesy of Pierpont Morgan Library, New York.

7. PAGE FROM THE TICKHILL PSALTER, *c.* 1300, New York Public Library.
> Phot. courtesy of New York Public Library.

8. *a.* PANEL OF *opus anglicanum*: THE ANGEL APPEARING TO THE SHEPHERDS, *c.* 1310. [10½ inches high.]
> *Victoria and Albert Museum. Crown copyright.*

   b. BORDER FROM QUEEN MARY'S PSALTER, *c.* 1308, B.M. Royal MS. 2BVII fol. 393V.
> Phot. courtesy of the Trustees of the British Museum.

9. *a.* PERSHORE ABBEY. THE CHOIR VAULT, begun soon after 1288.
   b. MALMESBURY ABBEY. THE NAVE VAULT.
> Phots. National Buildings Record.

10. WELLS CATHEDRAL. THE CENTRAL PILLAR OF THE CHAPTER HOUSE, begun *c.* 1290. *Phot. B.C. Phillips, City Studios, Wells.*

LIST OF FIGURES

*The arms on the title-page are taken from the Tomb of the Black Prince in
Canterbury Cathedral*

ABBREVIATIONS

Antiq. Journ.	*The Antiquaries' Journal*
Arch. Journ.	*The Archaeological Journal*
Bull. Mon.	*Bulletin Monumental*
Burl. Mag.	*Burlington Magazine*
Journ. Brit. Arch. Ass.	*Journal of the British Archaeological Association*
Proc. Soc. Ants.	*Proceedings of the Society of Antiquaries of London*
R.I.B.A. Journ.	*Journal of the Royal Institution of British Architects*
Trans. R. Hist. Soc.	*Transactions of the Royal Historical Society*

I

THE ORIGINS OF DECORATED STYLE

'MY harp is tuned to mourning.' So Edward I wrote to his bishops in 1290, asking for their prayers for his dead queen. In his reign of iron determination, keen legalism, and hard warfare, the epic gives place for a moment to a more lyric strain: the threnody for Eleanor of Castille, 'whom living I have dearly cherished and whom dead I shall not cease to love'.[1] Curiously enough it is this lyric outburst, which strikes so sharp a contrast with the background of sterner music, that sets the rhythm for the art of the next fifty years.

Queen Eleanor died in November 1290; for a time Edward shut himself away with his grief. Death was busy round him; his trusted advisers, Kirkby and Burnell, his mother, Eleanor of Provence, were called from his side. A new generation stood about the throne, but his daily companion was loneliness. There was no slackening in his tenacity of purpose, yet some vital fire had left him for ever. He now looked backward, as though to challenge Time by remembering things past. For his father's tomb he ordered a splendid effigy; for his wife he prepared a fullness of commemoration as yet unknown in England.

The grace and elegance of the monuments he erected in memory of Eleanor of Castille are not only a romantic remembrance of past beauty but also a challenge to Time in another fashion. When in 1271 the bones of Saint Louis had been carried from Paris to Notre-Dame on the shoulders of his son Philippe III, a cross had been set up at each resting-place: a crucifix with a pyramidal foot carved with the figures of the Three Kings.[2] One of these crosses

---

[1] H. Gough, *Itinerary of King Edward I*, London (1900), ii. 289.

[2] J. Doublat, *Histoire de l'Abbaye de Saint Denys en France* (1726). Le Nain de Tallemant, *Vie de Saint Louis*, ed. Soc. de l'hist. de France, Paris (1849), 202, says that a cross with four columns was set up outside Paris where the bearers were changed when the body of Philip Augustus was borne to Saint-Denis.

is, I think, represented in a miniature of the *Très Riches Heures* of the duc de Berri[1] as a spiry monument on a hexagonal plan, rising from a stepped base, with niches surmounted by double gables with pinnacles between.

In like manner Edward I determined to commemorate each resting-place of his beloved queen between Hardby in Lincolnshire where she died and Westminster where she was buried.[2] The crosses he set up were extraordinarily graceful and complicated in their design. Three that survive, not quite complete, at Hardingstone near Northampton, at Geddington near Kettering, and at Waltham Cross, show a marked resemblance to the monument represented in the *Très Riches Heures*. That at Hardingstone (Pl. 2) seems to have been the earliest.[3] It was begun in 1291; John of Battle, *cementarius*, was the architect. The stepped base and the arcaded pedestal are six-sided; the pedestal is hung with the shields of Ponthieu, Castille, Leon, and England. On three of the sides open books are represented as if upon a lectern: their inscriptions have vanished unrecorded. Above the pedestal three canopied niches, with ogival arches,[4] enshrine three statues of the queen. The records show these to have been carved in London[5] by William of Ireland, who is described both as *imaginator* and as *cementarius*. Above the niches rises a third stage, four-sided, which formed the base of the cross.

This many-sided composition is essentially conceived in the round, as a piece of free-standing sculpture might be. This plastic

---

[1] That representing the meeting of the Magi. See Joan Evans in *Burl. Mag.* xci.

[2] Stukeley, *Itinerarium Curiosum*, i. 36, says that the Eleanor crosses were set up at Lincoln, Grantham, Stamford, Geddington, Northampton (Hardingstone), Stony Stratford, Dunstable, St. Albans, Waltham, Cheapside, and Charing Cross. Gough, *Itinerary*, ii. 90, adds Woburn to the list.

[3] See Lovell, 26; Prior and Gardner, 98.

[4] I use ogival in the English, not the French, sense, to mean an arch struck from more than one centre, with its two upper curves struck from centres above the arch.

[5] At the same time the closest parallel to them in style would seem to be a work of the Northern school, the Virgin over the doorway in the north arch at York (Prior and Gardner, Fig. 366); a likeness which shows the difficulty of establishing local style. A statue in a niche in the façade of Saint-Jean-des-Vignes at Soissons (Gardner, *French Medieval Sculpture*, Fig. 370) affords a French comparison of much the same date. The treatment of drapery may also be compared with that of the Saint Paul in the south transept of Rheims, ibid., Fig. 293.

quality, and the decorative details—the foliage that fills the upper gables, the curious leaf-shaped tracery of the arcade, the elegant flowered cornice of the lower stage, the cusped ogival niches, the wave cresting, the pinnacles and finials—combined to set the standards of the new style. It has long been called the Decorated Style; and, though curvilinear may be a more exact epithet, none can be more descriptive.

That the nascent style was capable of variety is evident in the two remaining crosses, which increase our regret for the eight that have vanished. That at Waltham[1] was begun in 1291 under the superintendence of Nicholas Dymenge de Reyns—who must have been a Frenchman from Rheims—with Roger de Crundale, Alexander of Abingdon,[2] and Robert of Corfe to assist him. Like that at Hardingstone it is hexagonal in plan and designed in three stories, but the scheme is completely different. Here graduated buttresses with a foliage finial stand at every angle to enshrine three statues on the middle tier. Alexander of Abingdon's statues[3] have suffered a good deal of damage, but still show a deliberate skill in their elegant and dignified pose and in the contrast between the plain heavy folds of the dress and the slighter drapery of the cloak.

The third surviving cross, that at Geddington, was erected soon after 1294 (Pl. 1). Here the plan is triangular: gabled canopies rise over the three statues of the queen. The whole is of feminine elegance and metallic delicacy.

The Eleanor crosses were but a part of a great system of commemoration. According to the custom of the time the queen was embalmed, and some of the organs received separate interment. Her bowels were buried in the Lincoln Lady-chapel; the tomb, the work of Dymenge de Legeri (presumably the Nicholas Dymenge de Reyns who superintended the Waltham cross), had metal images of weepers. It was destroyed in 1641; a drawing of it made for Sir William Dugdale at this time[4] shows it to have had

---

[1] It is best represented in the engraving in *Vetusta Monumenta*, iii, London (1791), Pl. XVI, which represents it before its restoration by Blore in 1836.

[2] Also called the *imaginator*; he worked in stone here, but in metal at Charing Cross. See Prior and Gardner, 98.

[3] Illustrated in Prior and Gardner, Fig. 395.

[4] Now in the possession of Lord Winchilsea.

a gilt bronze effigy of the queen laid upon a stone chest of simple form. Her heart was enshrined in the Blackfriars church of Bridewell in London, where Adam the goldsmith made the figure of an angel to hold it, set upon a cenotaph with weepers by William of Suffolk.[1] Chantries were established at Hardby where she died, at Lincoln, at Peterborough, and at the London Blackfriars. Finally, a splendid tomb was erected for her at Westminster, and a perpetual and splendid commemoration of her endowed in that abbey.

This tomb still survives, though Time has blurred some of its details. The trees from which hang the shields of her descent on the arcaded front, which were once clearly differentiated as oaks and vines, are badly damaged; the painting on the base by Walter of Durham, of a kneeling knight, a woman with a child, and four pilgrims before the Holy Sepulchre (doubtless the record of a vicarious pilgrimage at the queen's expense), have grown dim; the canopy painted by Walter of Durham was destroyed when Henry V's chantry was built. Only the beautiful grill to the ambulatory, made by Master Thomas of Leighton Buzzard, the long Latin inscription of her genealogy ending

Femina consilio prudens, pia, prole beata,
Auxit amicitijs, auxit honore virum,

and the splendid gilt brass effigy by William Torel, citizen and goldsmith of London, who also made the effigy of Henry III, remain unblemished.

This effigy is of remarkable beauty. The severe stylization of face and hair is softened by the flow of her dress, that falls like a cascade to the feet; here is true accomplishment in the grand manner. It is more archaic than contemporary work in France—for instance the *Vierge Dorée* of Amiens—but it has a noble sweetness of its own. The effigy is crowned by a bronze canopy with wonderful naturalistic leaf-crockets and two head-corbels no less accomplished than the effigy.

The new Decorated style, thus triumphantly affirmed, was a

---

[1] *Arch. Journ.* xlix (1892), 17. The painted decoration was by Walter of Durham. The whole was destroyed at the Reformation.

natural growth. Edward I and Eleanor of Castille had known not
only the courts of France, the most civilized in Europe, but also
the half-oriental splendours of Cyprus, where they spent the
winter of 1271-2. On their way home they passed by way of
Sicily and Rome. Yet though royal standards of luxury and
ornament might be influenced by those of foreign courts, the
actual expression of luxury in England remained English.

A new decorative sense is evident in work at Westminster about
1240, in which diaper work is used as a background for sculpture
and a filling for spandrels in a way that finds no parallel in France.
The canopy over the tomb of Bishop Bridport of Salisbury, who
died in 1263, already heralds the new style in its rich and rather
heavy foliage and its pictorial use of figure work to fill the
spandrels; the north transept of Hereford cathedral, built about
1270, already shows the rose diaper that appears on the Geddington
cross; the angel choir at Lincoln is in its turn the evident precursor
of the new style. The Cantelupe shrine at Hereford, erected in
1286, is already beyond geometric style in its use of naturalistic
leafage and in its curiously lobed arcade. The same spirit may be
seen at work in the chapter-house at Southwell,[1] which was in
process of building six years later. The naturalistic leafage of its
capitals can only be rivalled in France, and the spandrel ornament
and the leafy crockets of the stalls show such sculpture spreading
to other fields.

Once the new style had been affirmed, it developed apace; but
the development was in the main confined to the parts of buildings
that were not purely structural.[2] The Decorated style, indeed, is
remarkable as the first medieval style that was not based on any
structural innovation. England had been less creative than France
in Romanesque architecture, and this inherited weakness had
curbed the scope and scale of English Gothic. This may help to
explain why the characteristic English development lay in decoration rather than in pure architecture, and why it was at first
worked out on a relatively small scale.

[1] See Pevsner, *Leaves of Southwell.*
[2] The ogival arch of the crosses is found in the same year—1292—in the under-
chapel of St. Stephen's, Westminster (M. Hastings).

Its best expression continued to be on tombs. Edmund Crouch-back, earl of Lancaster, brother of Edward I, died in 1296; his magnificent tomb in Westminster Abbey is probably a few years earlier in date (Pl. 3). It is still formally geometric in style; the ogival arch is not employed, the tracery is not flowing; but the peculiar richness of the cusping and recusping of the arches, of the many-storied pinnacles and multiple gables, and the elegant figures of mourners on the arcaded base, arranged as pairs half-facing each other, all link it with the style of the Eleanor crosses.[1] Compare it with the tomb of Aveline his wife, who died twenty years earlier, and the difference is plain. Yet for all the ornament, the gable figure of the knight praying on horseback—his hands and head given to God, and his knees still keeping a firm grip on his mount—has something of the touching simplicity of an earlier age.

The tomb of Edmund Crouchback is a peculiarly English monument. The more closely it is examined, the more evidently it is seen to be thought of in terms of enamelled gold. Every background is of gilt gesso;[2] the crestings and pinnacles are metallic in form and were once gilded; the lightness and the springing quality of the tabernacle belong rather to gold and silver than to stone. It has lost the architectural quality of emphasis by reservation and has gained instead a filigree richness. When all the images were still coloured, and the paintings on the plain parts were still visible,[3] when the details of the canopy were still inlaid with stained glass,[4] it could be seen to be a vastly enlarged shrine, translated from precious metal into stone, but with no modification in its decorative effect or indeed in its intention. The fact that the

---

[1] The cusped arch, the trefoil medallion on the gable, the crocketed cresting, and the storied pinnacles recurred in the tomb of Marie de Valois, d. 1331, in the church of Santa Chiara at Naples, destroyed by Allied bombing. The architect of the tomb was Gagliardo Primario.

[2] Stothard's drawing (p. 40) shows the rich diaper of quadrilobed medallions of foliage and eagles that diversified the ground of his surcoat.

[3] In 1723 the base on its unsculptured side showed a painting, already much defaced, of ten knights in surcoats of arms bearing banners. Dart, ii. 14. In its present state it is represented in Borenius and Tristram, Fig. 43. The whole still retains considerable traces of its original colour.

[4] Dart, ii. 11.

English goldwork of the time has not survived must not blind us to its achievements alike in skill and scale. The craft guild was recognized and the assay established in 1301. By 1309 Ralph of Baldock, bishop of London, was ordering from Richard Pickerell, citizen, a retable for the high altar in a painted frame 'variously adorned with many precious stones and enamelled work, and also with divers images of metal'.[1] Such composite pieces, of which the battered yet glorious Westminster retable still gives us an idea, must have formed an intermediate stage between works in precious metal and the painted and gilded tombs.

The success of Crouchback's tomb can be gauged by the number of its imitations. The closest is the tomb of William of Louth, bishop of Ely, who died in 1298;[2] it must surely have been the work of the same sculptor. It seems to have been as closely imitated on the lost tomb of Henry Lacy, earl of Lincoln, in old St. Paul's.[3] The canopy from an unidentified tomb—possibly Bishop Turvil's[4]—now in the chapel of St. James in Exeter cathedral, has a single gable, filled with an oval medallion of Christ showing His wounds, with censing angels in the spandrels. The cuspings are pierced; the pinnacles on either side are in gabled stories with statues of apostles in the niches. The whole has the same unmistakable metallic quality. The single gable, here more simply and architecturally treated, is used on the tomb of Archbishop William Greenfield in York Minster,[5] and the series is magnificently concluded by the tomb of Aymer de Valence, earl of Pembroke, at Westminster. He died in 1324, and the tomb was erected after his death. The imitation of Crouchback's is obvious and avowed, but a new note is struck in the ogival cuspings.[6]

It is not surprising that such art, essentially miniature in its

---

[1] Dugdale, *St. Paul's*, 11.

[2] Crossley, *Monuments*, 60. The canopy is almost intact but the tomb has gone.

[3] See Gough, ii. 81; Dugdale, *St. Paul's*, 84.

[4] Crossley, op. cit. 6; Evans, *Pattern*, Fig. 37.

[5] Crossley, op. cit. 61. He died in 1315. An intermediate example in the series is the tomb of Stephen Alard, admiral of the Cinque Ports, at Winchelsea; he died in 1324. Crossley, frontispiece.

[6] Its decoration was equally colourful, 'inlaid, after the mosaick manner, with stained glass'. Dart, ii. 11; Gough, ii. 86.

feeling, should have been produced at a time when decorative art on a small scale was notably developed. There is a certain artistic parity between the Eleanor crosses and an English ivory diptych in the Salting bequest[1] (Pl. 4). There is the same noble simplicity in some embroidery of the time, notably the panel of *opus anglicanum* by John of Thanet[2] and the splendid chasuble at Kloster Melk,[3] and in such illuminations as the psalter of Robert de Lisle.[4] All have the same gracious seriousness, the same contrast between rather expressionless faces and fluid draperies; the same pose under a cusped arch which emphasizes the affinity with the canopied tombs.

The psalter of Robert de Lisle deserves a more detailed study, for in it the characteristics of pictorial art of the years immediately before and immediately after 1300 can best be apprehended. The earlier miniatures (Pl. 5) are still dominated by architectural feeling; the later employ architectural elements purely decoratively. The compositions have the characteristic mixture of grace and serenity; the detail of the Visitation and Annunciation fitted into a geometrical scheme of devotional sentences shows the extraordinary sureness of line of which the English illuminator was capable about 1300.

The illustrations are interesting, too, for their schemes. The idea of correspondences dominates them: in one each of the Ten Plagues represents a punishment for a breach of one of the Ten Commandments; in another the eight beatitudes each find their reward in a grade of the celestial hierarchy; in a third the seven Offices of the

[1] Cf. the ivory figure of Christ from a crucifix in the same museum, Longhurst, *English Ivories*, Fig. 44.

[2] Evans, *Pattern*, Fig. 7. It is mentioned in an inventory of Canterbury cathedral made in 1321.

[3] See H. Kronberger-Frentzen in *Burl. Mag.* lxi (1932), 68.

[4] B.M. Arundel MS. 83. It contains two manuscripts, dividing at fol. 123v. See Millar, p. 4 and Pl. 7; Saunders, p. 150 and Fig. 43. The occurrence on one page of the arms of Howard and Fitton suggests that it was made for Sir William Howard, d. 1308, or for his wife Alice Fitton; the latter owner is the more probable as some pages seem to have been made for a woman's use. The psalter in the latter half of the book was given in 1339 by Robert de Lisle to his daughter Awdry. J. Noppen in *Burl. Mag.* lvii (1930), 72 allies it with the paintings of the Westminster School, especially with the retable and the sedilia paintings.

Hours are related with the seven scenes of the Passion and with the curiously assorted gifts of sight, smell, taste, hearing, touch, agreement, and liberty of judgement. The Cross is represented as the tree of Life; the ten stages of human life form a kind of wheel of Fortune.

In a page that illustrates the virtues of Love and Hate, first by symbolic figures and then by scenes of David kissing Jonathan and Saul attempting to murder David, the same parallelism is visible. There are affinities with the tombs in six well-differentiated little trees and a heading like an impossibly airy tomb canopy. Other miniatures are set in quadrilobed medallions with ogival petals at the corners, set six to a page with particoloured diapers to fill the spaces between; the effect is glittering and confused like that of a brilliant enamel. Similarly the noble and severe Crucifixion is incongruously set against lozenged backgrounds of the fleurs de lis of France and the leopards of England that find a parallel on French enamelled goldwork of the time of Philippe le Bel.

The later pages display a few marginal grotesques, a deer under a tree, and a birdcatcher at work, in a coat camouflaged with leaves, with his limed twig and an owl as his decoy. Such grotesques appear in even the noblest books of the time in that strangely English spirit that sets comic relief even in a tragedy.[1] They appear soon after 1250, for example, in a psalter now at Oscott College which has such marginal drawings as the fable of the cock who sang to the fox, and a monkey before a hooded centaur. The psalter of Edmund de Lacy, earl of Lincoln, who died in 1257,[2] has marginal grotesques of the Aesopic fox and crane, of a warrior attacking snails, of mice hanging a cat, and of an almost naked woman on all fours with a monkey-like devil on her back.

It has been pointed out[3] that such grotesques are not so sudden

---

[1] They are exceptionally found in French manuscripts (e.g. B.M. Add. MS. 38114, fol. 5) and are more common in the Netherlands (e.g. Bib. Roy. Brussels MS. 1175; B.M. Stowe MS. 17). A Spanish manuscript of the Fueros de Aragon in the Dyson Perrins collection, written after 1285, has grotesques that appear to have been painted by an English illuminator.

[2] Now in the collection of the duke of Rutland, *New Palaeographical Society*, Pls. 61–6. [3] F. Wormald in *Burl. Mag.* lxxix (1942), 134.

a phenomenon as it appears. In the margins, indeed, they are a novelty; but they arise naturally from fanciful ornamentation which had earlier been imprisoned in the initial spilling over into the vacant space. In such a book as the Peterborough Psalter[1] they appear as part of an ordered marginal decoration which gives them a factitious coherence, but in the psalters written about 1300 they are amazingly episodic. Their naturalistic development finds a literary parallel in the contemporary *Owl and the Nightingale*, where all the birds and beasts of the manuscripts appear.[2]

Their development reflects the constancy of English taste, that always enjoys amusing irrelevancies, but also is in a measure the result of the survival in England of the psalter as the most usual book of devotion. In France and the Low Countries its place had already been taken by the book of Hours, of which the content prescribed a new code of illustration. In England the psalter continued in use, and its illustration progressed from one irrelevancy to another.

The psalter written for Alphonso, second son of Edward I,[3] which may have been begun as a present for the marriage that was prevented by his death in 1284, is one of the earliest books to show this episodic tendency. The figure-work has a French elegance, and indeed affectation, of pose; the marginal decorations are wholly English, with nothing to hold them together but an occasional linear bar that breaks into a leafy ending. They include grotesque and sometimes obscene monsters, all the tribe of the dragons, the deer of English woods, and the lovely birds of the English hedgerow.

The style was developed in a group of manuscripts that are, perhaps, the most characteristic English creation of the years round 1300. Some, but not all, the evidence seems to indicate an East Anglian provenance. They are the work, so far as we can tell, not of one man but of a company of travelling illuminators

[1] Bib. Roy. Brussels, MSS. 9961–2; see Van den Gheyn. It is in relation with two manuscripts at Cambridge: another Peterborough Psalter (Corpus Christi MS. 53) written for Hugo de Stivede, prior of Peterborough 1299–1321 (Millar, p. 204), and a Sarum Missal (Camb. Univ. Library dd. 4. 17) written for Alice de Reydon, who died in 1310.

[2] See H. B. Hinckley in *P.M.L.A.* xlvii (1932), 303.

[3] B.M. Add. MS. 24686; sometimes called the Tenison Psalter.

whom the needs of patrons assembled from time to time into different groupings. Even when the scribe who wrote the text was a monk, the illuminators were laymen;[1] they had their own pattern books, and subjects drawn from these have made certain tentative identifications possible.

One of the earliest of the series is that known as the Ormesby Psalter.[2] It appears to have been written between 1285 and 1300; a stylus mark at 1289 in the calendar may indicate the date.[3] Its decoration was gradual. The first few pages are by the best artist and contain no evidence of ownership. Then it seems to have been continued by order of Sir Jordan Foliot, a tenant under the abbey of St. Edmund, for presentation to Gilbert de Clare, steward of the abbey. He died in 1295, and it was continued for a time without heraldic decoration, until Sir Jordan gave it to his kinsman Sir Hugh Bardolf, who had his arms, and those of his Foliot wife, inset. He died in 1299 and soon afterwards it seems to have been acquired by Robert of Ormesby, a monkish member of a neighbouring family, and given by him to the cathedral priory of Norwich. At this time portraits of the donor and the bishop of Norwich were added over some lines of the text on the Beatus page.[4]

Originally the psalter had eight bordered pages; their initials still contain the traditional subjects—Solomon and Marcolf, the legendary fool, for *Dixit insipiens* and Jonah for *Salvum me fac*— but 'a world of fine fabling' has peopled the margins. An extraordinary creative power has invaded the page; the subjects are fantastic and ill assorted, but they live and move and have their being. Every creature, man, monster, beast, bird, and insect, is vital and in action; we find ourselves in an impossible but incredibly real world where size and habitat have been abolished by the stroke of a magic quill. A page holds a D, enclosing figures of the Trinity in Majesty, ornamented with two seraphs and two even

[1] See Egbert, *Tickhill Psalter*, 3 and 81.

[2] Bodleian Library, MS. Douce 366; admirably published by Cockerell and James.

[3] See Nicholson in *Catalogue of Western MSS. in the Bodleian Library*.

[4] Dr. Egbert points out the likeness between the Jesse tree on a page with the Bardolf and Foliot arms, and that in the Tickhill Psalter (see below). They appear, indeed, to be by the same hand.

larger greenfinches. In the margin a monkey mounted on a hound pursues an owl on a rabbit; flies and ladybirds crawl over the border, where a man on a bear fights another on a lion, a peasant rests by the wayside, and a trumpeter blows a fanfare among a number of dragons.

Another page[1] besides an initial with a serious miniature of God anointing David, and an entwined border richly decorated with foliage and diapering, has a man slinging stones at a snail as big as himself; a butterfly that seems to have alighted on the page; a winged dragon chasing a centaur, who is shooting at the butterfly; a robin looking at a goldfinch, and a magpie looking at an owl; a hawk eating meat, and a man-headed bird preparing with targe and falchion to attack a squirrel. A man-headed quadruped combs his hair before a mirror, next to a C that enshrines a charming Virgin and Child.

Sometimes the intention is frankly narrative. A farmer's wife, armed with her distaff, pursues a fox who has carried off her cock; a fox, dressed like a friar and leaning on a crutch, comes to pay a friendly visit to a rather suspicious rabbit; a knight hunts a unicorn who takes refuge in a lady's lap. Sometimes the representation of nature is enough; there is a charming border of squirrels. Heraldry only appears in the line-endings; a fertile imagination did not find it interesting.

The Ormesby Psalter in many ways stands alone;[2] the psalter that belonged to Bromholm priory[3] is simpler and more serious. The Windmill Psalter[4] has an even finer page-plan than the Ormesby Psalter, but is more restrained in its ornament. There are a few grotesque line endings, and a few birds in the margins, but the illuminator's skill lies less in the exuberance of his fancy than in

[1] Fol. 38.

[2] I have not seen the Ramsay Psalter, now in the abbey of St. Paul in Lavanttal, Carinthia. It includes the portrait of a monk with the words 'Grafham honoretur'; they probably refer to William of Graffham who became cellarer of Ramsey abbey in 1297.

[3] Bodleian MS. Ashmole 1523. After fol. 168 the MS. dates from the end of the fourteenth century. See Millar, p. 4 and Pl. 6. He considers it to be by the same hand as Emmanuel College, Cambridge, MS. 112, *Moralia* of Gregory.

[4] Pierpont Morgan Library, New York, MS. 19. See James, *Catalogue* 41.

the incredible skill of his penwork,[1] which finds expression not only in the adventurous posing of his figures but also in the delicate scrolling ornament of the background. One page (Pl. 6) has a windmill at the top; this was probably the device of the man for whom it was made, but he has not so far been identified. Then comes the traditional subject of the Judgement of Solomon; the initial E against a superb penwork background; an angel flying down with a scroll; and, at the bottom of the page, a cock pheasant.

The next surviving English psalter of importance was written by John Tickhill, an Augustinian of Worksop priory in Nottinghamshire, and illuminated by other hands. Tickhill was prior of Worksop from 1303 to 1314, and it probably dates from this time. The manuscript[2] offers a number of unusual features. It is illustrated, for one thing, with 482 pictures of subjects from the Old Testament, partly taken directly from the Bible and partly from Peter Comestor's *Historia Scholastica*. Some are set in the large initials, more in the bottom margins of the manuscript. The illuminator had a great gift for setting out a monumental page; his work has the curiously inevitable quality of really fine design. Characteristic of the book are the extraordinary inscribed scrolls that spring out from the drawings and serve not only to tell their story but also to link the varied parts of the design into a whole (Pl. 7). A page has the marriage of David and Abigail represented inside the D of Psalm xxxviii in interlaced quatrefoils with backgrounds variously diapered. Eleven curving scrolls spring out from it into the margin. Even an ordinary page, with figures only in the bottom margin, has the scrolls flying out to curve and twist and give a curious dynamic force to the design. It is not surprising that some unfinished pages show that the scrolls are a fundamental part of the scheme and were put in at the very beginning. These unfinished pages show, too, how the team of craftsmen proceeded with the work. The figures, scrolls, and details were first lightly sketched in with very pale brown ink, then carefully—but still rather impressionistically—drawn with black ink by a draughtsman of extraordinary ability. Next, gold leaf was applied over

[1] Cf. Bodleian Auct. D 32.   [2] In the New York Public Library.

gesso to certain details and grounds and highly burnished. After the heavy body colours had been applied to the garments and backgrounds, final details were added; high lights in white, folds of drapery in black or white, the silhouettes of dark coloured areas refined and strengthened by black outlines, and the backgrounds softened by delicate diapering. The colouring is restricted in its gamut, but far removed from the heraldic simplicity of earlier work. The dominant colours are a greyish-blue, a pinkish-red, and a pale viridian green—composite colours like the leech and plonket, murrey and tawny, sinople and glaucus, that occur frequently in contemporary inventories.

In the Tickhill Psalter the fine fabling gives place to biblical narrative; there are no grotesques; and though there are a number of carefully drawn plant-forms,[1] they play an unimportant part in the whole design.

The remarkable differences between the Ormesby, the Windmill, and the Tickhill psalters show how difficult any classification of such manuscripts must be. The *magister* of the group of artists must have designed the page and drawn the chief outlines; but men working under him might employ in a corner of his manuscript a figure or a technical trick that they had used before under another master on a very different book.

Dr. Egbert in his admirable publication of the manuscript has grouped a certain number of early-fourteenth-century manuscripts round the Tickhill Psalter, and has found cause to link them with a small number of families, connected by marriage or ancestry, living in Nottinghamshire, and with Augustinian houses in the same district to which they were friends and benefactors. A brief study of the books he lists vividly shows the difficulty of disentangling such team-work. The Grey-FitzPayn Hours,[2] written between 1300 and the marriage of Sir Richard Grey to Joan FitzPayn which took place soon before 1308, has some links of detail with the Tickhill Psalter, but is unlike it fundamentally; it

---

[1] Dr. Egbert has identified columbine, ground ivy, herb robert, marsh mallow, germander veronica, hazel, vetch, sweet woodruff, box, forget-me-not, and quince.

[2] FitzWilliam Museum, Cambridge, MS. 242; it is an early example of an English book of Hours.

has no flying scrolls, the figure work is on a larger scale and is more archaic in style, there are far more grotesques in the Ormesby manner, and an important part is played by shields of arms. Some of the artists of the Tickhill Psalter may well have worked upon it, but they worked in quite a different concatenation. The psalter of Queen Isabella,[1] made for her in England on or before her marriage to Edward II in 1308, was, like the Tickhill Psalter, written by a religious, probably an Augustinian, and illustrated by a group of laymen. Some of them seem to have been men who worked on the Tickhill Psalter, as some grotesques are identical and come out of the same pattern book; there are a number of illustrations of the history of David out of the same cycle. But the whole is weaker and more pastoral in feeling; the dynamism is missing. There are no flying scrolls and more monsters.

There is, indeed, in the psalter of Queen Isabella a measure of French courtly elegance, and the manuscript, though its illuminations seem certainly to be by English hands, was written in Paris.[2] This elegance finds yet fuller expression in the slightly later book known as Queen Mary's Psalter[3] that may likewise have been written for Edward II's queen.[4] The errors which occasionally occur in the text suggest that it was written by a lay scribe; many inscriptions are in Anglo-Norman verse. It has a long series of Old and New Testament illustrations; 203 drawings cover the period from the Fall of Lucifer to the Death of Solomon, followed by a calendar with the Labours of the Months. The psalter proper has miniatures of the life of Christ, and the litany that follows is accompanied by scenes from the lives of the saints,

[1] Munich Stadtsbibliothek Cod. Gall. 16; Egbert 82. He also includes in the group the Greenfield Apocalypse (Brit. Mus. Royal MS. 15 D 11); the Bardolf-Vaux Psalter (Lambeth Palace MS. 233) which has some grotesques identical with the Grey-FitzPayn Hours; the Guisborough Breviary, Missal, and Psalter (Douai abbey, Woolhampton); and the Commentaries and Decretals (St. John's Coll., Cambridge, A. 4).

[2] Durrieu 14. Another French MS., Bib. nat. lat. 3893, dated 1314, is by an English scribe although the illuminations are French. Thomas of Wymonduswold was a scribe who worked in Paris; he probably came from Wymeswold, Leics.

[3] B.M. Royal MS. 2 B VII. See Warner. It is so called because Queen Mary acquired it in 1553.

[4] Edward II appears in gold in the calendar. Another work by the same hand is a psalter of a monk of Canterbury in the Dyson Perrins collection.

including twenty-two from the life of St. Thomas of Canterbury. The bottom margins have over 450 miniatures. There are no grotesques, monsters, animals, or flowers, but there are some charming sketches from life (Pl. 8 *b*): a band of pilgrims and a country dance led by a man playing the vielle. A nun, a Franciscan, another nun, and a Dominican walking together in a kind of stately dance may be symbolically interpreted; but what are we to think of a minoress playing a psalterion accompanied by a Franciscan friar on the mandoline? A few pages have quadri-lobed medallions in the rather heavier tradition of the Lisle Psalter; the calendar and a few full-page illustrations have their scenes set against a lozenged ground; but most of the illustrations are of a feminine lightness. Many are pen drawings very lightly washed with colour,[1] with a curiously sketchy effect.

The treatment of the figures offers an obvious parallel with some French work of slightly later date;[2] it is perhaps worth remembering that in 1308 Simon of Bordeaux figures among the king's painters.[3]

In Queen Mary's Psalter we begin to feel the independent pictorial artist at work. It must be remembered that by this date scribe and illuminator were different craftsmen; the discipline of calligraphy was no longer that in which the painter of the illu-minations had necessarily been trained. The differentiation was perpetuated in the ordinance of the craft guild in 1403, which decreed that the 'lymenours' or illuminators were to elect one warden and the writers of text letters a second.[4] A craft which had originated in the cloister had reached the stage of the technical differentiation of production on a commercial scale.

A parallel with the organization of the craft of illumination, and many parallels with its style, may be found in the other English craft of embroidery, *opus anglicanum*.[5] It has, like English illumina-

---

[1] This style of decoration is used in more archaic fashion in a rather earlier English psalter, Brit. Mus. Add. MS. 28681.

[2] e.g. B.M. Royal MS. 19 B XV and B.M. Harl. MS. 2891. B.M. Egerton MS. 1894 (published by M. R. James, Roxburghe Club, 1921) seems to be half-French and half-English.

[3] Lethaby in *Walpole Soc.* i (1911–12), 71.   [4] Riley, 557.

[5] The whole subject has been well studied in the magnificent volume of Mrs. A. G. J. Christie.

tion, a long history behind it. Like illumination it had begun in the cloister; to embroider was as natural an occupation for a nun as to write and draw was for a monk. Like illumination it was passing into the hands of lay craftsmen, though as late as 1314 an injunction had to be sent to the nuns of Nunkeeling, Yedingham, and Wykeham in Yorkshire forbidding them from absenting themselves from divine service *propter occupacionem operis de serico*.[1] Embroidery had long been dealt with by lay middlemen;[2] a quit-claim exists, for example, made by Thomas Gaydichon of Lucca to Alice Darcy of London for his share in a piece of cloth embroidered by her.[3]

Like illumination, embroidery design, which was doubtless drawn by other artists than those who executed the embroidery, was shifting from a series of geometrical panels[4] to freer compositions, often set under architectural arcades and canopies. Such familiar psalter compositions as the tree of Jesse had by 1295 already appeared on copes;[5] one of a few years later still survives in part.[6] Such a panel as that in the British Museum with scenes of Christ's Commission to the Apostles and Betrayal under an ogival arcade, has an evident likeness with such illuminations as those of the Lisle Psalter.

Copes of this English embroidery, worked in split-stitch on grounds of dark silk, were not only used in English churches[7] but were also exported to France and Italy. They were recognized, indeed, as the most splendid and appropriate present that England could offer to a foreign prelate. Pope Clement V[8] had at least three English embroidered copes that were probably gifts; Pope John XXII received three, one from Queen Isabella, one from the

---

[1] Power, 255. A hundred years ago Lord Willoughby de Broke owned a panel of embroidery signed DOM'NA JOHANNA DE BEVERLEI MONACA ME FECIT. *Arch. Journ.* vi (1849), 290.   [2] Saunders, 226.

[3] Riley, 52.   [4] e.g. the Syon and Ascoli copes.

[5] Inventory of St. Paul's Cathedral, Dugdale, 316.

[6] Cf. an orphrey of *c.* 1300 with the same subject once in the Spitzer collection, Cat. *Étoffes*, Pl. III.

[7] e.g. in 1307 the archdeacon of Lichfield bought an embroidered choir cope from Alexander le Settere of London (Riley, 60) and in 1308 the city of London presented an embroidered cope to the bishop of Worcester.

[8] 1305–16. See Christie, 3.

archbishop of Canterbury, and one from John Hotham, bishop of Ely.

Pope Clement V gave two of his English copes to the cathedral of Saint-Bertrand-de-Comminges in 1309; they are still preserved in the sacristy. One represents the story of the Virgin;[1] the other is embroidered with scenes of the Passion of Christ divided by medallions of birds, remarkably like those in the margins of the Ormesby Psalter. The interstices are filled by little figures of dogs, foxes, lions, sheep, rabbits, and squirrels, that recall alike the beasts of the marginal decorations and those of which Chaucer sings in the *Parlement of Foules*:

> *On every bough the briddes herde I singe,*
> *With voys of aungel in hir armonye,*
> *Some besyd hem hir briddes forth to bringe;*
> *The litel conyes to hir pley gunne hye,*
> *And further al aboute I gan espye*
> *The dredful roo, the buk, the hert and hinde,*
> *Squerels, and bestes smale of gentil kinde.*

The Pienza cope is very little later in date.[2] It is arranged in three tiers of arcading; in the lowest are figures of saints, with apostles in the spandrels of the arcade; in the next are scenes from the life of the Virgin, with her ancestors in the spandrels, and in the uppermost are the Annunciation, and the Death, Assumption, and Coronation of the Virgin, with censing angels above. The orphreys are embroidered with medallions of pelican, cock, peacock, falcon, hawk, heron, partridge, pheasant, thrush, finches, magpies, and a pair of swallows.

The finest cope of all has an unknown history; it is now in the Museo Civico of Bologna. It is, perhaps, the most architecturally conceived of all the copes, but its architecture is thought of in terms of illumination. The two tiers of arcading are all filled with

---

[1] Cf. the 1404 inventory of Philippe le Hardi of Burgundy. 'Une chappe a prelat de brodeure d'or a plusieurs ystoires de la vie Nostre Dame en tabernacles, par maniere de lasseure ou est escrit Ave Maria, et en la bordeure dessoutz est escript Salve Regina . . . et dist on qu'elle fut faicte en Angleterre.' Dehaisnes, ii. 835.

[2] M. Morris, *Burl. Mag.* vii (1905), 54. She suggests it may have been that given to the pope by the queen of England in 1317. It was left to Pienza by Pius II in 1410.

scenes of the life of Christ, except for one that shows the martyrdom of St. Thomas of Canterbury. Between the arcades run
friezes with medallions of strongly characterized heads;[1] in the
spandrels a great choir of angels play instruments of music.[2]

All these embroideries are near to the Lisle Psalter in the style
of their figures and their architecture, and to the Ormesby Psalter
in their birds and beasts. A long velvet band[3] embroidered with
scenes from the childhood of Christ (Pl. 8 a) is closer to the Tickhill
Psalter in its style. In the spandrels are shields of Bardolf and the
Poyntz family of Gloucestershire. A similar use of shields of arms—
recalling those in the Bardolf-Vaux Hours—occurs on a splendid
cross-shaped orphrey from a chasuble with scenes of the Crucifixion culminating in a representation of the risen Christ.

By a fortunate chance a pattern book used by a group of the
artists who designed these copes still survives.[4] It appears to be
by as many as eight hands, to have been begun soon after 1280,
and to have continued in use until at least the end of the fourteenth
century, facts which in themselves are evidence of the continuity
of workshop tradition. It includes some excellent sketches of birds
and beasts, some of which recur in the embroideries; there is the
landrail and the tabby cat of the Comminges cope, the long-tailed
parakeet of the Butler-Bowden cope, and the rabbit bolting into
its burrow that appears on the panel in the British Museum.[5]

What is particularly interesting is that the pattern book might
equally well have been used for certain fourteenth-century manuscripts,[6] while certain designs, such as brocade-like patterns for

---

[1] Cf. the slightly later psalters, p. 41. Similar heads occur on a cope belonging to
Señor Luis Planidura, Christie, Pl. LXVII.

[2] With it may be compared another cope in St. John Lateran with zones of arcading
and angel musicians; the Butler-Bowden cope, and the cope of Cardinal Carrillo de
Albernoz at Toledo, arcaded with large birds instead of angels; a cope in the museum
of Vich, Catalonia; and that at Skå in Sweden, with scenes of the Passion under
canopies. See Lindblom in *Burl. Mag.* x (1915), 178.

[3] Acquired by the Victoria and Albert Museum in 1936 from the Roman Catholic
community of Marnhull, Dorset.

[4] Magdalene College, Cambridge, MS. 1916. Published by Dr. M. R. James in
Walpole Soc. xiii. 1. Manuscript illuminations may occasionally have served as models;
a dragon in Bodleian MS. 614 has been pricked for pouncing.

[5] See Christie, 11.   [6] e.g. the Lovel lectionary, see p. 98.

gesso backgrounds and mouldings for frames, suggest that it was also used by painters of retables and panel pictures. It reminds us that the crafts of illumination and embroidery design did not stand alone, though they were the most characteristic decorative arts of the years round 1300. They find parallels in the minor sculptures of the cathedrals: in the corbels of Exeter; in the misericords of Wells; in the bosses of the cloister at Norwich, and of the vault of Exeter; and behind them lies the tradition of paintings on a small scale that are now lost to us.

II

THE DECORATED STYLE IN ARCHITECTURE

THE death of Edward I in 1307 marks a real change in the colour of English history. His personal ascendancy had continued to the last: his death was the signal for reaction and relaxation. Everything was suddenly on a smaller and more personal scale. The change is as great as that between the France of Saint Louis and the France of Philippe le Bel; in both countries the new era was marked by the growth of a court that had its influence on artistic as well as on constitutional history.

The fundamentals of the new Decorated Style were a purely decorative use of architectural forms, a strong three-dimensional sense, a love of graceful and flowing line, and of amusing and sometimes irrelevant detail. These last were exactly congenial to the England of Edward II. The new king, handsome, wayward, and young, had long been out of sympathy with his father's austere preoccupation with affairs of state. The second Edward found his pleasures in country pursuits, whether in racing or hunting or in the labourer's tasks of hedging and ditching. In the evenings he worked at his own anvil, learning the techniques of work in metal. He was a man of his hands, not of his head. The main source of his troubles lay in his obstinate devotion to his friends: friends chosen with as little regard for the dignity of rank as were his favourite pursuits. His court, where manners and costume assumed a new quality at once soft and fantastical, reflects the exuberance of a release from strict control. More than half French and a quarter Spanish, he had a natural taste for elegance and luxury that was intensified by his marriage to a daughter of Philippe le Bel. Nothing but his inherent want of purpose prevented him from being as closely identified with the new style as Louis XIV is with the art of Versailles. Even wealth was not lacking: on his accession in 1307 he seized no less than fifty thousand pounds in silver, besides gold and jewels, that had been deposited with the Templars. Yet no great work of building is associated with his name; and of surviving work we can ascribe little to his direct patronage but the sedilia paintings at Westminster.[1]

His reign, however, is remarkable for the building carried on in many of the great churches of England, in cathedrals such as York and Worcester, in Benedictine cathedrals such as Norwich and Ely, and in cathedrals of secular canons such as Exeter, Lichfield, Wells, and St. Paul's.

It was, indeed, an age when a king who was not interested in affairs allowed a great amount of power and wealth to slip into the hands of ecclesiastics who were both statesmen and adminis-trators. The religious houses had received a considerable shock in 1297 when the king's commissioners visited them to take inventories of their treasures, in case Edward I should need them for his wars in France. They may well have considered that buildings which could not profitably be sequestrated were a better investment than more portable forms of riches. At all events the last fifteen years of Edward I's reign saw the planning of an unusual amount of ecclesiastical building, much of which was carried to its completion in the reign of his son.

At the same time several Orders had passed their prime and no longer had to build: the Gilbertines, for example, have left no important building in Decorated style. Temple Balsall church in Warwickshire, dating from just before the suppression of the Templars in 1312, is remarkable for the fine tracery of its windows, but it is the last church that the Order built in England. The Cluniac houses were under the shadow of sequestration as alien priories, and their priors built little. The Cistercians had built so much in the generations before that their current needs were met, and only the royal foundation of St. Mary's Eastminster falls within our period.

The considerable number of friars' churches that were erected at this time are lost to us. Margaret of France, the second queen of

---

[1] Made in 1308, when Master Thomas of Westminster was the king's painter. They represent Edward the Confessor and another king. See Lethaby in *Walpole Soc.* i (1911–12), 70.

Edward I, began in 1306 the building of the Grey Friars at London, where she was buried: a church that, Weever tells us, held nine alabaster and marble tombs in the choir and innumerable lesser monuments.[1] It followed the French Franciscan plan of two aisled parallelograms separated by a passage. Edward II himself, for once roused from indolence by the beheading of his favourite Piers Gaveston, founded a noviciate house for the Dominicans at King's Langley[2] to enshrine the victim's tomb; little now remains. At the same time a number of Carmelite churches were built, at Plymouth in 1314, at Gloucester little later, at Blakeney in Norfolk in 1321.[3] Stukeley's engraving of the Whitefriars at Gloucester[4] shows a detached bell tower and two equal naves, each with its gable and a great east window: the traditional friars' church beautified by the new style. The London Austin Friars, begun in 1354, continued the Decorated tradition into the second half of the century.

Other fourteenth-century churches were largely built because economic prosperity had brought fresh life to their region.[5] The Channel trade caused those at Winchelsea, Rye, and Deal to be built; the Avon trade, the Bristol churches; the Baltic trade, Boston; the Trent trade, Newark; the Humber trade, Hull, Patrington, and Beverley; and already Lincolnshire and the west of England were profiting by the trade in wool.

The new style began as a style of detail, and brought no change in ground plan into the tradition of church building. The ogival arch which was its keynote could not be used for structural arches of any great span,[6] and did not hold within it the germ of any new vaulting system. Yet gradually many of the essentials of Gothic construction came to be modified under the influence of the new style: vaulting, tracery, and bay design.

Vaulting was not structurally changed, but became frankly

---

[1] Weever, 388. 'All of which were pulled downe, taken away and sold for fiftie pounds or thereabouts by Sir Martin Bows, Maior of London, an. 1545.' The church was built under the supervision of Master Walter of Hereford. Harvey, *Yevele*, 4.   [2] Jarrett, 5.   [3] Weever, 813.
[4] i, Fig. 32.   [5] See Prior, *Eight Chapters*, 110.
[6] It is exceptionally used for windows by a school of masons in Northamptonshire who seem also to have worked at Llandaff.

decorative in intention. The use in England of wooden vaults imitating those of stone, but freed from many problems of weight and stress, naturally fostered the view of ribs and bosses as decorative rather than purely structural elements. As early as 1240 the transept of Lichfield received a sham stone vault in wood, later replaced by one in stone; and the wooden groining of the choir of St. Albans dates from not long after 1280. The roofs of York and Selby choirs, erected in the years round about 1340, show a many-ribbed vault with heavy bosses that expressed in an exaggerated form a style achieved with difficulty in stone. Already, too, the vault of Lincoln nave had shown a use of tiercerons that had in it the germ of the decorative vault. The thirteenth-century development of chapter-houses with a central column likewise helped to break up the traditional vaulting bay-systems and to develop the use of a multiplicity of ribs.

Meanwhile a different system was being worked out from structural developments in stone. The vault set up at Pershore abbey after the fire of 1288 is a landmark (Pl. 9 a); it has a peculiar beauty both in its linear pattern and in the play of light upon its varied facets. From this to the use of liernes to form a tracery vault is an easy step. It can be followed in Malmesbury nave (Pl. 9 b) and Tewkesbury presbytery, in Bishop Gower's work at St. David's, and in lesser churches.

The multiple vaulting ribs were naturally married to a pier of complex design. Exeter cathedral is the classic instance of a pier and archmould of extraordinary complexity. In the south transept at Gloucester the nine ribs of the vaulting are reflected in nine 'beads' in the wall pier. After about 1380 this complexity was exchanged for a simpler scheme of four semicircular columns set widely apart and separated by a moulded member, as at Thaxted, Howden, and St. Mary's, Beverley, and in many parish churches.[1]

The English triforium, that had played a large part in the development of the earlier Gothic style, was in some buildings abruptly superseded. The simple arcaded triforium found at Beverley about 1229 was at Exeter soon after 1280 treated as a blind arcade with

---

[1] At Holbeach in Lincolnshire the half-columns of the quadrilobe are stressed by being edged, centred, and collared by little rounded beadings.

a balustrade of pierced quatrefoils above, while in the nave of
York it became the lower story of the great traceried window,
keeping its canopied heads to crown its lights and divided from the
main window by a transom pierced like the Exeter balustrades.
At Guisborough a few years later these canopies and transom are
further merged into the window tracery. In the choir of Selby
about 1340 the acceptance of the two-story scheme is complete,
and all that remains of the triforium is a low pierced balustrade
beneath the great window.

This amalgamation lessened the previously existing analogy
between the window tracery and the architectural tracery of the
triforium, and made the many-mullioned windows the key of the
structure and its chief decoration. Consequently the development
of window tracery was free to follow less architectural and more
decorative lines.

Instead of 'geometrical' tracery, in which circles and other
figures are complete, linked only where they touch tangentially,
a new flowing curvilinear style was achieved by omitting parts
of the circle and merging the lines into ogival forms. The fine
east window at Mildenhall, dating from just before 1300, has its
seven main lights surmounted by a complex tracery of this kind
with a central mandorla for the figure of Christ in Majesty.

At the same time the area of the tracery was greatly increased,
so that in many fourteenth-century windows its spread covers
at least half of the field. The geometric 'wheel' in the head of
the window was merged into the curves of the sub-arches to
create the great ogees that appear at Selby, at Howden, and in
Lincolnshire, and most beautifully of all in the west window
at York (Pl. 20) and its northern derivatives. About 1340 this
developed into a foliate tracery such as is found at Patrington,
Beverley, and York.[1] The central light, characteristic of the earlier
English work, was commonly renounced; instead, the tracery
radiates from a central mullion like the branches of a tree from its
trunk.

In southern and western England the tendency was rather

[1] And less often in the midlands, e.g. at Wymington, Beds., and Castle Ashby,
Northants.

towards a reticulated type of ogival tracery, a delicately cusped network derived from the multiplication of the circles in the head of the Early English window. Early examples occur in Tintern chapter-house and in the north transept of Hereford; the most typical are the windows of Wells choir. The comparatively simple lines of such tracery were commonly enriched with foiling, as in the windows of Bishop Lucy's chapel at Oxford (about 1320), the Hereford chapels, and the windows of Malmesbury clerestory.

Such reticulated tracery, primarily designed as *cloisons* for glass, was applied to cloister arcades (notably at Westminster[1]) and even to vaulting. It only needed foiling to be applied to a lierne vault, as at Bristol and Sherborne, for the analogy with reticulated tracery to be evident. Similarly a graceful foiled tracery was applied to pierced balustrades to form the wave parapets that were to be one of the most enduring features of the style.

While it is broadly true to say that foliate tracery originated in the north, and reticulated in the west, nothing is more striking in the Decorated style than the freedom with which different systems of tracery are combined in the same edifice. At Olney in Buckinghamshire the south side of the chancel, dating from about 1330, has three windows each with a different kind of tracery: one is foliate, one wheel-headed, and one reticulated. At Lawford in Essex the four splendid windows of the south side of the nave are no less individual. A style of which the origins lay in pure ornament could permit of variety even in fenestration.

The first breath of the new style may perhaps be felt in the chapter-house at Wells, begun about 1290 and finished in 1319. Its doorway is purely geometric in line, and yet a certain plasticity of feeling heralds the new style. The incredible palm-tree vault of the central pier (Pl. 10) strikes an entirely new note; architectural form here passes into something far closer to natural growth. The same feeling inspires the capital of the shaft, which has a wholly different feeling for leafage than that shown in the capitals of the nave. A curious creative gaiety pervades the room; most of the

---

[1] The east cloister was designed by the master mason Walter de la Bole, the west and north by John Palterton. The new work was begun in 1344. See Rackham in *Arch. Journ.* lxvii (1910), 259.

corbel heads are smiling or laughing.[1] The polygonal Lady chapel, begun soon after 1300 and finished in 1326, applies the multiple palm-vaulting to a more complex space, with effects of extreme elegance and grace (Pl. 12).

The rebuilding of Exeter cathedral, which had been envisaged by Bishop Peter Turvil, owed something of its execution to the work at Wells. It was initiated under Thomas de Bitton, who was promoted from the deanery of Wells to the see of Exeter in 1292. The inspiration of his work, however, seems to be drawn less from Wells than from Pershore, of which the choir had been reconstructed after a fire in 1288. The marriage of piers of multiple and varied mouldings (here sixteenfold) with a strongly ribbed vault of complex design is the same in both. At Exeter, however, the vault does not form a starry web as at Pershore, but springs out like a palm in the manner of Wells, in a lovely multiplicity that is a denial of pure structure (Pl. 11). A balustraded triforium gives a rather unexpected emphasis on horizontal line. Some of the windows of the choir already display tracery that is passing from geometric forms into a more flowing line. The design, like that of some work in Normandy, depends upon architectural multiplicity for its effect, but it does not exclude sculptural detail. The roofs, including those of chapels and porches, have no less than 374 bosses and 147 half-bosses, all carved between 1301 and 1338.[2] In the fifteen years of his episcopate Thomas de Bitton completed the whole of the presbytery and aisles and began the transformation of the Norman choir. His successor, Walter Stapeldon, prosecuted the work during his episcopate, which lasted from 1308 to 1326. In his time the church was ready to receive its fittings: the throne in 1312, the reredos, sedilia, and pulpit in 1316–17, and the choir-screen in the years immediately following.

The throne (Pl. 13) and sedilia show the airy quality of the tomb canopies applied to less incidental work, and treated in a new way in a tiered structure. The sedilia have front and back finials and richly ornamented pinnacles. From among these springs a second story of

---

[1] See Prior and Gardner, Fig. 444.

[2] Bishop and Prideaux, *Building of Exeter Cathedral,* give an admirable account of the way the work was carried on and of the carvers employed.

extremely slender arcading surmounted by an airy pyramid of five tiers of pinnacles held together by buttress-like struts. The great oak throne has the same system, with an added story and additional links. A curious and interesting contrast is evident in the two constructions. Both use tiers of canopied arcading, and both use the ogival line in their arcades; but while the stone sedilia treats it in one plane in the usual fashion, the wooden throne thrusts out the line to form a 'nodding arch'. This curious denial of the existence of any plane in the design is one of the most remarkable architectural inventions of the fourteenth century; it is the hall-mark of an English Gothic that can only be compared with eighteenth-century *rococo* in its fluid sense of architecture as a sculptural creation in three dimensions.

Both the throne and the sedilia have foliage sculpture of remarkable quality; but the best expression of it at Exeter is in the choir-screen begun in 1318. The gracefully cusped spandrels are filled with bryony foliage of the greatest accomplishment. The upper arcade was originally filled with figure sculpture: the side altars under the screen had statues of the Virgin and St. Peter. When the high altar had been completed by Bishop Grandisson in 1328, with a silver retable and a reredos with nearly fifty statues, he could well write to Pope John XXII: 'Ecclesia Exoniensis . . . mirabili super ceteras in genere suo Anglie vel Francie, si perficiatur, pulchritudine renitebit.'[1]

The history of the expansion of the style in the west is now an imperfect and broken record. Of the great chapter-house at Evesham, which Abbot John de Brockhampton built in 1316,[2] nothing remains but a battered doorway with figures under niches following the line of the arch in the French manner. Little is left of the abbey of Tavistock, largely rebuilt under Abbot Robert de Champeaux at some time near 1320. The towers at Wells, which date from 1320, have a new lightness, but seem to be politely conscious of the nearness of the nave. At Salisbury, however, where the tower and spire were erected in the same year under the supervision of Master Richard of

[1] Oliver, 129. When he wrote, the nave was half finished.
[2] He also built cloister, library, great hall, abbot's hall, and kitchen. Dugdale, ii. 6.

Farleigh,[1] they dominate the whole. It is they, and they alone, that add a crowning touch of poetry to what would otherwise be a remarkably prosaic building. They are a piece of pure architectural luxury; the tower did not house the bells, nor serve any purpose but that of beauty.

In the west of England the regular lines of globular buds known as ball-flower soon became one of the characteristic motives of the Decorated style.[2] The church of Badgworth in Gloucestershire, consecrated in 1315, has the cornice under the roof and the jambs of the windows and door richly studded with it; at Gloucester cathedral itself the south aisle, built between 1318 and 1325, is all budded over within and without with the same ornament. An even more filigree richness is achieved by the use of ball-flower ornament at Ledbury, where the rather hesitant Gloucester tracery is splendidly developed into quatrefoils; at Leominster[3] ball-flower is applied to a system of roses, and it blossoms all over the square central tower of Hereford that dates from the tower-building year of 1320.[4] At Gloucester the effect of the ball-flower is enhanced by the elaboration of the buttresses between the windows; a gabled base supports a richly cusped and gabled pinnacle, set cross-wise, with two pedestals for statues. Above it rises a canopied niche. Such statues as remain, battered though they are, are remarkable for their naturalistic draperies.

In the comparatively small church of Sparsholt in Berkshire, dating from about 1330, all the hall-marks of the style are to be met, including a wave-moulding parapet, reticulated tracery, and corner buttresses set diagonally. A like integration is achieved in the parish church of Bishopstone in Wiltshire.[5] At Oxford

[1] Richard of Farleigh was engaged at the same time on work at Bath and Reading and went from one to the other (Prior, 429); the transition is being made from the *magister operis* to the architect.

[2] It is also characteristic of a small group of midland churches: Raunds, Ringstead, and Byfield, Northants., and North Luffenham, Rutland. Other Decorated churches in the area are Stoke Bruern and Harleston, Northants.

[3] A Benedictine priory dependent on Reading abbey.

[4] Another west country instance is Ludlow.

[5] The only hesitation here is in the east window, which is planned as two small windows with foliate tracery set side by side with no important development in the head.

cathedral, especially in the Latin chapel, finished by 1355, there is a number of fine reticulated windows; and in the spire of St. Mary's a monument that has achieved a merited fame.[1]

At Winchester work of peculiar beauty was wrought in the arcade at the back of the choir enclosure (Pl. 14). Nowhere is the contrast between the straight lines of the gables and the complex ogival line of the arches, conceived in three dimensions, more elegantly exploited; the gables have crockets and finials of fantastic richness, the arcade, mouldings that by their very simplicity mark the subtle transitions of the curving line.[2] Here is decorative art of infinite accomplishment and sophistication.

In London and its neighbourhood the emphasis lay rather on the ornamental redundancies of the new style than on development of tracery. Hollar's drawing of the old St. Paul's depicts a rose window of great beauty in the flat east end; its tracery, rather French in style, shows the beginning of foliate feeling, though it presumably dates from about 1285. At Canterbury the screen set up by Prior d'Estria in 1306[3] has the ogival line applied to the five gables that surmount it. A flowing tracery fills these gables, and in the arcades below the tracery is arranged in quatrefoil reticulations. The Lady chapel of St. Albans, dating from about 1310, combines reticulated and foliate tracery (and a very early instance of flowing tracery) with sculptured decoration of an unusual kind. Figures of English saints in niches are set on the mullion of the window and in the embrasure; the hood moulds are sculptured with naturalistic foliage.[4] The same marriage between sculpture and window tracery is effected even more completely on the well-known windows at Dorchester in Oxfordshire. The first shows the tree of Jesse with the stem and branches formed by the tracery, with sculptured figures standing upon them to complement those that appear in the lights. The second window is almost wholly

---

[1] It dates from about 1300; for details of the sculpture see Prior and Gardner, Fig. 376.

[2] They are notably better designed, though no more rich, than the contemporary sedilia at Dorchester, Oxfordshire.

[3] Dart, 13. Evans, *Pattern*, Fig. 42.

[4] Cf. the windows at Maldon in Essex, which have a traceried blind arcade between them and a continuous arcaded dado below.

filled with reticulated tracery, with sculptured groups of Passion scenes at the intersections.

Farther to the east, in the south aisle at Waltham abbey, the chapel, which can be dated to 1318, shows the flowing line gradually creeping into the tracery. In the Lady chapel, of about 1330, a wholly new note is struck by the square-set quatrefoils of the tracery and by the light arcade with soufflets on the spandrels that is set in front of it.[1] The contemporary east window of Tilty priory, not far away, is equally original; nowhere is a rose more elegantly welded into a flowing scheme (Fig. 1).

FIG. 1. *Tilty, Essex.*
The Chancel Window, c. 1330

In Norfolk the new style first appears in the less structural work. At Norwich the cloister begun in 1297[2] (Fig. 2) has its vault planned something after the Wells fashion. The prior's door is of rather startling originality. A lace-like arcade, alternately of gables and ogival arches, heavily crocketed, radiates across the voussoirs, its niches filled with saints and angels standing round a seated Christ (Pl. 15).

At Lincoln the main work of construction was already accomplished; the only large-scale expression of the new style is in the central tower (Pl. 17) begun in 1307 under the direction of Richard of Stowe, who had designed the Lincoln Eleanor cross.[3] The Decorated style, however, is admirably represented by a group of churches in Lincolnshire, many of which depended on religious houses. Heckington[4] and Sleaford are remarkable for the abun-

[1] Prior, Fig. 271.
[2] The treatment may be compared with that in the slightly later south aisle of Little Dunmow, added to the Augustinian priory about 1370.
[3] See Harvey in *Journ. Brit. Arch. Ass.* vi (1941), 20.
[4] After 1310 Heckington belonged to the great family of Beaumont, but after

dance of their exterior sculpture[1] and Sleaford for the beauty and variety of its flowing tracery; Swineshead for the fine architectural

FIG. 2. *Norwich Cathedral—Cloisters, 1297–1325*

quality of its nave arcade and for the consistent use of reticulated tracery in its windows.[2] Here, too, some remarkably fine towers

1345 to the abbey of Bardney. The choir was built by the vicar, Richard de Potesgrove.

[1] Heckington has 31 niches for statues, 80 carved corbels, and 198 gargoyles.

[2] Others are Gaddesby, Billingborough, Claypole, Ewerby, Donington (the nave, which dates from 1351, has crenellated capitals), Haconby (about 1325), Helpringham, Holbeach, Leadenham, Leake, Leverton, Pickforth, Swaton, Brant Broughton, and Newark.

were erected: Donington, Brant Broughton, and Grantham in Lincolnshire; Ketton in Rutland; and Newark in Nottinghamshire are worthy of mention.[1] None are buildings absolutely of the first class, yet they are not only picturesque but also significant in indicating the spread of the new style.

In the great Benedictine house of Ely, however, work of the first importance was initiated in 1321, when the Lady chapel was begun.[2] (Pl. 16.) Here for the first time a considerable architectural ensemble is dominated by the contrast between the angular gable and the nodding arch. This three-dimensional arcade is used not only for the sedilia that run all round the chapel but also for the niches on the pilasters between the windows. The building is the largest Lady chapel in England and has the widest span of vaulting: vaulting which springs out like that of Exeter to merge into a starry net-work of tracery. This simplicity of plan finds ample compensation; few architectural rectangles can be more richly decorated. The elaborate arcading is but the frame for a life of the Virgin told in sculpture: sculpture that when it was undamaged[3] and still coloured must have closely resembled an illuminated manuscript.[4] The group in the middle niche of the east end completed the whole with a larger composition of the Coronation of the Virgin. The foliage is for the most part rather seaweedy,[5] but one gable on the south side is filled with hops and one on the north with chestnuts.

The Lady chapel had only just been begun when disaster befell the main fabric of the abbey. The central tower fell in February 1322, and Prior Alan of Walsingham at once set about restoring the damage.[6] The tower was rebuilt as an octagonal lantern (Pl. 18)

---

[1] For a detailed study of fourteenth-century spires see Prior, 372 et seqq.; for towers and spires, Bond, ii. 873 et seqq.

[2] Dugdale, *Monasticon*, i. 464. It was finished in 1349, thanks to the munificence of Bishop Simon de Montacute. The east window dates from 1373.

[3] Every head was knocked off at the Reformation.

[4] See M. R. James, *Sculptures of Lady Chapel at Ely*. The story is largely drawn from the apocryphal gospels: the life and death of the Virgin from the *Protevangelium*, the infancy of Christ from the *Gospel of Thomas* and the *Miracles*. Dr. James (8) established a definite similarity of subject between the sculptures and the Carew-Poyntz Hours (Fitzwilliam Museum), Queen Mary's Psalter (see p. 15), and a Dominican MS., Brit. Mus. Royal MS. 10 E IV. [5] See, e.g., *Pattern*, Fig. 95.

[6] It was finished in 1342: the stone work took six years and the wood fourteen.

that fits into the crossing by the aid of four windows with flowing tracery. The interior capitals which support the elegant wooden ceiling are carved with the story of St. Etheldreda.[1] The result is remarkable for its apparent inevitability.

The choir had been seriously damaged when the tower fell; some of the bays were rebuilt and the north aisle revaulted about 1338, with a complete modernization of the tracery[2] and interior decoration. Rich though it is, the effect is disappointing; the Decorated style had by now achieved a scale and proportion of its own and could not satisfactorily be applied to an earlier structure.

In the north Guisborough, a priory of Austin Canons, had its choir rebuilt soon after a serious fire in 1289. It remains rather archaic in style,[3] with geometrical tracery; but the influence of the new style is seen in the merging of the triforium and its balustrade into the window scheme, and in the ornamental treatment of the gabled square buttresses, with a traceried blind window in the head and a niche for a statue in the foot. Bishop Walter de Langton brought something of the elegance of the new style to the presbytery and Lady chapel of his cathedral at Lichfield. The Lady chapel, which was begun in 1310, was still incomplete when he died in 1321 and was finished with the aid of his bequests.[4] It (Pl. 19) clearly shows the influence of Exeter; it gains by the omission of the triforium arcade. The exterior is notable for the two superposed niches, each occupied by a statue, that adorn the buttresses, and for the rather metallic clarity of the design.

At Selby the work done between 1300 and 1340 also shows a carefully composed external buttress system, with crocketed gables. The open parapets are adorned with wave mouldings with little figures above. To contrast its east front with that of Ripon, dating

[1] See Prior and Gardner, Fig. 65.

[2] At St. Albans, however, where the eastern half of the nave was rebuilt by Henry Wy, the design follows that of the earlier western half. *Roy. Com. Hist. Mon.* 181.

[3] At Howden, again, the fine west front is predominantly archaic in its inspiration; its pinnacled turrets give it breadth and solidity but are not essentials of the design. Even in the choir screen at Southwell, erected between 1335 and 1340, there is no Decorated element except the ogival line of the cusping.

[4] The master mason was William de Ramsay. Harvey, *Yevele,* 13.

from just before 1300, is to see what richness and solidity the gabled and pinnacled buttress can give.[1]

The work at York Minster was initiated in 1290, when the chapter-house was begun. This belongs altogether to the Early English style; its geometrical tracery is richly cusped, its detail is elaborately sculptured, yet there is nothing that could be called Decorated unless it be the bowed plan of the sedilia, and the swaying pose and notably rich drapery of the Virgin of the doorway.[2]

The same slightly archaic quality reigns in the nave, of which the first stone was laid in 1291. The varied planes of the triforium show a new plastic sense, but the style is still strongly geometrical. The reigning archbishop, John le Romeyn, a man of Italian descent, had been to Rome to receive his pallium and had travelled to Aragon with Edward I; yet his nave is entirely English and notably lacking in any evidence of Latin taste.

The work was paid for by all sorts of voluntary taxes on the prebends, by the sale of indulgences, and by great personal gifts, especially by the archbishops and by the families of Vavasour, Percy, and Scrope. The nave walls were finished by 1324; the west front was erected by 1338. A stone vault was planned, but was not executed because in 1344 a quarrel arose and a long strike paralysed the work. In 1346 the nave was summarily completed by a wooden roof.[3]

It is in the west front that the new style finds magnificent expression (Pls. 20, 21); original[4] and beautiful both within and without, it is the only English façade that can challenge even if it can hardly stand comparison with Rheims. The pointed gables that appear in every stage of its canopy work set off the flowing line of its window tracery; the occasional use of the nodding arch in the

[1] Gardner, *Handbook*, Fig. 244; Prior and Gardner, Fig. 367. It was finished slowly; the parapet is carved with the bears of Francis Fitzurse, who became treasurer of the Minster in 1337. Raine, *Fabric Rolls*, xiv.

[2] Within, the corbels of the vaulting are formed as finials to canopies over statues in the spandrels of the arches.

[3] This was destroyed in the fire of 1840, but is reproduced as nearly as may be in the existing roof. Some interesting later fabric rolls have been published by Raine.

[4] Though it owes something to the late thirteenth-century façade of St. Mary's abbey, York.

upper tiers of niches gives depth to the whole. It is rare to find so
great a wall equally beautiful within and without. Originally the
interior mullion wall was completed by much statuary. In the gable
over the west doorway was a seated figure of Archbishop Melton
holding a representation of the church, with two knightly benefactors on either side; a statue of St. Peter stood below and the three
deep niches above held statues of the Virgin and St. John on either
side of a crucifixion. The spandrels were filled with sculptures of
Samson, David, and Jacob wrestling with the angel: scenes glorifying fortitude and strength. The six niches to either side held statues
of the apostles; the niches in the upper tiers those of saints.[1] A similar system of tiers of canopied niches is applied to the glass of the
nave and aisle windows, dating from 1306 and later.

It is not always recognized how long the Decorated style continued in use, especially in the east and north. It is easy to say that
its knell was sounded beside the plague-pits of 1349, but it is not
true. Even in the west it is not hard to find survivals, as in the
ogival framing of the great west window of Shrewsbury tower,
or in the whole building of Chaddesley Corbet church in
Worcestershire. In woodwork, too, the style lingered on; a screen
as late as that of Totnes, set up in 1459 (Pl. 23), is wholly of the
Decorated style in its ogival arcades, its recusped cuspings, and its
superposed tiers of arches with nothing to break their vertical line.[2]

In the north the great east window of Carlisle, erected between
1363 and 1382, is Decorated in style and not even particularly advanced. At Durham the reredos, given by John, Lord Neville of
Raby, in 1379,[3] has the same sort of tiered and spiring canopy work
as the Exeter sedilia;[4] the loss of its 107 alabaster statuettes brings
out the essential similarity of line.

The most striking survivals, however, are in East Anglia, which
received the style late and cherished it long. A perfect instance
is the slipper chapel at Houghton-le-Dale, where the pilgrims to

[1] Browne, i. 139.
[2] Cf. the simpler wooden screen at Southacre, Norfolk. Decorated tracery in iron-
work survived as late as the iron gates given by Edward IV to the lower chapel of
St. George's, Windsor.
[3] See Cox, *Chancel of English Church*, 99, for a good drawing of what remains.
[4] So, too, has the throne set up by Bishop Hatfield soon after 1362.

Walsingham left their shoes to proceed barefoot to the shrine. The west front has deep ogival-headed niches on either side of a great window filled with foliate tracery; the gable is set off by two niched pinnacles facing north and south. There are no battlements, but a quatrefoiled balustrade. Only a certain rigidity and squareness of proportion betrays the late date of a perfect Decorated ensemble. Another instance is St. Botolph's church, Boston, which dates from the second half of the fourteenth century. But for its quadrangular outline it is of pure Decorated style, but a Decorated that is a little thin and rigid. The sap no longer rises; the bare and rigid beauty of Autumn has come. Yet none could deny dignity or grace to the nave with its elegant tracery, or to the porch with its rich cusping[1] (Pl. 22). North Walsham, again, is a Decorated church dating from 1381, with the peculiarity that the chancel is the same breadth and height as the nave, from which it is divided only by a screen. Wigenhale is another Norfolk church in a belated Decorated style. Walpole St. Peter is yet more remarkable in that it was rebuilt between 1423 and 1425 in a fine and ornate version of Decorated architecture. Decorated elements, indeed, continued to enrich the English late Gothic tradition until alien influences brought it to an end.

[1] The cusping may be compared with that on the stall work of Norwich cathedral, though this is notably less beautiful.

III

DECORATED ART

*B*ABUINARE, we are told,[1] meant in the middle ages to paint marginal figures in manuscripts; and Chaucer sums up the decoration of his day as

> *subtil compassinges . . .*
> *Babewinnes and pinacles,*
> *Imageries and tabernacles . . .*[2]

The connexion with the Italian *babuino*—baboon—is obvious; in the fourteenth century monkeys were imported from Italy to serve as pets. One of the ladies who figure as mourners on the tomb of Philippa of Hainault carries a little one attached to her girdle by a chain. Artistic 'babwyneries'—as Wyclif calls them[3]—are no more strictly confined to monkeys than are the *singeries* of the eighteenth century. A lady's girdle (that now forms part of William of Wykeham's mitre) is set with enamels with monkeys walking on all fours and blowing horns, hares, stags, and dogs, and the same variety will be found in the manuscripts. More significantly, monkeys sometimes appear in schemes where one would not expect them: the window which Richard Tunnoc gave to York Minster soon after 1320 has a border of monkeys playing wind-instruments, and a corbel of the same date at Dorchester has a monkey blowing a horn beside the crouching figures of monks with which it is carved (Pl. 24 *a*). Queen Isabella had in her chapel cushions worked with monkeys and butterflies,[4] and Westminster abbey albs embroidered with golden vines on which 'babewyns' were fighting with axes.[5]

In general, however, we may take babewyns to be grotesques, of whatever subject. It is a measure of the importance of such

[1] Daunon, *Hist. Lit.* xvi. 39; *O.E.D.*
[2] *Hous of Fame*, iii. 1186, Skeat, iii. 36; written *c.* 1384. *Compas* is the contemporary word for a quatrefoil. [3] *Works*, i (1880), 8; *O.E.D.*
[4] Palgrave, iii. 245. [5] Legg in *Arch.* lii (1888), 249.

ornament in the early fourteenth century that it achieved a
name.[1]

The dawn of a style is apt to be marked by a few unusual works
of exceptional quality that are succeeded by a greater quantity of
work in which the characteristics of the style are more strongly
marked but less exquisitely expressed. Thus the Ormesby Psalter
is succeeded by a number of works in which its characteristics are
exaggerated, with an increase in technical skill rather than in artistic
achievement. The moment of creation has passed into an epoch
of *genre*.

Such a psalter as Queen Mary's still has a lengthy series of Old
and New Testament illustrations, but most of the next series of
manuscripts have only a few full-page illustrations. There is often
a Crucifixion and a Virgin and Child; *Salvum me fac* has David
praying for help; *Cantate Deo* a choir of monks singing; and *Dixit
Dominus* a representation of the Trinity. All the interest, however,
has shifted to the marginal decorations.

The evolution may be said to begin in the Gorleston Psalter,[2]
which may have been written for or at Gorleston, a Norfolk house
of Augustinian friars: the dedication feast of the church is recorded
in the calendar in gold. Later it seems to have belonged to Norwich
cathedral. Its owner, a middle-aged man, is represented from time
to time;[3] one initial shows six friars praying. Sir Sydney Cockerell,
who has made a detailed study of the manuscript, thinks he identifies four painters (of whom one is a much better artist than the
rest) and five figure-draughtsmen. The great Crucifixion page
seems to show the influence of the Italian Trecento in the calm
dignity of its composition[4] and its heavy frame, but the influence
is not that of a manuscript but of a panel picture. The most
characteristic work lies in such minute miniatures as frame the
Beatus page, but much of the charm of the book lies in the babe-
wyneries of the margins. There are monkeys and there are

[1] e.g. six pieces of plate 'taillés de babewyns' in the 1324 inventory of Edward II.
Palgrave, iii. 125.

[2] In the Dyson Perrins collection. See Cockerell, *Gorleston Psalter*; Maunde
Thompson in *Burl. Mag.* xiii (1908), 146; Millar, 5 and Pls. 14–18.

[3] A layman is represented with the shield of Robert Bigod, earl of Norfolk, d. 1306.

[4] See Paecht in *Journ. Warburg and Courtauld Institutes*, vi (1943), 51.

monsters; there is a duck being carried off by a fox and saying
'queck'; but the best of all are the rabbits who conduct a funeral with
all possible ceremony (Pl. 23 *b*). Besides these there are delightful
scenes of everyday life such as had already appeared in the Ormesby
Psalter: the arrest of a cutpurse, a plough, and a blacksmith's forge.
We are reminded that in fourteenth-century England, as in eighteenth-century France, agricultural pursuits were in fashion at the
court of a king who himself pursued them. Edward II enjoyed
farming, smith's work, thatching, and digging,[1] and it does not
seem idle to relate his tastes with the decorations of the psalters.

The Gorleston Psalter, if its exact history is unknown, is certainly a Norfolk manuscript. It does not stand alone; a group of
East Anglian books are the best representatives of English illumination in the years between 1320 and 1340 and the finest before it was
ruined by damp when it was buried for safety in the First World
War is that, now at Douai, given by Thomas, vicar of Gorleston,
to an Abbot John, probably John of Aylsham who was abbot of
Hulme in Norfolk between 1325 and 1346.[2] This, too, seems to
show the influence of panel painting in its larger compositions,
which are set against beautiful backgrounds of punctated gold. The
full-page miniatures of the Virgin and Child and of the Crucifixion
have all the qualities of art on a greater scale. The elaborate and
rather fussy borders, the heraldic ornament, and the general confused
richness of the lesser pages are, however, typically East Anglian.

The next in the series, and the finest now surviving, the Saint
Omer Psalter,[3] seems also to have been the work of the same
school (Pl. 26 *b*). It was probably begun about 1325 for a member
of the family of Saint Omer of Mulbarton in Norfolk, but it was
not finished until it was completed for Humphrey, duke of
Gloucester, in the fifteenth century. The medallion borders are
here the most important part of the decoration; their miniatures
are of incredible minuteness. Babewyns take a secondary place:
the Passion page, for example, has nothing irrelevant in its decoration but a pair of wrestlers at the top. The Beatus page is more
eclectic. The B is duly filled with a Jesse tree and angels, and the

[1] Tout, 9.   [2] Douai, Bibliothèque publique, MS. 171.
[3] B.M. Add. 39810.

main medallions with subjects from Genesis; but the interstices between them have extraordinarily varied decorations. There are quatrefoils of heads; peacocks and waterfowl, rabbits and monkeys, bears and stags, hedgehogs and snails, pigs and unicorns; a knight and his wife kneel in adoration, people fight pick-a-back, climb ladders, cut down trees, and saw logs; all are painted with incredible skill and minuteness. There is much observation and some fancy, but little conscious humour.

The next grand East Anglian psalter is that written about 1340 for Sir Geoffrey Luttrell of Irnham, Lincolnshire.[1] The general style shows a measure of decadence; the babewyns have got the upper hand. A surly monkey cracks his whip as he drives the baggage wagon (Pl. 24 b); there is far more movement and skill in his portrayal than in the more formal picture of four queens in a coach. There are sketches of men sowing and threshing with flails; there are pictures of the English saints, St. Thomas, St. Dunstan, St. George, St. Edmund the King, and that strange candidate for canonization, Thomas earl of Lancaster, mostly enlivened by adjacent monsters; there are the women saints, Katharine and Margaret, and the foreign ones St. Martin of Tours, St. Eloi, St. Giles, and St. Francis preaching to the birds. There are cooking scenes, a castle of Love, and a view of Constantinople; and all are large in size and comparatively heavy-handed in style. Even the unusually graceful lady who turns her back to us has the hands of a peasant.[2]

A similar trend can be followed in manuscripts with a London background. A copy of decretals[3] written in Italy, but ornamented in England, has a certain charm in some of its pictures; the rabbit who thumbs his nose at the hound who has been hanged, the friar and the lady who make polite conversation even sitting in the stocks, show a turn of wit; but all the trees and grounds and many of the figures are put in with a clumsy pen. A treatise on nobility,[4]

[1] B.M. His splendid tomb is still in Irnham church, together with the Easter Sepulchre he gave. See Pl. 77 b.

[2] Other East Anglian MSS. are the Tiptoft Missal, before 1322, in the Pierpont Morgan Library, and B.M. Stowe MS. 12, 1322–5, perhaps written at Norwich.   [3] B.M. Royal MS. 10 E IV.

[4] Christ Church, Oxford.

written for Walter de Milemete between 1326 and 1327 for presentation to the king, shows the same degeneration; some of its illustrations have a rough vigour, but its grotesques are notable only for their hideousness.[1]

These babewyns, to give them their old name, are a peculiarly English development. I have already said that they are found at the end of the thirteenth century in a few manuscripts from the Low Countries.[2] In a rather different form they appear in quatrefoils on the Portail des Libraires at Rouen[3] and on the west door of the cathedral of Lyons about 1290, and in the fourteenth century on the capitals of the cloister at Santes Creus in Catalonia. They recur in a few French manuscripts of about 1320, but these are exceptional, and may even be the work of some wandering Englishman; we know that more than fifteen English copyists were employed by the University of Paris between 1316 and 1350, and some illuminators from this country may well have worked there also.[4] In spite of these exceptions, babewyns remain a characteristic English production of the reign of Edward II and the years immediately before and after it.

While they are most characteristic of the art of illumination, they are found almost as often in carving. Capitals in the chapterhouse at York already show the episodic influence at work; one is carved with vine branches laden with grapes, which two men are cutting with their curved knives; another has a branch of oak, with squirrels taking the acorns from their cups, and swine feeding on those that have fallen to the ground. At Henham church in Essex a bell capital of the usual kind is enlivened with heads and grotesque figures; at Henwell in Oxfordshire[5] the capitals are formed of four crouching human busts.[6] At Winchester, in the

---

[1] A manuscript of this kind, exceptional because it was made for an Augustinian house in the north of England, is Bodley Liturg. 198. Its marginal paintings include two knights, two fools, and a peasant.

[2] e.g. B.M. Add. 30029; from St. Peter's, Ghent.   [3] Evans, *Pattern*, Fig. 191.

[4] The *Bréviare de Belleville*, written before 1343, has some East Anglian elements in its decoration, notably in its birds and beasts, and we know that its scribe was an Englishman, Robert de Billyng, though its chief illuminators were Jean Pucelle and Jaquet Maci. Durrieu, 17; Saunders, i. 108.   [5] Prior and Gardner, Fig. 442.

[6] Cf. the capitals at Adderbury and elsewhere in the Banbury district. See Keynes, though his association of them with William of Wykeham is untenable.

north transept built about 1320, a capital is carved with a monk holding a draught-board.[1] Perhaps the most characteristic English architectural grotesque is the foliate mask that seems to bring to life the fabled creatures of the English woods.[2]

Even more episodic grotesques were carved on the seats of misericords. Those at Wells (Pl. 25 b, c) have all the charming inconsequence of a manuscript illumination. The scene of the little birds who are mobbing the owl occurs at Gloucester, Norwich, and Beverley; monkeys rifling a pedlar's pack at Beverley and Manchester; rats, mice, weevils, and woodlice at All Saints, Hereford; the fox preaching to a congregation of hens and geese at Whalley.[3] The nave windows at York, set up between 1306 and 1338, have motives that are in evident relation with the babewyns of the psalters, notably a monkey's funeral with a cock reading the service. In all of them we see the influence of naturalism at work in style, even when the subject is fanciful and literary; a fresh inspiration has changed the ancient bestiary tradition into something new and living.

The records seem to show that similar subjects were employed in all the arts. To embroidery the transition was easy, as on Edmund Mortimer's wall-hangings embroidered with children chasing butterflies,[4] and the bed of Thomas, duke of Gloucester, embroidered with woodwoses jousting.[5] The birds of the marginal paintings were particularly congenial to the embroiderers. Witness the 'grant sale de worstede, le champ tanne ove papejayes et cokerele de blu', which Elizabeth de Burgh, Lady Clare, left to her daughter in 1355.[6]

Edward III owned plate decorated with babewyns: a ewer with

---

[1] Prior and Gardner, Fig. 26. In citizen work they remained in use longer. The Fromond chantry at Winchester, for example, has bosses carved with grotesques about 1445.

[2] It is found at Winchelsea, Norwich, Ely, Beverley, Worcester, Oxford, Dorchester (Oxon.), and St. Mary's Minster, Thanet. In France it appears in the English domain at Rouen cathedral and on the stalls at Poitiers. It is found in Spain at Leon and is fairly common in the Rhineland.

[3] The misericord is now at Blackburn. Whalley abbey was a Cistercian house.

[4] 1332; Palgrave, iii. 164.

[5] Seized at Pleshey in 1397. *Arch. Journ.* liv (1897), 290.

[6] Nichols, 35.

a monkey playing a harp, a hanap with swans and ladies bathing, a cup and ewer enamelled with children riding pick-a-back, and a cup 'ove diverse babwynerie'.[1] Similarly Walter Skirlawe, bishop of Durham, had a great silver-gilt cup enamelled with babewyns and a knop formed as a bird's nest with three men climbing up to steal the young birds.[2]

In goldwork the existing example is the famous Lynn cup, that offers certain parallels with the contemporary Luttrell Psalter (Pl. 26 a).[3] The coconut cup with a tree mount at New College must have provided another parallel when its foot still had little rabbits playing at the foot of the tree. The Bruce horn,[4] too, has hunting-scenes and figures of a bishop, a king, and a forester that recall marginal decorations.

If the irrelevant babewyns are the characteristic art of the reign of Edward II, a serious religious art, balanced by secular decoration mainly heraldic in inspiration, is characteristic of the active reign of his successor, which began when Mortimer fell in 1330. Both were, in a sense, an assertion of stability; the incompetence of Edward II, the years of pestilence and famine that had succeeded the defeat of Bannockburn, the choice by parliament of Edward III as king while his father was yet alive, and Edward II's ignominious and pitiful end, had to be forgotten. They could best be hid behind a façade of dignified beauty. Edward II, therefore, was enshrined as a saint,[5] the Gothic rococo of his age went out of fashion, and the patrons of art turned to more serious things.

Edward III was himself familiar with French and Flemish standards of luxury. He had been in France with his mother in 1325, and went again in 1329 when he did homage for his French possessions to Philippe de Valois in the choir of Amiens cathedral. The vagaries of English politics had in 1326 removed foreign merchants, with a few insignificant exceptions, from the freedom of the city of London;[6] the policy of Edward III both encouraged foreign mer-

---

[1] Palgrave, iii. 262, 264. In my own view the monkey salt at New College, commonly dated to 1500, is at least sixty years earlier. It is defaced by a later guilloche moulding added under the cushion.　　　　　[2] Test. Ebor. 317.

[3] See Penzer. Nothing definite is known of its history.

[4] Belonging to the marquess of Ailesbury.　　　　　[5] See p. 164.

[6] Riley, 149.

chants and made him dependent upon them. His marriage with a
Hainault princess encouraged the entry into England of Flemish
weavers. In 1331 John Kempe of Flanders, a weaver, was given a
letter of special protection: colonies of Flemings were established
at Cranbrook in Kent and in the neighbourhood of Norwich;
others set up their looms in London, two at least in York, while
at Bristol Thomas Blanket established the first regular factory.[1]
The complicated foreign and fiscal policy that Edward III embarked on in 1337 led to alliances with all the Netherlands pro-
vinces, the Palatinate and Bavaria, that were effective not only in
his attacks on France but also in the development of the export
trade in English wool through which he hoped to finance them.
In 1338 he sailed for the Netherlands with a great entourage, and
visited their prosperous cities and the shrines of Cologne. At the
same time the Italians lost their dominance among the foreign
merchants of London to the Flemings. In 1343 Edward III struck
his gold noble, to circulate both in England and Flanders, and made
it the only money that might be taken out of the country. In 1345
the Bardi and the other leading Italian merchants went bankrupt,
and their place was to a great extent taken by men from Louvain
and Flanders. Most of their wares were for current use and had no
artistic significance, but a few imports of carved furniture were
made, such as a chest carved with the story of St. George in York
Minster.[2]

The campaigns in France did not drain the country of men. It
seems that not more than 4,000 men were ever in arms; and at first
the war brought glory to those who waged it. When they re-
turned in 1340, the country enjoyed five years of peace. At the
same time the abolition of the royal right of tallage and the
stabilization of the tenth and fifteenth that parliament could levy
on movables as well as real property to a fixed local assessment that
was not revised, did much to encourage display.

[1] Cunningham, *Alien Immigrants*, 106.
[2] The York chest is probably the 'Archa de Flaundres' for vestments recorded in
the inventory of the chapel of St. Paulinus and St. Chad in 1388. Raine, 300. Another
with the same subject reversed, said to have come from Rufford abbey, is in the
Victoria and Albert Museum (W 82.1893) as well as another (W 15.1920) with the
Magi, Annunciation, and Coronation of the Virgin.

Not even the years of plague could make much difference; they were the years of Edward III's greatest personal glory. There is no special break in the fabric rolls at Westminster;[1] masons were employed from 1350 to 1360 much as in the decade before and the decade after. At York the nave was given its vault in 1354, and the choir went on forthwith, and the story is the same at Exeter, Ely, Winchester, and Gloucester. The Black Death might sweep away half a generation of craftsmen, and necessitate legislation to make stonemasons, jewellers, and other skilled artisans to work at the rates current before the plague,[2] but it did little or nothing to change the standards of artistic luxury. From 1330 until 1360 England was dominated by a man whose selfish ambition required a background of formal and costly display, and even in the eight years after 1369 when the glory had departed the tradition lived on, though hardly any new work was initiated.

Of the king's two personal foundations, the Cistercian house of St. Mary's Eastminster, and the house of nuns at Dartford, founded in 1355,[3] not a stone remains. Yet we still know something of the architecture and more of the decoration of St. Stephen's chapel at Westminster, of which the main upper chapel was begun in 1327 and finished nearly fifty years later under the provisions of Edward III's will.[4] It was as richly decorated as any of the French *saintes chapelles* that it rivalled; every surface was enriched with gilt gesso, painting, or glass inlay. The accounts show that some of the workmen who built and carved the Lady chapel at Ely were also engaged on St. Stephen's.[5] The gable was set on its inner face with statues of St. Stephen and his executioners. The outer wall bore sculptures of St. Edward the Confessor and St. John with the ring, carved by Master Richard of Reading.[6] They represent one

---

[1] Prior, *Eight Chapters*, 118.

[2] The Statute of Labourers was extended to cover them in 1351.

[3] First Augustinian and later Dominican. It was famed as a place of education for great ladies. The original foundation goes back to a vow of Eleanor of Castille. Jarrett, 9.

[4] See Maurice Hastings, *St. Stephen's Chapel and the Architecture of the 14th Century in London* (1949). He points out that Carter is an unreliable authority, and that Mackenzie is only to be trusted on matters visible to him.

[5] Bentham (Stevenson), 64.   [6] Brayley and Britton, 15.

of the royal attempts to rival the house of Valois; Edward III everywhere tried to exploit Edward the Confessor as the English rival of Saint Louis. He had his image carved over the courts of King's Bench and Common Pleas in Westminster Hall, over the gate into Dean's Yard, and in relief on the back of the screen in the saint's chapel; wrought in the hangings of the choir and in a window on the south side of the abbey.[1] At St. Stephen's it is set as the seal of the royal builder on the wall of his own chapel.

The inside walls were richly painted between 1350 and 1363 by a team of painters, all of whom had English names, under the supervision of Hugh of St. Albans.[2] The western wall had a series of pinnacled canopies surmounted by a frieze of shields interspersed with babewyns. Beneath the canopy a series of angels was painted by William of Walsingham and Gilbert Puckeridge. They were robed in liturgical vestments, and had great peacock wings that filled all the background. They held up mantles of oriental brocade to form a dado of drapery.[3] Above this arcade were smaller paintings of the story of Job and Tobit,[4] with Latin verses to explain them; the text and pictures are in the proportions they would have in an illuminated manuscript. On another wall the Adoration of the Magi was represented (Pl. 27) with members of the royal family kneeling below under a richly painted arcade. The surviving fragments[5] have heavy and varied grounds and borders of gilt gesso. The colouring is more subtle than appears at first sight; there is no heraldic simplicity of blue and red, but a sophisticated arrangement of vermilion and maroon, olive-green and grey. All the figures wear contemporary court dress; the Magi come as if robed for the court of Westminster. The king's inventories give some indication of the rich chapel furniture which added to the brilliance of the whole: a folding retable with silver-gilt images of St. Edward giving St. John the Evangelist his ring,

[1] Dart, *Westmonasterium*, i. 57. The subject also occurs in glass in Romford church.

[2] Smith, *Antiquities of Westminster*, 202. See also Borenius and Tristram, *English Medieval Paintings*, 22.   [3] Evans, *Pattern*, Fig. 100.

[4] J. J. Smith, *Ants. of Westminster* (1807), has a plate opposite 153 which shows the architectural framing better than the drawing by Leonard Barnard.

[5] In the British Museum. Borenius, *English Primitives*, Pl. 9.

a silver gilt reliquary shaped like a shrine borne by two angels, eight silver-gilt-images of saints, each containing a relic of the saint represented,[1] and a great illuminated missal and antiphonal.[2] The further entry of a folding 'tabula' painted in colours with various images points to the development of panel painting in England.

Very little remains of such painting that can be dated to the reign of Edward III and is definitely English. A long narrow picture, now in the Cluny Museum, with four scenes from the life of the Virgin (Pl. 29) and almost certainly of English origin, may well belong to the later years of the reign of Edward II.[3] Its combination of simplicity of feeling and mannerism of pose is characteristically English; the little lions that powder the background recall those on the sedilia paintings at Westminster. The lid of a chest given to Winchester cathedral by Sir William de Lillebonne between 1320 and 1335[4] has little paintings of the donor and his wife, the Crucifixion and the Coronation of the Virgin. It is not an important work of art, but it shows such painting well established in this country. More significant is the contemporary retable now in the little church of Thornham Parva in Suffolk.[5] It represents the Crucifixion (Pl. 28), with St. Peter and St. Paul, on a gold ground; the predominant colours are green, purple, and red. On the outside panels St. Dominic, St. Katharine, and St. John the Baptist are represented to the left, St. Edmund the King, St. Margaret, and St. Peter Martyr to the right. The presence of St. Dominic and St. Peter Martyr suggests a Dominican origin; it is possible that it was painted for their church at Yarmouth.[6] The

---

[1] Palgrave, iii. 206-7. The gold offered by Edward II at his coronation was shaped as a similar group. Dart, *Westmonasterium*, i. 51.

[2] Devon, *Issue of the Exchequer*, 177; bought in 1363.

[3] Cf. will of Humphrey de Bohun (1322), 'j table de fust depeynt pur un autel', *Arch. Journ.* ii. 349.

[4] Now in the north presbytery aisle. See A. R. Green in *Hants Field Club*, x (1926-31), 220.   [5] See Lillie in *Suff. Inst.* xxi (1933), 153, and *Burl. Mag.* lxiii (1933), 99.

[6] The Estouteville triptych in the collection of the late Lord Lee of Fareham has English connexions, but its concatenation of saints, notably St. Louis of Toulouse, are not English. See Borenius, *English Primitives*, 91; Borenius and Tristram, Pl. 62. It represents the Crucifixion in the middle, with scenes of the Passion beneath and the life of the Virgin in the wings. On the exterior are St. Anselm, St. Louis of Toulouse,

study of English painting at this time is made more difficult by a comparative dearth of manuscripts.[1] A psalter written for Queen Philippa between 1328 and 1340[2] has delicate miniatures on patterned gold grounds; it carries on the courtly tradition of feminine elegance.

The *Sainte Chapelle* of St. Stephen's, like a magnified jewelled shrine, is a typical production of royal patronage; it was rivalled by some of the work ordered by the courtly prelates. The bishops played no less important a part in the affairs of the realm than they had under Edward II, and continued to be great builders and patrons of the arts.

After the reign of Edward I no monk was archbishop of Canterbury, and any shadow of monastic poverty gradually faded from the idea of a prelate. Between 1325 and 1350 the highest offices in the realm were held by ecclesiastics:[3] John Stratford, archbishop of Canterbury, was lord treasurer to Edward II and lord chancellor to Edward III; bishops of Hereford, Chichester, Lincoln, and Rochester were high officers of state; William Edington, bishop of Winchester, was lord treasurer and lord chancellor of England at the time of the Black Death.

One of the most magnificent of the bishops was John Grandisson, who was elected to the see of Exeter in 1327. He had studied theology at Paris, and had negotiated peace in Gascony; he had been consecrated bishop in the Dominican church at Avignon. His own tastes were as luxurious as those of any French prelate. Three ivories still exist that once belonged to him.[4] In one triptych (Pl. 31) the Coronation of the Virgin and the Crucifixion

St. Paul, and St. Clare. The Estouteville arms (which look as if they had been added by another hand) may refer either to the English or the Norman branch. The picture was long at Woodendean manor, Sussex. It may be remembered that when King John of France was in England in 1359 he had with him three painters: Girart d'Orleans, Giles de Melun, and Copin. Doüet d'Arcq, 264.

[1] Dr. Eric Millar indeed, *English Illuminated Manuscripts*, 24, goes so far as to say that from about 1340 to about 1360 there is a complete gap in the series of English manuscripts caused by the Black Death. There is no such gap in France, which suffered equally from plague.

[2] B.M. Harley MS. 2899. [3] See Prior, *Eight Chapters*, 103.

[4] See Longhurst, 44 and 105. Bishop Bitton, who died in 1307, left three ivory tabernacles, two of which were given to his successor. Camden Soc. (1872), 5.

are carved in the central panel; St. Peter and St. Stephen on the left wing, and St. Paul and St. Thomas of Canterbury, whose life Grandisson wrote, on the right; a shield of Grandisson with a mitre confirms the ownership. The triptych is interesting because it is, devotionally speaking, a miniature version of the high altar at Exeter, which had the Coronation of the Virgin between figures of St. Peter and St. Paul, with collateral altars to St. Stephen and St. John, who is here replaced by Thomas Becket. A second Grandisson triptych, also in the British Museum,[1] with a similar iconographic scheme is curious in that the Virgin and Child seem to have been copied from a Sienese picture; perhaps the bishop had brought such a picture with him from Avignon. The Exeter inventory of 1506[2] shows that Grandisson gave or left to his cathedral silver-gilt statues of St. Peter and St. Paul, a silver-gilt cross resting on four lions, standing on a great enamelled foot with figures of two angels, the Virgin and St. John, for use as a processional monstrance; an enamelled tablet with the Crucifixion, the twelve apostles, and other figures; as well as illuminated books and embroidered frontals and vestments. He left to Pope Urban V his purple velvet cope embroidered with figures.[3]

His patronage was far from ending with such portable works of art. It was in his time, and probably by his munificence, that the musicians' gallery with angels was added to the nave of Exeter (Pl. 30 b). He continued Stapeldon's work, and completed the nave,[4] and started in 1330 on the great west front,[5] which was finished by Bishop Brantyngham between 1370 and 1394. A curious note, characteristic of Grandisson's time, is struck by the intense 'Penseur' poses of the statues that adorn it; the kings and warriors sit with crossed legs and contorted arms, in an agony of thought, that seems denied by their blunt-featured faces. The same poses and intensity are seen in the contemporary reredos at Christchurch in Hamp-

---

[1] See Dalton in *Burl. Mag.* xlix (1926), 74. The third ivory, a diptych, is divided between the British Museum and the Louvre. It represents the Annunciation and the Coronation of the Virgin with the two St. Johns who were John Grandisson's patrons.

[2] Oliver, 321. [3] Christie, 3.

[4] Bishop and Prideaux, p. 82. Thomas of Witney was his master mason. His piers may be distinguished by their having a seat at the base.

[5] Prior and Gardner, Fig. 397.

shire,[1] in the surviving figures of the ancestors of Christ. Here, however, they are balanced by a beautiful verticality of line in the architectural framing that gives a soaring quality that Exeter lacks. The two lower niches were originally filled by statues of wood plated with silver.[2] Something of the same quality, with less intensity, is represented in the line of kings who were set a little later over the main door at Lincoln (Pl. 30 b), and in the figure of David added to the Ormesby Psalter after it was given to Norwich.

Grandisson did not stand alone. At Rochester Bishop John of Sheppey, who ruled from 1332 to 1360, built a new refectory and in 1344 remade the shrines of St. Michael, St. Paul, and St. Ythamar in marble and alabaster. To him, too, must be due the chapter doorway dating from 1352, with its figures of Church and Synagogue and its seated doctors beneath canopies that follow the curve of the arch, that is one of the English sculptures in which French influence is most evident.[3] William Bateman, bishop of Norwich in 1343, gave to the high altar two images of the Trinity, one in a tabernacle of silver-gilt;[4] it was in his time that the south walk of the cloister received its bosses, on which apocalyptic scenes are represented with extraordinary force, movement, and terseness. He, or his immediate successor, gave the cathedral its famous lectern shaped as a pelican.[5]

The enrichment of cathedral interiors by carved woodwork in Decorated style, that had begun with Bishop Stapeldon's work at Exeter, continued everywhere.[6] The development from Geometric tracery, as used at Winchester about 1300, to Decorated, is well shown in the stalls at Lancaster, which must date from about

---

[1] In the middle ages it retained its old name of Twynham.

[2] A fragment from the screen now in the Lady chapel comes from a Coronation of the Virgin.

[3] S. Gardner, *Guide to English Gothic Arch.* 130. A. Gardner, *Handbook*, Fig. 263. It has been much restored. It may be compared with the battered ruins of the chapter-house door at Evesham. A French parallel is the cloister door at Saint-Wandrille.

[4] Blomefield, ii. 364.

[5] Cf. Fowler, *Rites of Durham*, 13: 'At the north end of the high altar there was a goodly fine letteron of brasse where they sunge the epistle and the gospell, with a gret pelican on the height of it finely gilded pullinge her bloud out hir breast to hir young ones and winges spread abroade wheron did lye the book. . . .'

[6] See Crossley for admirable illustrations.

1340, and are said to have come from Cockermouth abbey. The Gloucester stall canopies of a few years later show a stronger three-dimensional sense, which is expressed at Hereford about 1380 with all the curving grace of the Ely stone-work. At Lincoln about 1370 a great change appears. The canopies are magnificently transmuted into tabernacles, worthy to stand beside the bishop's throne at Exeter. A new type had been founded, and was followed all over the north, at Chester, Nantwich, Whalley abbey,[1] and York.[2]

So, too, the cathedrals were enriched with sculpture and goldwork, though the sculpture is for the most part known to us in a fragmentary state,[3] and the goldwork has vanished. A charming sculptured fragment is the Virgin and Child from Winchester cathedral, which has a modest grace that can challenge comparison with the more sophisticated contemporary Madonnas of France (Pl. 32). The Reformation inventories include an incredible amount of sculpture in precious metal, of which a good deal must date from this time. At Lincoln, for example,[4] there was a silver-gilt Christ and a great silver-gilt seated figure of the Virgin; and at York[5] three such Virgins and one of gold, and silver-gilt figures of St. Peter, St. Paul, St. John, St. Margaret, and an Annunciation group. At Winchester one description deserves quotation:[6] 'the nether part of the High Altar, being of plate of gold, garnished with stones. The front above being of broidering work and pearls, and above that a table of images of silver and gilt, garnished with stones. Behind the high altar St. Swithin's shrine, being of plate, silver and gilt garnished with stones.' The silver-gilt censer found in draining Whittlesey Mere must stand as the example of the lost goldwork; it probably came from Ramsey abbey (Pl. 34 a).

One of the great works of the bishops in the reign of Edward III was to fill the windows of their cathedrals with stained glass. They gave important windows themselves, and they forced,

---

[1] Now in the parish church: c. 1430. See Cross in *Lancs. and Ches. Hist. Soc.* lxx (1918), 22.   [2] And in the wooden sedilia at Beverley.
[3] See Prior and Gardner.   [4] Dugdale, *Monasticon*, vi. 3. 1279.
[5] Ibid. vi. 3. 1204.   [6] Ibid. i. 202.

cajoled, and encouraged others to give the rest. York Minster has no less than forty-three windows of the Decorated period, though comparatively few of them are now complete.[1] The great west window, with the Coronation of the Virgin, Annunciation, Nativity, Resurrection, and Ascension was given in 1338 by Archbishop Melton; he appears at the bottom with his seven predecessors. A window in the Lady chapel celebrates Edward III, who appears between St. Peter and Samuel against a background powdered with garters. At the foot Archbishop Sutton, the donor, and some of his canons, are represented in prayer. The bell-founders' windows, given by Richard Tunnoc of that craft, not long before 1330, and the contemporary Penancers' window, commemorate the occupations of men attached to the minster. The Penancers' window has scenes in the lowest tier of people confessing, doing penance, and receiving absolution. Exceptionally an individual gave a window in performance of a vow or in vicarious performance of a pilgrimage. Agnes de Holme, of Burton-in-Lonsdale, in 1361 left to York Minster as much money as it would cost to send two men on pilgrimage to Compostella, for a choir window with St. James in one light and St. Katherine in the other.[2] Sometimes, too, the purpose was commemorative; the great east window at Gloucester, datable on heraldic grounds between 1347 and 1349,[3] is a memorial of Crécy. It was given by Lord Bradeston, who commanded a fifth part of the king's division, and was probably carried out by Thomas Glasswright of Gloucester, who was working there between 1330 and 1340 and was engaged on the glass in Westminster abbey in 1355.[4]

The craft of stained-glass making was beginning to be fully organized in England. The ordinances of the London glass painters date from 1364–5.[5] Only white glass was produced in England, and even this was made at Chiddingfold about 1350 by a German, John de Alemagne.[6] He provided the white glass for

---

[1] Benson, *Yorkshire Philosophical Soc. Ann. Rep.* (1914), 81. The Lady chapel windows were badly damaged in the fire of 1829.

[2] Raine, *Test. Ebor.*, p. xii note.

[3] See Grimké–Drayton in *Bristol and Gloucester Arch. Soc. Trans.* xxxviii (1915), 78.

[4] Ibid. 97.   [5] Knowles in *R.I.B.A. Journ.* xxiv (1926–7), 263.

[6] Le Couteur, 6.

St. Stephen's chapel; the coloured glass was bought from the London office of the Hanseatic merchants in Thames Street. All the sheet glass for Exeter cathedral came from Rouen. As late as 1458 the *custos vitri* of York Minster bought his glass from Peter Faudkent, 'Dochman', and had it brought from Hull.[1] About 1449, however, a Fleming called Utinam came to England to make coloured glass and obtained a contract for the materials for the windows of the King's chapels of King's College and Eton.[2]

The actual technique was changing a little. In 1351 six master glaziers were employed at Westminster palace to draw and paint the images for the St. Stephen's windows on whitened wooden tables, but by 1389 the cartoon for the east windows at Exeter was drawn on parchment.[3] The use of such a cartoon meant that a design could be used more than once; it was the beginning of a measure of mass production. Less than a century later a window at Great Malvern[4] would show six bishops and archbishops all produced from the same cartoon, in two instances reversed, and another at Margaretting in Essex would depict most of the kings of the tree of Jesse drawn from one cartoon, occasionally reversed, and changed in colour and detail.

The canopied niche that dominated sculptured work in the time of Edward III came in great measure to dominate window design also. A figure under a canopy might well fill even a large window; in the three windows at the west end of York nave, made by Robert the Glazier in 1338, half the space is taken up by the canopies that stand out in white and gold against a background of colour. For yet larger windows, such schemes as those of the west front of Exeter and the Christchurch reredos were easily translatable into stained glass.

The tree of Jesse, indeed, that was figured in stone and silver at Christchurch was the first design to be integrated in England to fill a large window.[5] It had been a characteristic feature of the English psalters of the first years of the century, and models were not far

---

[1] Raine, 69.   [2] Tipping, ii. 173.
[3] Le Couteur, 10; Oliver, 206; Prideaux and Bishop, 93.
[4] Middle window of north choir clerestory.   [5] Le Couteur, 52.

to seek. At least fifteen Jesse windows have been counted,[1] of
which the best date from the years round 1340. One of the oldest
is the great east window of the choir at Wells, fitly called the
Golden Window. Jesse lies at the foot, and scrolls lead from his
body to the kings of Judah in the side lights. In the middle is the
Virgin and Child; above them, dominating the whole window,
the Crucifixion. The little lights above once held the Doom. The
strongly architectonic scheme was followed with varying closeness
at Ludlow, Selby, the Grey Friars at Shrewsbury,[2] and Carlisle.
The tree of Jesse plays a more important part at Shrewsbury and
Selby, the Doom at Carlisle,[3] but the affiliation is evident and close.
At Tewkesbury the Doom fills the great east window, and the
Kings and Prophets are relegated to two side windows; the third
on each side holds four figures of the knights who gave it.[4]

Other details of the stained glass likewise recall the babewyns of
the psalters of slightly earlier date. At York there is a monkey's
funeral, knights and ladies, squirrels and falcons, and canons in
their stalls; at Gloucester many natural plants—spotted medick,
ivy, bluebell, wood-violet, lesser celandine, white bryony, and
wild rose—that recall those of the Tickhill Psalter; at Carlisle there
is a border of squirrels cracking nuts. Naturalistic leafage was also
used, as in France, to cover whole backgrounds; a window at
Wells[5] has a background of large maple leaves, and one at Harlow
in Essex a ground of trailing sprays of oak and ivy set against a
light-golden glass.

The heraldic decoration that had sufficed to fill a line-ending or
adorn a margin in the psalters was developed to form a genre of
decoration of its own which reflects the new importance of tourna-

[1] Woodforde, *Journ. Brit. Master Glass Painters*, vi (1935), 184. He thinks eight
may come from one workshop. He cites as particularly fine a window at Lowick,
Northants.
[2] Given by Sir John Charlton between 1351 and 1355 and now in St. Mary's.
[3] And in the later window at Winchester college, 1393. Another Jesse window,
with accompanying windows of saints, was given by an abbot of Waltham who died
in 1371 to Wrangle church, Lincolnshire.
[4] G. McN. Rushforth on heraldic grounds dated these side windows as about 1340
and before 1344. *Bristol and Gloucester Arch. Soc. Trans.* xlvi (1924), 316.
[5] Middle window, north side of choir.

ments in English courtly life. With the reign of Edward II, said Stubbs,[1] we pass from the age of heroism to the age of chivalry. The remembering eye of history sees Edward I on the battlefield and Edward II in the tiltyard. The change of background necessarily brought a change into heraldic art; from the martial austerity of practical use it passed into the decorative richness of adornment and display. Tournaments, that earlier had been mimic mellays, became a series of single combats, and heraldry reached a new stage as the mark of the individual displaying his individuality.

The portrayal of battle-scenes became a recognized genre in English art; the Painted Chamber at Westminster was painted with 'all the warlike pictures of the whole Bible',[2] and the 1295 inventory of St. Paul's includes two copes embroidered with figures of knights fighting.[3] The magnificent tournament held at Windsor under the auspices of Queen Margaret in 1306, to celebrate the knighting of Edward of Caernarvon, marks the beginning of the age when tournaments inherited the prestige of battle. In 1313 Edward II and his queen crossed to France with an immense retinue to assist at the knighting of the three sons of Philippe le Bel and the consequent tournaments, just at the time when the English strongholds in Scotland were falling. Soon we find tournament themes appearing in the minor arts, as on the 'coupe doore eymelle od chivalrotz' and the ewer to match that appear in the royal inventory of 1324.[4]

The vogue for tournaments only increased under Edward III, a king who found endless satisfaction in pomp and display, chase and tournament. During the early years of his minority French romanticism invaded the tiltyard and gave to the tourney the further glamour of dramatic make-believe. In 1328 Mortimer held a series of Round Tables at Bedford, assemblies at which knights played the parts of Arthur and his peers, and mimic warfare followed upon the feasting. By 1330 the king was old enough to joust himself. In one tournament, held in Cheapside between the Eleanor cross and the Great Conduit, he and his

[1] Const. Hist. ii. 317.   [2] Lethaby in Burl. Mag. vii (1905), 263.
[3] Dugdale, 317.   [4] Palgrave, iii. 125.

friends paraded the city dressed as Tartars on the Sunday before the lists were opened. Each knight had a lady on his right hand, robed in ruby velvet and led by a silver chain. The great tournament of the Round Table in 1344 was marked by the making of a huge round table for the knights to sit at, by the beginning of a great round tower to hold it,[1] and by the taking of a vow by the king to restore the Round Table in its glory. A certain number of barons and knights were sworn in as companions of the Round Table, and regulations for the observances of the brotherhood drawn up, providing for an annual feast at Whitsuntide.

The successful phase of the French War was followed by an infinity of tournaments in 1347 and 1348, in some of which the Scottish prisoner knights took part. Nineteen were appointed by the king, eight at Westminster and the rest at Bury, Eltham, Windsor, Canterbury, Lichfield, and Lincoln. For the Eltham tournament in January 1348 mantles and garters with the motto *Honi soit qui mal y pense* were ordered for the king and twelve companions,[2] and later in the year the new Order was more formally established. The chapel of St. Edward in Windsor castle was redecorated as the chapel of St. Edward and St. George; the eight canons endowed by Henry I were increased by a warden, fifteen canons, and twenty-four alms-knights; a chapter-house, cloister, and lodgings for their use were built;[3] and a great tournament was held there on St. George's Day, 1349. Thus a romantic fancy, even a little tawdry in its conception, was gradually and almost unconsciously transmuted into a great Order of knighthood, linked with the church as with the monarchy to the glory of England. In 1358 it held the most splendid of its jousts, a Table Round on St. George's Day that was graced by the presence of the two captive kings, John of France and David Bruce of Scotland. We may find a reflection of it in a ewer in the king's treasury enamelled *ove les Chivalers de la rounde table*.[4] As late as 1374 the king held another great tournament at Smithfield, at which Alice Perrers appeared as the Lady of the Sun.[5]

---

[1] W. St. John Hope, *Windsor*, i. 111 and 128; the tower was never finished.
[2] Ramsay, i. 357.
[3] W. St. John Hope, *Windsor*, i. 129.
[4] Inventory of 1370; Palgrave, iii. 264.
[5] Stow, i. 717.

Comparatively little remains to us of all these glories. The forty-six stall plates of knights of the Garter at Windsor that are anterior to 1421 show heraldic art at its best, depending only on the pageantry of helm, crest and mantling, shield and scroll for their effect.[1] Not less beautiful, if less severe, is a horse trapping embroidered with the leopards of England (Pl. 34) against a background of red velvet covered with delicate sprays of foliage, with knights and ladies playing amongst them.[2] The same fanciful gaiety is evident in an embroidery of the same kind recorded among the goods left by Edward Mortimer in his castle of Wigmore: 'une cote pour les joustes de rouge velvet ove une frette dargent ove papillons des armes de Mortemer.'[3]

The prestige of the tiltyard brought new subjects into art, and new developments into heraldic decoration. Figures of knights engaged in single combat were carved on the fronts of English chests[4] (Pl. 36 a), and on the misereres of Worcester cathedral, and enamelled on perfume cases.[5] Sir Geoffrey Luttrell being armed for the lists by his wife and daughter was painted in his book of psalms (Pl. 36 b). The nave windows of York, dating from 1306 to 1338, have figures of knights and ladies, like those on the dorsal described in the will of Matilda of Kirkbride in 1347.[6] Such figures were even used to teach morality; the fall of Pride is represented on a Lincoln misericord by a knight riding in the lists whose horse has crossed his feet and gone down.

More important than this, the shield of arms itself assumed a new importance. As the mark of the donor it passed even into ecclesiastical use. The 1295 inventory of St. Paul's includes a cushion de serico scutellato.[7] The Syon cope has forty-six coats of arms on the stole and eighteen on the maniple, significantly rather later in date than the cope itself. The 1315 inventory of Christchurch,

---

[1] See W. St. John Hope, *Stall Plates*.

[2] It was later made up into a chasuble, but has recently been remounted.

[3] Palgrave, iii. 164; 1332.

[4] Another is in the Saffron Walden Museum. A later chest with subsidiary figures is in the parish church, Harty, Isle of Sheppey.

[5] A knight fighting a wild man armed with a club on V. and A.M. 218, 1874, middle of the fourteenth century.

[6] *Test. Ebor.* 37.

[7] The gift of Dean William de Montfort. Dugdale, 316.

Canterbury, includes a white cope with the arms of the king of Scotland, three copes with the arms of bishops, and five with the bearings of other persons.[1] At St. Augustine's, Bristol, the high altar itself was framed in heraldic ornament (Pl. 35 a).[2]

Similarly coats of arms began to play a larger part in the decoration of illuminated manuscripts. The Tiptoft Psalter has shields in the framing of its great initials; and the Gorleston Psalter has its miniature of the Crucifixion bordered with panels of the arms of France and England. Even more natural was the use of shields of arms on tombs and memorials such as the Eleanor crosses; and from these it was an easy transition to their use in greater architecture, as, for instance, on the spandrels of the wall arcade of the aisles at Westminster under Robert of Beverley. The ten triangular shields which fill the spandrels of the gabled arcading on the gateway of Kirkham priory in Yorkshire, built between 1289 and 1296, are succeeded by the great armorial that adorns the gateway of Butley priory in Suffolk, built about 1320 (Pl. 35 b).[3] The keep at South Kyme in Lincolnshire, dating from the middle of the century, has the keystone of the vault of the windowless ground floor carved with the arms of Umfraville, who held the barony.

The story is continued to the end of the century in the sixteen shields of noble descent that adorn the inner side of the gatehouse at Lumley castle begun in 1389; in the rich vault of Canterbury cloisters, begun in 1397, of which every boss is a shield of arms,[4] and in the still later vaulting of the Chichele porch of the same cathedral.

Within the churches the old fashion of shields hanging straight upon a tomb chest continued, since it could hardly be bettered. The tomb of Edmund of Langley at King's Langley, set up in 1391,[5] has twenty shields carved round its alabaster sides; those of a man and his wife at Little Baddow in Essex each have eight shields in

---

[1] W. St. John Hope, *Heraldry*, 321. For Westminster carpets of heraldic design in 1388, see ibid. 322.

[2] The work appears to have been begun under Abbot Knowles and completed under Abbot Bolton.   [3] The spaces are filled in with babewyns.

[4] The fashion was introduced at Canterbury on the bosses of the Black Prince's chapel in the crypt in 1363.

[5] Devon, 244; and see John Evans, *Edmund of Langley and his Tomb*. It is now in the parish church.

quatrefoils on the front, making a continuous frieze of sixteen shields. Elsewhere new fashions were found to bring the shield of arms more closely into the decorative scheme. The shield was often set within a cusped border,[1] as it is, for example, on the tombs of the two great men who died in 1376: the Black Prince, who lies at Canterbury, and Cardinal Simon Langham, who lies at Westminster. The tomb of Simon Burley, who died in 1388 and was buried in old St. Paul's, had the four gables of its wall canopy each filled with a shield of arms, and eight more shields on the base of the tomb.[2] Monumental brasses, too, were often studded with shields of arms. The fine brass at Balsham[3] of John Sleford, who was chaplain to Queen Philippa, master of the wardrobe to Edward III, and archdeacon of Wells, and died in 1401, has shields of France, Hainault, Flanders, Ely, and another.

The spandrels of the Percy Tomb at Beverley are carved with delightful little figures of Lady Idoine Percy and her husband (Pl. 33), each holding shields of their arms. At Ottery St. Mary a leafy stem is used to hang a series of shields from, so that they follow the curve of the arch (Fig. 3): a rather unarchitectural device that did not find imitators.

A happier invention was that of using figures of angels to hold the shield: a symbol no doubt of angelic protection for its bearer. The scheme, first adopted by the royal house of France, is found about 1390 on the boss of Worcester cloister[4] and on the canopy of Richard II's tomb. Great angels holding shields stand at the ends of the hammer-beams of Westminster Hall, set up between 1394 and 1398, and on the roof of the Law Library at Exeter. Two angels hold shields of Neville and Longespée on the seal which Richard Neville, earl of Salisbury, used in 1429; and similar shield-holding angels appear on the tombs of Henry IV at Canterbury and on many other monuments of the fifteenth century.[5]

---

[1] The device is first found on the gold denier of Saint Louis, struck between 1266 and 1270.

[2] A sketch by Sir William Dugdale made in 1640–1 is in Lord Winchelsea's album, fol. 181v.

[3] Cambridgeshire. It lies inside the screen he gave to the church.

[4] Prior and Gardner, Fig. 599; and see ibid. 84, 260, 329, and 515.

[5] See below, p. 166.

Meanwhile the shield itself was playing a less important part in warfare. The Aldeburgh brass of 1360 at Aldeburgh, Yorkshire,

FIG. 3. *Ottery St. Mary, Devon. Detail of Arch, c. 1350*

is probably the last English effigy on which the shield appears as part of the martial equipment, while the Wantone brass of 1347 at Wimbish, Essex, is the first on which the effigy bears no shield. The shield of war was giving place to all the varied usages of the tournament of chivalry. How complicated these might become may be seen from the shields which Richard Beauchamp, earl of

Warwick, had made for a tournament at Calais in 1422.[1] Three shields were each painted with the figure of a lady. On the first she sat on a couch playing a harp; her knight, the Green Knight, was ready to joust twelve courses with any knight of France. On the second she was seated at an embroidery frame, sewing pearls; her knight, Chevalier Vert, would joust fifteen courses. On the third she was sitting in a garden weaving a chaplet; her knight, Chevalier Attendant, challenged in like fashion. French knights accepted the challenges and the earl fought them for three days.

The greatest development in the fanciful use of heraldry took place in the reign of Edward III, in the age in which the tournament reached the zenith of its factitious glory. Every device of the joust found a place in decoration. He had his motto, *It is as it is*, embroidered on a white linen doublet worked at sleeve and hem with devices of clouds and vines;[2] he had his sejant crowned leopard, in a cloak of the royal arms, set upon the half-florin;[3] he had his plate not only enamelled with shields of arms, but also diapered with heraldic lozenges and powdered with badges.[4] He and his followers wore brooches in the form of his badges of the fetterlock and the white greyhound,[5] and in his reign a powdering of badges was a common form of ornament, especially for hangings. Edmund Mortimer had beds powdered with his badge of butterflies;[6] the Black Prince beds with his badges of golden roses and ostrich feathers, as well as hangings with the heraldic charges of eagles and griffins and the Bohun swans;[7] while John of Gaunt owned plate adorned with his collar of SS,[8] and left to St. Paul's copes with orphreys adorned with his collar of SS encircling his badge of the stag.[9]

---

[1] Blore, 9.   [2] W. St. John Hope, *Heraldry*, 325.
[3] Cf. a cup belonging to Charles V in 1381 that may have been a gift from him: a goblet with 'ung lyon ou couvescle emmantelé des armes de France et d'Angleterre'. Labarte, *Inventaire du mobilier de Charles V*, 72.   [4] See Palgrave, iii. 126, 166.
[5] Ibid. iii. 345.   [6] Ibid. iii. 164.
[7] Nichols, *Wills*, 72, 78; Nicholas in *Arch.* xxi (1846), 350. Cf. the seventeen carpets and bankers of green powdered with swans left by Humphrey de Bohun in 1322. *Arch.* xxi (1846), 349.
[8] 'Un paire de basynys ... ove un coler gravez ove letres de S del livere de Mosr. de Lancastre'; Palgrave, iii. 322.   [9] *Arch.* l (1901), 502.

The usage of the tournament by which the shield of challenge was hung on a tree is represented on the seal of Thomas, Lord Holand and Wake of about 1353; the tree is represented growing in a rabbit-warren.[1] That used by Thomas of Woodstock about 1385 shows his own shield, and two shields of his wife's, hanging from a tree set within a paling surrounded by water on which float two of her Bohun swans.[2]

Richard II continued the tradition of his house; his admiration for his father was boundless, and with it went an admiration for his father's feasts and jousts, his extravagance, and his rather purposeless wars. Born in France and reared by French people, he brought something of French magnificence into English heraldic decoration. His colours of red and white were everywhere in his palaces, and many of his belongings were powdered, like his robe on his effigy, with his badges. The string moulding under the windows of Westminster Hall is still studded with his helm, crown, and leopard crest, and his badge of the white hart; the glass that he gave to Gloucester cloister was sprigged with his broom pods.[3] In his day English nobles—Nottingham, Huntingdon, Clifford, and Courtenay—went over to take part in the jousts of Saint-Inglevert, and the usages of the English tourneys were hardly less splendid. Hall has left a description[4] of a single combat between Henry of Lancaster, duke of Hereford, and Thomas Mowbray, duke of Norfolk, the first 'on a white corser barbed with blewe and grene velvet embrodered sumpteously with swannes and antelopes of goldsmith's work', and the second with trappings of crimson velvet embroidered with silver lions and the mulberry trees that were his canting device.

As Bolingbroke, Henry IV had played his part in European chivalry, both as a challenger in the lists and a crusader in the armies of the Teutonic Knights. The elaborate Italian armour prepared for his judicial combat against Norfolk suggests a full appreciation of martial splendour and style; the friendship with Jean, duc de Berry, which lightened his exile, suggests a knowledge

[1] W. St. John Hope, *Heraldry*, 211. [2] Ibid. 213.
[3] J. T. Niblett, *Records of Gloucester Cathedral*, i. 114.
[4] *Chronicle*, 1809, ed. 4.

of a lavish way of life. Yet as king, he appears as an uneasy and sombre man, continuing the Plantagenet tradition of pageantry in the tiltyard from policy rather than pleasure. The institution of the Order of the Bath on the eve of his coronation and the holding of a great tournament at Smithfield in 1402 were calculated rather than spontaneous events.

To Henry V such matters were more congenial; he had his motto, *une sans plus*, 'flourished upon leech damask' for his queen's coronation,[1] and when he took '6 vallectz peintours' with him to France in 1415 it was to paint heraldic devices.[2] His carver, Robert Broune, specialized in heraldic work; he carved the swan and antelope for the king's ship, *The Holy Ghost*, as well as swans in the king's chamber at Sheen.[3] For Henry's interview with the king of France his tent of blue velvet was embroidered with fanciful devices of antelopes and the motto 'After busie labour cometh victorious rest'.[4] Such pageantry was even introduced into the service of the Church. On Trinity Sunday, 1413, Henry had the hearse at Becket's tomb set out with innumerable candles and with ninety banners painted with the arms of all the kings of Christendom, with multitudes of fanons, streamers, and valances.[5]

Banners, indeed, were one of the most characteristic fields of heraldic display in the fifteenth century. Though they were used in the lists, they seem first to appear on English seals in token of their owner's rights of justice; Walter Lord Hungerford, on the seal he used about 1420, has his shield flanked by banners of his lordships of Heytesbury and Hussey. The banner held by an heraldic beast, however, was the characteristic pinnacle of a jousting pavilion. It appears on the Westminster tomb of Lewis Robsart, Lord Bourchier, the standard-bearer of Agincourt who died in 1431, and in greater architecture at the very end of our period. At Nevill Holt, for example, the buttresses are shafted columns of which the capitals serve as pedestals for sejant lions and antelopes of York and Lancaster, that once held banner vanes. To the same period belongs the decorative use of diagonal stripes of

[1] Palliser, *Historic Badges*, 368.   [2] Waugh, *Henry V*, ii. 30.
[3] Devon, 338, 357.   [4] Hall, *Chronicle*, 90.   [5] Waugh, i. 48.

colour, banner fashion,[1] and the introduction into decoration of the jousting shield, with its deep notch for the spear on the dexter side,[2] that was to become a characteristic decorative motive in the reign of Edward IV.

[1] e.g. on the Windsor stall-plate of Sir John Beaufort, earl of Kendall and duke of Somerset, c. 1440.

[2] e.g. seals of John Tiptoft, earl of Worcester, 1449; William Herbert, earl of Huntingdon, 1479.

IV

PERPENDICULAR STYLE

EVERY style in which decoration plays a predominant part
is the prelude to a severer mode. Rococo came before the
classicism of Louis XVI; and the Decorated style found its
counterpoise in the rectilinear purity of the Perpendicular.

The basis of Decorated style was the flowing curve of the
Gothic arch, endlessly multiplied, and, where it served no structural
purpose, transmuted into new ogival forms. The first denial of
this line is found at St. Augustine's, Bristol, a house of Black
Canons of the Order of St. Victor, in the work done under Abbot
Edmund Knowle. It was begun at some date after 1298, when he
became treasurer, and finished, after his death in 1332, in 1341. The
great east window omits the arms of Piers Gaveston from among
the donors but includes that of Humphrey de Bohun, earl of
Hereford; it therefore seems likely that it was set up after the
death of Gaveston in 1312 and before the death of Bohun in 1322.[1]
The use of white vine-scrolls on a red ground invites comparison
with the windows in the chapter-house at Wells, set up before 1320.
It is therefore reasonable to suppose that the architectural work was
nearing completion at this time (Pl. 38 a).[2]

The work is full of originality. The pier arcade is the loftiest in
England, with the crown of the arch 51 feet from the floor. The
vertical mouldings of the pier are stressed to give a curious linear
quality strangely different from the plastic roundness of Exeter.
The aisles are of equal height with the nave, the transom across
them, which gives a rectangular line, being in fact an internal
flying buttress that conveys the thrust of the nave to a heavy
buttress outside the church; a use that had been preluded a century

---

[1] G. McN. Rushforth in *Bristol and Gloucester Arch. Soc. Trans.* liv (1932), 41.

[2] The choir alone is original; the modern nave copies it. It is noteworthy that the
Berkeley chapel, built in 1348, is in ordinary western Decorated style with foliage
capitals and ball-flower ornament.

earlier in the lower *Sainte Chapelle* at Paris. The conception is one more natural to wood than to stone. The result is almost disconcerting in its logic; it seems nearer to engineering than to architecture. The vault over the high altar minimizes the rib-line by the use of liernes in a rhomboid scheme, in what may well be the earliest lierne vault in England. The sacristy, a little later, continues the engineering style of the nave in an extraordinary vault in which the ribs are left in a skeleton state.

The denial of the arch line—a denial which cannot be more than partial in a Gothic church—is continued in the addition of pierced transoms to the windows, by the omission of a triforium or clerestory,[1] and by the framing of the sedilia with reversed arches touching the arcade at the crown to give a series of quatrefoils.[2] Abbot Knowle's friend, Bishop Gower, copied this arcade at St. David's and Llandaff, and used a skeleton vault like that of the Bristol sacristy for his screen at St. David's before 1347.

The evidence seems to show that this new emphasis on horizontal line begins at Bristol,[3] but it is found at little later date in other great churches in the west of England. In these, however, it is used not for fundamentally new work but to mask the rotundities of an earlier style. The casing of the triforium of the choir at Wells by Bishop Ralph of Shrewsbury, who held the see between 1329 and 1363, seems to have set a fashion, though his work, in its emphasis on a vertical line melting into an ogival arcade, belongs to the earlier tradition.

The abbey of Gloucester was vastly enriched after the fall of Mortimer in 1330 by the pilgrims to the tomb of the murdered Edward II, the king to whose body Abbot Knowle had not dared give shelter at Bristol.[4] Here the casing of the choir and south transept by Abbot Wigmore between 1329 and 1337 marks a

---

[1] The first step had already been taken in York and Guisborough naves, where clerestory and window are merged to give two stories instead of three and a window with a median division.

[2] See Evans, *Pattern*, Fig. 49.

[3] Mr. Maurice Hastings is, however, of the opinion that a rectilinear quality is characteristic of the London Decorated style, notably in St. Stephen's chapel.

[4] See *Chronicle of Gloucester Abbey*, Rolls Series (1863), 44. The chronicle says that Abbot Wigmore was a practising craftsman: but what does this mean?

definite shift to a new style. In this work quadrangular panelling, with no more than a reminiscence of the arcade in its cusping, dominates the design;[1] the broad Norman proportion of the bays behind is echoed in the rather wide oblongs of the panelling (Pl. 38 b).

For the first time a rectangle of panelling is seen as the unit for the composition of a wall, whether the panel be left empty or filled with stone or with glass. The Gloucester choir is reduced to a scheme of seven tiers of such units, with shadowy arches behind and above; the east end to nine tiers, solid or glazed but for the screen and entrance to the Lady chapel at the foot. The origin of the scheme is clearly to be sought in window tracery, where the rectangular panel of glass forms a natural element; but the aesthetic basis of the innovation, as at Bristol, is the denial of the arch-line as the conditioning motive. The scheme is continued at Gloucester on the outside of the east end, perhaps the first Perpendicular exterior to be planned in England. It is remarkable in its attempt to treat the whole as a wall, panelled in stone or glass indifferently, with its buttresses and finials as important features and the arch of the great east window given as little emphasis as may be. Only in the gable over the window and in the pierced balustrade is the ogival line retained.

The chronicle of Gloucester abbey[2] tells us that it was in the time of Abbot Adam de Staunton, who ruled the abbey from 1337 to 1357, that 'the great vault of the choir was built, at great and sumptuous expence . . . from the offerings of the faithful who flocked to the tomb'. Here again the essential lines of the vault are hidden by a complex reticulation of liernes (Pl. 39) studded with heavy bosses carved with angel musicians (Pl. 37).[3] The result is very different from the engineering austerity of Bristol,

---

[1] Harvey (*Yevele*, 8) ascribes the work on stylistic grounds to Master William Ramsey. I have found instances of it abroad that are not many years later than the English examples, for instance, at St. Peter's in Leiden and in the cathedral at Antwerp.

[2] loc. cit. 48. Mr. Sydney Pitcher has raised the interesting problem of how this was done with the old tower *in situ* and the new tower built afterwards without revaulting.

[3] See Prior and Gardner, Fig. 84. A similar vault, one degree more structural in its design, was set over the north transept before 1377.

but both are equally far removed from the palm-like vaulting, serene and calm, of Exeter cathedral.

The final development of the new style at Gloucester was in the cloisters[1] (Pl. 41), begun by Abbot Thomas Horton, who ruled the abbey from 1351 to 1377, and finished by his successor Abbot Frocester, who died in 1407. They are the largest in England, and it is not without reason that Stukeley wrote of them:[2] 'the cloysters in this cathedral are beautiful, beyond anything I ever saw.' Here the arch-line is for the first time removed from the vaulting. A fan vault springs as a traceried half-cone from either side, just touching in the middle, with a traceried quatrefoil to fill the space between the conoids. The whole Gothic conception of a structural rib-vault is given up; there is a return to the Romanesque system of a vault of intersecting surfaces, though these are now beautified and given an apparent integration by the decorative tracery that covers them. It is not vaulting as the Gothic architects envisaged it; rather, one feels, has a system of tracery been strengthened and filled in to span a limited space.

Gloucestershire was the only county in England with four mitred abbeys: Gloucester, Tewkesbury, Winchcombe, and Cirencester. The Lady chapel at Tewkesbury is lost; the whole abbey has been destroyed at Winchcombe and Cirencester. We do not know what part they played in the dissemination of the Perpendicular style. Yet we can still see that the Gloucester style by its very beauty conquered the west. Stukeley's drawing shows that the Hereford chapter-house[3]—ruined even in his day—had a fan vault; it was begun in 1359 and must have been one of the first buildings to be influenced by the Gloucester cloisters. The interior of the lantern at Pershore shows a similar panelled scheme to that of Gloucester choir; the choir at Tewkesbury is vaulted in a system that combines the liernes of the Gloucester choir vault with the traceried conoids of its cloister vault (Pl. 40). The intrusion of the style into lesser work can likewise be studied at Tewkesbury. The

---

[1] The first cloister had been burned in 1300. See W. St. John Hope in *Arch. Journ.* liv (1897), 97. [2] i. 67.

[3] I owe the information to the kindness of Sir Alfred Clapham. The drawing is reproduced in the publications of the Anastatic Drawing Society.

screen of the Trinity chapel, begun about 1390, has rather rigid and severe tracery, but the arcade and gable are still ogival; the Fitz-Hamon chantry, begun about five years later, has similar tracery but instead of an arcaded base is set above cusped rectangular panels of Perpendicular style. At Llantwit Major, a dependency of Tewkesbury, the great reredos, for all its high gables and spiry pinnacles, shows an unusual stress on horizontal line.

At Lacock abbey the cloister, that had been begun with a wooden roof, was completed about 1420 with a fan vault that is a miniature version of the Gloucester theme, with an octagonal net of liernes between the fans. The choir of Ottery St. Mary achieves a yet closer approximation to the prototype.

When Bishop Edington founded a collegiate church in his native village of Edington in Wiltshire, he intended it to be a college of canons, and began to build it with this intention in 1352. Before it was finished in 1361 the Black Prince, who favoured the Order of Bonshommes, persuaded him to transfer it to this order under the guidance of two Bonshommes brought from Ashridge.[1] The church is a landmark in the history of the Perpendicular style. The chancel and transept are in a slightly rigid Decorated, with reticulated windows, and niches enshrining fine statues, supported by consoles carved with varied and interesting figures. The nave, however, is entirely Perpendicular in style, with uniform triple windows with almost square heads, such as are also found in Bishop Edington's work on the west front at Winchester, and quadruple piers with angular capitals. In the exterior (Pl. 42) the two styles are skilfully married; the chancel alone has pinnacles and carved gargoyles, but the strong embattled cornices that it shares with the nave serve to unite the whole. The west front, presumably the last part of the church to be built, has the linear tracery of its great window echoed in the door beneath. The side pinnacles are small; the flowing tracery of the side windows is all that remains of the earlier style. The whole is noteworthy for a massive breadth of scheme; the soaring quality of Gothic is here subdued to a static solidity. The new style may have been worked out as

[1] Leland, iv. 23.

a tracery to mask other work, but here it achieves a strong architectural expression.

Bishop Edington began to remodel the presbytery of Winchester between 1345 and 1366; his work was continued in the nave by William of Wykeham, and finished, partly under the provisions of Wykeham's will made in 1403, by Cardinal Beaufort, whose arms appear in the vaulting of the nave.[1] Here more than masking is achieved; without complete rebuilding, a Norman shell has been transformed into work in the new style. The two-storied scheme, the horizontal line below the windows, and the netted roof have a magnificent if superficial unity (Pl. 43).

The story is carried on at Sherborne abbey, of which the choir was rebuilt between 1436 and 1459. The structural likeness with Winchester is evident in the exterior; the buttresses are no longer crocketed, and the horizontal line is further stressed by a pierced balustrade to aisle and nave roofs, but the general scheme and proportion are the same. The interior shows an extremely rich fan vault, with a starry network of cusped liernes to fill the space between the conoids:[2] a scheme that combines those of the Gloucester cloister and choir vault. In the west of England, indeed, the style was now fixed; St. Mary Redcliffe shows a difference in proportion but hardly in style from Winchester that was planned more than a century before.[3]

Outside its cradle in the west of England the development of the style was more spasmodic. Something of its linear quality seems evident in the drawings of the lost hexagonal chapter-house of old St. Paul's, begun in 1332 under the mason Master William de Ramsay,[4] though the likeness is of quality rather than style. In the Dean's cloister at Windsor, however, designed by John Sponlee in 1353,[5] this linear quality is fulfilled with quatrefoils in

[1] The master mason William Wynford, who was at Windsor 1360–6, Wells 1364 (for the western towers), Abingdon 1375, supervised the nave 1394–1403. Harvey in *Brit. Arch. Ass.* vi (1941), 43.   [2] It may be compared with that at Milton Abbas.

[3] On the dating of the church see Brakspear in *Bristol and Gloucester Arch. Soc. Trans.* xliv (1922), 274.

[4] Dugdale, 87; Riley, 185; Harvey in *Burl. Mag.* lxxxix (1946), 192; *Yevele*, 7.

[5] William de Ramsey was also working at Windsor about this time. Harvey in *Brit. Arch. Ass.* vi (1941), 40.

the heads of the arches and trefoils in the spandrels in a rather unimaginative version of Perpendicular style.

When the new nave of Westminster was begun in 1376, it followed Henry III's style in every essential,[1] though its master masons[2] were distinguished men fully capable of original creation. The west front, however, seems to have felt the breath of the new style; there are still remains of Perpendicular panelling on its inner face, and the mullions and transoms of the window are designed to continue its lines.[3]

The nave of Canterbury, rebuilt between 1377 and 1391 by Archbishops Arundel and Chichele, is in most respects close to Winchester in its scheme, though freedom from the limitations of an earlier structure has resulted in a more elegant pier design and a greater impression of lightness (Pl. 44). A characteristic Perpendicular note is struck by the quatrefoils in the spandrels of the arch. The vault shows a simplification in its network; the ribs are less strongly denied; and the network of the crown is simpler in its form. The great windows of the aisles flood the lower part of the building with light, and change the dramatic emphasis of the whole composition.

Meanwhile the style had begun to find its own expression in the north of England. A new choir was begun by Archbishop Thoresby at York in 1361,[4] following the main lines of the nave. The Gloucester panelling system, however, appears immediately above the arch, as it does in the north transept.[5] The choir vault displays a particularly beautiful version of lierne vaulting: it is far

[1] Rackham, Nave of Westminster, 35; Lethaby, Westminster Abbey Re-examined, 138. It was not finished until 1528.

[2] Henry Yevele, Robert Kentbury, and Thomas Paddington. On Yevele see articles by J. G. Nichols in Gentleman's Magazine, xix (1842), 38; N. Wonnacott in Ars Quatuor Coronatorum, xxi. 244; Knoop and Jones, Mediaeval Mason, 23, and J. H. Harvey, Yevele.

[3] Lethaby, loc. cit., points out its likeness to Winchester, which was by William Wynford who was working with Yevele in 1370.

[4] Raine, xiv. It was partly built by the sale of indulgences obtained from Rome in 1396, but was not finished much before 1423.

[5] William de Hoton the younger was appointed master mason in 1351. He was succeeded by Robert de Patrington, 1368–71; Hugh de Hedon, 1399–1401; William Colchester, 1415; John Long, 1421, and Thomas Pak, 1433. Raine, xix.

more elegant than the heavily ribbed vault of the central tower, built between 1400 and 1423. The great east window, glazed between 1405 and 1408, maintains the ogival tradition in its tracery; but the 117 rectangular panels of its glass show how far the Perpendicular style was dominating design.[1]

The splendid west front at St. Mary's, Beverley, begun about 1380, shows the panelled system successfully applied to a façade; the scale is notably more lofty, and the style more light than in the comparable façade at Edington. The contemporary octagonal chapter-house at Howden, the gift of Walter Skirlawe, bishop of Durham and once canon of the house, displays the only lierne and fan vault in the north, but it is a simple one of relatively small span.

The Decorated style was based upon variety, the Perpendicular upon uniformity. A Decorated church may have windows with varied systems of tracery to give richness, a Perpendicular church has windows designed upon a single system to give dignity. Castle Ashby in Northamptonshire, for example, has four windows in the nave, six in the chancel, and the east window all traceried alike. The regular succession of identical clerestory windows is one of the hall-marks of the style. Perpendicular architecture, indeed, progressed in the direction of simplicity and uniformity. Finally, in the north aisle at Crowland, built between 1392 and 1427, a new version of the style is achieved, infinitely simpler and more lucid than Decorated, but accepting the flowing line of arch and vault with candour. There are no liernes to break the flow of the vault, no capitals to break the flow of the arch; the Gothic scheme is reduced to an austere abstraction, and its beauty yet survives.[2] The same logical simplification finds another and very different expression in the nave of Chipping Campden in Gloucestershire (Pl. 45), built just before 1401. Here again the style is developed in a purely structural form. The arches of the nave arcade are struck from four centres; their form for the first time renounces the true pointed arch which is the basis of Gothic construction.

---

[1] See J. A. Knowles, *York Glass-painters.*
[2] The style may owe something to Low Country influences; uncapitalled piers occur in Antwerp cathedral, begun in 1352, and in that of Utrecht. Saint Maclou at Rouen followed the scheme in 1437.

The piers have straight sides separated by concave mouldings of equal width. The moulded capitals, also eight-sided, have all their sides concave. The flattened arches are heavily moulded; between them pilasters rise to frame the great windows of the clerestory.[1] The form of the aisle windows echoes that of the arches of the nave; they are filled with cusped tracery of a rectilinear form. The whole may stand as the completed Perpendicular achievement in pure architecture.

It is a remarkable fact that it has been possible to give a continuous history of the early Perpendicular style without reference to the national disasters which occurred in its years of growth. Yet these were so great that it seems miraculous that they did not leave a greater scar upon the art of England. The reason lay, perhaps, in a different regard for the value of architecture. In our utilitarian and hard-pressed times anything larger than a Council cottage appears to be in some measure a work of luxury which stands in need of moral justification. To the men of the fourteenth and fifteenth centuries building was in itself a good act; if ecclesiastical, it glorified God, if secular, it was a part of good administration. In times of stress and shortage, to build might, indeed, be a doubly virtuous act, since it would provide work for the unemployed and would benefit the country by a nobler scale of construction made possible by the lower building costs.

A good deal of work was begun and almost if not quite completed in the years of the Scottish wars. The nave, west front, and chapter-house of York, the choir of Bristol, the west steeples of Lichfield, the chapter-house of St. Paul's, the south transept at Gloucester, the vault of Pershore, were all in hand by 1348. The cloisters at Westminster were, we know, finished before Abbot Simon de Bercheston died of plague in 1349. Then in 1348-9 the Black Death brought terror and tragedy to England. Legal and judicial work ceased for two years, even war was discontinued until 1355. It is hard to estimate the loss of life, and of life in its prime. Four wardens of the Worshipful Company of Goldsmiths died within the year. Two archbishops of Canterbury

---

[1] The whole scheme is followed with little variation at Northleach, that must surely have been built by the same master mason.

—John Ufford and Thomas Bradwardine—were preferred to the dignity and died before they could be enthroned: two-thirds of the clergy of Norfolk died,[1] and about half the priests of the rest of the country. The monastic dormitories were ravaged by the infection: at St. Albans out of sixty monks, forty-seven died; the Dominicans suffered so severely that they never again held quite the same place in the life of England. Yet at such centres as Gloucester architectural creation continued with undiminished vitality; only in glass-painting is there any noticeable lag,[2] and glass-painting was always one of the least progressive of the arts. It is rare to find a church that shows any direct effect of the Black Death, though the cathedrals of Worcester and Chester show clear breaks in their construction for which it would seem an obvious explanation. The church of Cley in Norfolk is an East Anglian exception to prove the rule; begun about 1330, its building was interrupted by the plague, and it was nearly a century before the aisle walls and the western end were finished and the roofs put on. The transept chapels, indeed, remain uncompleted to this day.[3]

There was, moreover, no appreciable slowing down in the work of church building in the years following the Black Death. The building of the Lady chapel at Tewkesbury, the remodelling of Winchester, the erection of the church and college at Edington, the royal foundation of St. Mary's Eastminster, the marvellous creation of the cloisters at Gloucester, the new work at Windsor, all belong to the decade that followed the two years of plague, and were all built in undiminished splendour.[4]

Nor were many foundations the result of vows made in terror or of thank-offerings for deliverance. Seven Charterhouses, it is true, were founded in England between 1343 and 1414,[5] but the earliest

---

[1] In the diocese of Norwich 863 incumbents; in that of Ely the holders of 92 out of 145 benefices. [2] See Knowles, *York Glass-painters*.

[3] It is said that work at St. Nicholas, Great Yarmouth, was also interrupted, but not for long.

[4] Archbishop Thoresby's wooden ceiling of York nave represents a local style rather than financial economy.

[5] Beauvale, Gresley, Notts., 1343; London, 1349 and 1371; Kingston upon Hull, 1378; St. Anne's, near Coventry, 1381; Mountgrace, Yorkshire, 1397-8; and Sheen, 1414. Little or nothing remains save at Mountgrace, which shows a cruciform church, aisleless, with the nave and presbytery separated by a passage under the central tower.

of these antedated the plague, and of the rest only one was directly inspired by the Black Death. This was the London Charterhouse, originally a chapel built in 1349 by the Hainaulter Watelet de Mauny—a denizen as Sir Walter Manny—over a plague-pit where thousands of the citizens of London were buried.[1] It was not until 1371 that he founded a house of Carthusians here, under the name of the Salutation, and built dwellings for them under the supervision of Yevele.[2] Similarly the churchyard of the Trinity in East Smithfield became the foundation of Eastminster in 1359; but the royal vow to found it arose not from the fear of plague but from peril of shipwreck.[3]

The turn of the mid-century saw the building trade in course of reorganization[4] and much work in view. The Premonstratensian abbey of Leiston in Suffolk was built;[5] and a crown or lantern story was added to innumerable towers to form the first stage of a spire: witness Patrington, Grantham, Norwich, and Worcester cathedrals. In 1361 the foundation-stone of York choir was laid and the Lady chapel planned. Edward III might be fighting in France, but he had no more than 6,000 men with him and in England the dominance of William of Wykeham assured a surface tranquillity and laid the foundations of an administrative reconstruction.

From 1368 onwards famine and plague walked hand in hand with defeat and decay. The ill-starred war with France lost the European dominions of the Crown; by 1374 only Calais, Brest, Bordeaux, and Bayonne were left to England. The political life of the country at home was rent over the question whether churchmen or laymen should control the State; illness had stricken the heir to the throne, who in 1371 was so poor that for a time he

---

[1] Weever, 432.

[2] Barnes, 435. Lethaby, *Westminster Abbey Re-examined*, 149; Harvey, *Yevele*, who gives a ground plan. [3] Barnes, 435.

[4] In 1356 London regulations were made to settle dissensions between the hewers, the light-masons, and the setters. Twelve men were chosen to regulate the craft: Walter de Sallynge, Richard de Sallynge, Thomas de Bredone, John de Tyringtone, Thomas de Gloucestre, and Henry de Yevele, for the master masons; Richard Joye, Simon de Bartone, John de Estone, John Wylot, Thomas Hardegray, and Richard de Cornewayle for the light-masons and setters. Riley, 280.

[5] *c.* 1363; it is plainly designed with a façade panelled in flint.

could not pay his men. From 1377 England was drearily and incompetently governed by a 'Continual Council': the war ingloriously dragged on; and there seemed a real danger that the French and Spanish fleets which were cruising in the Channel were there as the heralds of an invasion. South coast towns, indeed, were taken and sacked; the Isle of Wight was occupied, and an army landed in Sussex. In England a growing murmur of anger and frustration made a solemn bourdon to disaster: the prelude to the Peasants' Revolt of 1381 was being played. England's support of the Roman Urban VI brought heavy papal taxation on the land. In 1376 the Commons complained that the taxes paid to the pope amounted yearly to five times those paid to the Crown; the proportion of aliens to natives among deans and archdeacons was one to three, and many were cardinals and prelates living abroad.

Yet these were the years in which Glastonbury nave was remodelled and the cloister rebuilt; when the nave of Westminster was rebuilt and the cloister finished; when Norwich cloister was completed, when the vaults of Worcester cloister were built, and adorned with peculiarly rich and heavy bosses, and the window jambs beautified with quatrefoil tracery.[1] In 1376 Archbishop Simon Sudbury took down and rebuilt the north and south transepts at Canterbury and pulled down the body of the church. Then he was seized by Kentish rebels and murdered with the lord chancellor of England on Tower Hill; but the rebuilding went on under Archbishops Courtenay and Arundel, who added the great tower and rebuilt the cloisters.[2]

The reign of Richard II, indeed, saw a vast amount of ecclesiastical building, encouraged no doubt by the confiscation of the property of the alien priories. The choir clerestory at Norwich, the west front of Beverley, the chapter-house at Howden, were all erected soon after 1380; the cloister at Durham, the cloister and Lady chapel at Crowland, were only a few years later in date. A

---

[1] Harvey (*Yevele*, p. 70) ascribes them to *c.* 1372 and to the design of John Clyve. The same heavy proportion of the bosses will be found in the westernmost bay but one in Gloucester cathedral.

[2] Dugdale, *Monasticon*, i. 86; Dart, *Canterbury*, 37.

wave of lesser church building spread over the country;[1] in Cheshire, for example, few medieval churches are without some work of the date.[2] Yet in 1390–1 the plague was so bad that it was compared with the Black Death.[3]

In 1399 Henry of Lancaster landed, and the *éternel recommencement* of history made the revolution of 1326 repeat itself. The usurper was a soured and disappointed man, too deeply preoccupied with politics to be a patron of the arts; his wealth was rapidly reduced to indebtedness by the wars against Scotland and France. The Lollards were busy sowing dissension in the land; in 1404 the Commons, under Wycliffite influence, proposed a measure that was not far from an expropriation of Church property. Yet in that very year the transformation of the Norman nave of Winchester was begun; and in the next year the splendid Perpendicular choir of the church of canons regular at Christchurch in Hampshire was being built.[4] In 1407 there was a severe outbreak of plague in England, yet the great tower of York[5] was begun, to be quickly followed by the north-west tower of Wells. In 1410 the Lollards are said by Walsingham to have demanded the expropriation of episcopal and monastic lands[6] in favour of lay barons, knights, esquires, and a hundred hospitals: an absurd demand, but that it could be formulated was ominous. Yet just then Archbishop Arundel, their chief opponent, began the Arundel steeple at Canterbury,[7] and in 1414 Henry V established three new foundations: houses of Carthusians and Celestines at Sheen, and

---

[1] An interesting contemporary manuscript in the British Museum—*Construciones artis geometriae secundum Euclydem*, 1390—shows the established custom of masonic lodges or workshops. See Knoop and Jones, 169.

[2] See Crossley in *Journ. Chester and N. Wales Arch. and Hist. Soc.* xxiii (1937), 5.

[3] It is noteworthy that the old church of St. Peter Mancroft at Norwich was pulled down in 1390 but that its successor was not built until 1455.

[4] As appears from the will of Sir Thomas West. *Test. Vet.* i. 167. The old name of Twynham is now dropped.

[5] Henry IV sent William of Colchester, one of his own masons, to supervise it. The local masons objected and killed his assistant, but he probably designed the tower that now stands.

[6] Stubbs, iii. 65.

[7] Dart, *Canterbury*, 26, thinks it was not begun until after 1449; but Arundel gave the bells in 1408.

Brigittines at Sion, largely endowed out of the properties of the alien priories that parliament had finally put into his hands.[1]

Building, too, continued in the older foundations. Robert Mascall, bishop of Hereford, built a new choir, presbytery, and steeple for the London White Friars before his death in 1416;[2] Abbot Newton vaulted the transept of Pershore; the church of Forde abbey was newly built in 1419.[3] The west front and porch of Gloucester was put up by John Morwent, prior from 1420 to 1437,[4] and the Lady chapel at Lacock is of the same date.

Henry V's early death in 1422 brought his triumphs in France to an end. The mockery of Henry VI's coronation at Saint-Denis by Cardinal Beaufort did little but mark the end of English dominion in France. A few years later the cardinal's own city of Winchester held nearly a thousand houses that were uninhabited and seventeen parish churches that were unserved.[5] For a time the tide of building flowed less strongly; when something important was done it was to repair a catastrophe or to finish work already begun. The east part of Sherborne was rebuilt after it had been burned by the townspeople; Norwich nave was vaulted after the fire of 1463 had destroyed the wooden roof. The tower of Gloucester was built to complete the whole by Thomas Seabroke, abbot from 1450 to 1457.[6] It is rare, outside the universities, to find a new foundation, like the priory of Austin Canons at Staverdale in Somerset, founded by Sir John Stourton and consecrated in 1443.[7] At this time, indeed, the supply of stonemasons was inadequate. When in 1441-2 the king's chief mason started to impress fifty skilled men for the work at Eton, he went to Burford and Oxford to get them. His proceedings at once threatened to put a stop to the work at All Souls, and Chichele had to offer twelve of his men to buy off the rest.

---

[1] By this time, too, Perpendicular panelling is found as far away as the Rathaus of Cologne, on a tower built between 1407 and 1414.   [2] Weever, 436.

[3] See will of Edward Courtenay, earl of Devon, *Test. Vet.* i. 197.

[4] Dugdale, i. 535.

[5] In 1430. Salzman, quoted Harvey, *Gothic Eng.* 106.

[6] So there are few whole parish churches, but such parts as the chancel at Luton, built between 1430 and 1440.

[7] Like most of the new churches of the fifteenth century the Church is aisleless.

The years after 1450 offer a yet more melancholy political
picture. Jack Cade's rebellion, successful enough to gain control of
the capital, was an organized protest against incompetent government. The childless king was mad; and by 1455 the wars of the
Roses had begun. Not till about 1465 did Yorkist rule bring about
more stable conditions. In the intervening years political conditions at last brought a certain lull in building: the Lady chapel at
Canterbury and the south tower at York seem just to have pre-
ceded them;[1] the central tower at Durham was begun as they ended.
Only a few smaller churches, notably in Norfolk, can be ascribed to
them. The great *floraison* of late Gothic that followed more stable
political conditions after 1471 lies outside the scope of this volume.[2]

[1] Dart, 29.

[2] So, too, does the question of the influence of English Perpendicular on the French
flamboyant style. On this see R. de Lasteyrie, *L'Architecture religieuse en France à
l'époque gothique*, Paris (1926), chap. xiii.

V

ART AFTER THE BLACK DEATH

WHEN in 1354 the Lord Chamberlain asked the Commons: 'Donques vous voillez assentir au Tretee de pees perpetuele si homme la puisse avoir?', the Commons replied with one voice, 'Oil, oil'.[1] Never had England more profoundly desired peace than after the ravages of plague and famine. But peace was not yet; 1355 witnessed the ravaging of Languedoc, 1356 the victory of Poitiers. The spoils of war might come to England, but she could not yet enjoy tranquillity. Edward III might give Westminster a relic of St. Benedict stolen from Fleury, the prisoner king of France might make offerings at the London shrines,[2] but the regular pilgrimages were not yet restored nor the regular flow of offerings re-established. Though building continued, creation in the minor arts was at a low ebb. Men were glad to buy things overseas. It is significant that the cup given by William Bateman, bishop of Norwich, to his new foundation of Trinity Hall, should be Avignon work of 1352,[3] and that Master Hugh of St. Albans, the king's painter, should by his will of 1361 have left his wife 'unam tabulam de VII peces de Lumbardy'.[4] John of Gaunt bought a golden chalice made at Bordeaux and a golden retable made at Amiens.[5] Even the famous crozier of William of Wykeham,[6] probably acquired soon after his election to the see of Winchester in 1366, is remarkably Italianate. By 1378 Southampton was formally established as the staple for the Mediterranean trade, while Calais was retained for that with the north and east.

---

[1] *Rot. Parl.* 262.

[2] See Doüet d'Arcq, *Comptes des rois de France au XIVᵉ siècle*, 255, 265. He offered at the Sepulchre, and the Three Kings at Bermondsey, and to the relics behind the high altar, the image of Our Lady in the choir, and the crucifix in St. Paul's.

[3] See *Burl. Mag.* lxi (1935), 287.   [4] Lethaby in *Walpole Soc.* i. 71.

[5] *Arch. Journ.* xxxvi (1869), 317.

[6] Bequeathed by him to New College, Oxford, where it still is; see W. St. John Hope in *Arch.* lx (1906), 465.

The Italian trade might be less highly organized than that of the Germanic Hanse, but the *Libelle of Englyshe Polycye* complained that it brought in useless luxuries.

> *The grete gallees of Venees and Fflorence,*
> *Be wel ladene with thynges of complacence . . .*
> *Apes and japes and marmusettes taylede*
> *Nifles, trifles, that litell have availed—*[1]

and in return they took from England good English cloth that could have been used at home. It was of greater ultimate importance to England that Englishmen were going more and more to Italy, and that Chaucer was at Genoa and Florence in 1372.

Charles V succeeded to the throne of France in 1364: 'a man who never took the field himself nor allowed his armies to fight.' He was the antithesis of Edward III, who fought too much; but he brought victory and prosperity to France, whereas Edward III's campaigns ended with nothing to show for them but Berwick and Calais. Charles was a great builder materially as a part of his effort to rebuild his country spiritually, and his sons and grandsons and nephews carried on the tradition into the lesser details of courtly life, to create a tradition of personal magnificence hardly paralleled even under Louis XIV. For a considerable time France set the standard of luxury for Europe, whether her styles were followed or no; England was long to feel conscious of her inferiority.

The first years of the young Richard II were years of incompetent government and dragging war. Yet already there was cause for hope; his long minority fostered the power of the great territorial lords, his uncles first among them, and it was through their patronage that the arts once more began to flourish. The benefactions of John Lord Neville to Durham cathedral between 1372 and 1380 may stand as examples. He gave the windows of the south aisle, with the Trinity, the Annunciation, and many saints,[2] and a statue of Our Lady of Bolton which opened on two leaves below the breast to reveal an image of the Trinity.[3] In 1379 he

---

[1] J. Warner, *Libelle of Englyshe Polycye* (1926) 18, l. 344.
[2] Fowler, *Rites of Durham*, 110.   [3] Ibid. 30.

gave the famous Neville screen to the cathedral, which renewed the Decorated tradition of metallic splendour expressed in stone.

At Westminster Abbot Nicholas Litlyngton was not only accumulating a store of personal treasures—at his death he left over 120 pieces of silver plate[1]—but also building and decorating the Jerusalem Chamber. At Exeter Bishop Brantyngham was filling the upper tiers of the west front with statues of prophets and saints; and at Worcester the north walk of the cloister was being completed with bold and interesting sculptured bosses, albeit of rather archaic style.[2]

Yet now, for the first time, a murmur was arising even against such beauties as these. Wyclif by 1383 was denouncing those who 'drawen þe peple by coryosite of gaye wyndowes . . . peyntings and babwynerie'.[3] Four years later two men at Leicester broke up a wooden image of St. Katharine to boil their broth;[4] and others were found who could call Our Lady in her English shrines 'the witch of Walsingham' and 'the witch of Lincoln'. The feeling of the time was still more favourable to destruction than to creation.

The turn of the tide came in 1389, when Richard took the government into his own hands. He tried to rule as an autocrat; and whatever effect autocracy may have upon the public weal, it is usually the form of government most favourable to the courtly arts. Richard had not the physical strength of his father and grand-father, but was rather a throw-back to a Valois ancestress. He was a dilettante of taste, with a passion for the pageantry of kingship. Under his leadership all the arts in England entered upon a phase of fruition.

His marriage in 1382 to Anne of Bohemia made closer the links that already existed between England and northern and central Europe. Bohemia was in the fourteenth century an artistic centre, especially in illumination,[5] that owed its inspiration to Paris and Avignon, with side-currents from Cologne and Italy. Its level was

---

[1] Dart, i. 31. For his pastoral staff see *Arch.* lii. 221.
[2] Prior and Gardner, Fig. 511.   [3] *Works* (1880 ed.), i. 8.
[4] Ramsay, ii. 283.
[5] See Dvořák, 'Die Illuminatoren des Johann von Neumarkt', in *Gesammelte Aufsätze*, Munich (1929).

at least equal with that of England, and some influence from it might be expected. Yet no influx of artists from Bohemia into England can be proved, nor any specific influence demonstrated. The one certain fact is that more German artists came to work in England about this time.[1]

In 1389 Richard concluded a truce with France that was to continue for many years. Two years later both Froissart and Walsingham made note of the natural friendliness that existed between Frenchmen and Englishmen of all classes. Stephen Vyne, the king's embroiderer, came to him on the recommendation of the duc de Berry,[2] and Froissart records that André Beauneveu worked for a time in England.[3]

The twelve years of Richard's marriage with Anne of Bohemia were years of pageantry and pleasure. His household included a band of minstrels and a number of artists;[4] his wardrobe such garments as a dress of white satin, embroidered with leeches, water, and rocks, hung with fifteen silver-gilt whelks, fifteen silver-gilt mussels, and fifteen cockles of white silver, the doublet embroidered with gold orange-trees on which were set a hundred silver-gilt oranges.[5]

The death of Anne in 1394 brought about a crisis in Richard's life; thereafter he seems a neurotic character, alternating between bouts of melancholy and bouts of extravagance, capable of energy and determination, but quick to despair when faced by reverses. The good understanding with France was sealed by his marriage to the child Isabella in 1396, but his extravagance and his increasing autocracy began to alienate his own subjects. By 1398 his court in peace was costing as much as his grandfather's had done in war, and from the country's point of view there was little to show for it. His deposition in 1399 had the inevitability of high tragedy. Historians of art cannot but regard it with a certain regret. A highly civilized court may not be the best thing for a country's political welfare, but it helps to polish and refine a native art as

---

[1] e.g. Hermann Scheerre: see below, p. 98.
[2] Devon, 285.   [3] *Chroniques*, ed. Buchon, iv. 4.
[4] Tout, *Chapters in Administrative History*, iv. 54.
[5] *Arch.* lxii, pt. 2 (1911), 503.

nothing else can. Whatever a usurper may bring to his kingdom, it cannot be the irreplaceable continuity and security which make it possible for men to turn from fighting to think of beauty. The objects which Henry IV found in the royal treasury[1] are the measure of how far Richard had succeeded in rivalling the court of France. Many of them were imported. There was a triptych of enamelled silver gilt, adorned with 'diverses ymageries' of Spanish work, and a great nef of silver gilt on lion feet, chased with moresque letters, with the forecastle manned by eight men holding banners and pennons of France. Others suggest a French origin by their likeness to objects described in contemporary French inventories. There was an ivory mirror standing on a castellated base with figures, another with the back enamelled with St. George and the cover with a mermaid; another in a golden frame, set with jewelled and enamelled roses, standing in a tree, the back enamelled with the figure of a queen. There was a ewer, engraved and enamelled with birds, with a lady on the knop seated on a mound within a paling, and another shaped as a dragon with a crowned queen riding upon it. There was a salt-cellar formed as a whelk shell with a dragon coming out of it, and a pair of silver-gilt basins 'embosez de roses ove les buddes enaymelez ove babwyns et en le fons un soleyl ovesque les armes le Roy et le Royne partiez et gravez en bordure ovesque un traile de vyn . . .'.

These treasures have vanished, and of all the king's embroideries none remains. Our estimate of the art of his court must rest on a few pictures, of which the Wilton diptych is far the finest,[2] a few illuminated manuscripts, remarkable for their technical rather than their artistic excellence, and a few scattered objects such as the Studley Royal bowl. This modest example of secular plate, chased with the A B C among Gothic foliage, is of the utmost elegance; rarely has a more perfectly harmonious outline been achieved. It must have been completely insignificant when it was made, yet to-day it can stand as a witness to one of the great periods of English Decorated art. In other arts a high level is shown by such chance survivals as an ivory Virgin and Child,[3] and the fine latten

[1] Palgrave, iii. 317–37.   [2] See below, p. 102.
[3] Victoria and Albert Museum, 202.1867.

chandelier of the Temple church at Bristol, with its statuettes of the Virgin and Child and St. George.

Henry IV had far less natural taste for the arts than the man he supplanted, though he was an accomplished musician. The art of his time is largely an official art, designed to express the prestige of the monarchy rather than to give the monarch himself any personal pleasure. The first important work of the kind seems to have been the great choir-screen set up at Canterbury when the nave was finished about 1400. It is completed by six portrait statues of English kings, about 7 feet high and of a higher standard of accomplishment than any portrait sculpture hitherto achieved in England (Pl. 46). Iconographically it is an expression of the Lancastrian emphasis on their hereditary claims.

The Canterbury screen set a fashion which endured for some seventy years. It was followed by a very fine screen at St. Paul's, with four kings under a double arcade on either side of the central door: an ensemble only now known to us from the plate in Dugdale's book after a drawing by Hollar. The screen with the statues of kings that once stood at Wells has wholly vanished; that at Durham, which had statues of the kings of England from the Conqueror to Henry V, with a few Scottish royal benefactors thrown in, is only known to us from a written description.[1] A fine head of a king at Winchester[2] suggests the possibility that a like monument was once erected there. The series closes with the magnificent screen at York with figures of fifteen kings from the Conqueror to Henry VI; it may be as late as 1472 when William Hyndeley was master mason.[3] The series of screens, which has no parallel in France, represents a Lancastrian attempt to bring the English monarchy within the received iconography of the Universal Church.[4]

---

[1] *Rites of Durham*, ed. Fowler, 20.

[2] Prior and Gardner, Fig. 479; it seems to show the Burgundian influence of the school of Claus Sluter.

[3] Raine, *Fabric Rolls*, xx. Seventeen statuettes of kings remain on the south front of Duke Humphrey's chantry at St. Albans, *c.* 1440.

[4] It must, however, be remembered that as early as the time of Edward II the refectory of Gloucester abbey was adorned with paintings of the kings of England. *Chron. of Glos. Abbey*, Rolls Series (1863), 44.

Such historical statues, indeed, may have been welcome in an age when men were beginning to be self-conscious about the worship of cult images. The Lollards declared that 'preyeris and offeringis made to blynde rodys and deve images of tre and ston ben nere of kyn to ydolatrie'.[1] In 1413 the trial of Oldcastle brought the whole question of the worship of images into the open. His profession was:

'As to images he understood that these were not of faith but ordained by the Church to be calendars to lay and ignorant folk to bring to mind the Passion of Christ and the martyrdom and good living of other saints, but if a man did the worship to dead images that is due to God or put such hope and trust in them as he should do towards God, he did in that the great sin of maumetry or idolatry.'

The looting and destruction of the London friaries was one of the aims of the Lollard rising of 1414.

Yet windows were still being set up to glorify at once the local saints and their donors. The great east window of York, with its 117 square panels, filled with the Doom in the middle, Old Testament scenes above, and a row of kings, popes, and bishops below, was commissioned in 1405 and finished in 1408.[2] A few years later Archbishop Thomas Langley gave the cathedral a St. Cuthbert window, in memory of his see of Durham, and the de Roos family of Helmsley castle gave a St. William window.[3] At the same time Thomas Langley gave Durham windows to St. Oswald and St. Cuthbert,[4] and Bishop Stafford one to St. Mary Magdalene in her chapel in Exeter cathedral. The series continues in the great east window at Malvern priory[5] set up about 1440, probably by Margaret Lady de Roos, a north-country woman who seems to have employed a York glazier. Here it is the story

---

[1] Waugh, Henry V, i. 251.
[2] It was made by a protégé of the Scropes, John Thornton of Coventry, probably a son of the John Coventre who worked at St. Stephen's chapel. Knowles in N. & Q. (1920), 481; Benson, 86.
[3] Two of the miracles of St. William are produced from the same cartoon with only the sick person the saint is healing changed.
[4] Fowler, Rites of Durham, 110. Another series of windows to the two saints was in the vestry. Ibid. 117.
[5] For a detailed study see G. McN. Rushforth, Mediaeval Christian Imagery.

of the Passion that is told, with the apostles and four saints as ancillary figures, and the Annunciation and Coronation of the Virgin in the tracery lights. The subjects here are purely devotional; but in a window given the Austin Friars at Norwich by Sir Thomas Erpingham the intention was purely historical. The antiquary Blomefield[1] had a roll which showed that it was filled with the portraits and shields of arms of the Norfolk knights who had died without male issue between the coronation of Edward III and the year 1419 when it was set up.

There was, however, little iconographic creation of a devotional kind. The French theme of the Virgin of Pity—Our Lady holding the body of her dead Son across her knees—was introduced early in the fifteenth century. A rude wooden version of the subject is in the church of Battlefield in Shropshire that commemorates those who fell in the battle of Shrewsbury;[2] Margery Kempe saw one in St. Stephen's, Norwich, about 1425,[3] and one was set up in London Blackfriars before 1433.[4] The other new scheme was that of the Five Joys of the Virgin, a devotion which seems to have been particularly followed in the northern province. In 1404 William Skirlawe, bishop of Durham, left to his cathedral an altar frontal embroidered with the subject,[5] and twenty years later Thomas Haxey, treasurer of York Minster, left to Lincoln cathedral a silver-gilt chalice with the Five Joys of the Virgin upon the foot.

The Church had long been the home of literary culture; Richard de Bury, bishop of Durham, lord chancellor of England, and one of the great bibliophiles of Europe, may stand as an example of ecclesiastical scholarship in the fourteenth century. That age, too, and especially the reign of Edward III, was marked by the appearance of the *miles litteratus*, the educated layman, who might not even be a lawyer. The change was emphasized by an increasing use of the English language for official purposes and for pure literature. 1362, the year of the first appearance of the first version of *Piers Plowman*, was also the year of the

---

[1] ii. 549. [2] See below, p. 185.
[3] W. Butler Bowden, *Book of Margery Kempe* (1936), 222.
[4] Jarrett, 1433. [5] *Test. Ebor.* 309.

first speech from the throne to parliament in English. By 1399 Henry IV could claim the throne before parliament in English. By 1408 even the king of England wrote his testament in that tongue.[1]

The growth of literacy and of literary interests was paralleled by the growth of decoration that was literary either in form or in subject. Just as jousting mottoes were used in secular embroidery, so sacred names were used for church work: witness the vestments of red velvet at St. Paul's *pulverizatae cum vocabulo Jhesu*,[2] and the duke of Gloucester's tapestry with angels in blue clouds holding scrolls of *Jhu miserere*.[3] Plate was commonly inscribed, and cups were often known by pet names arising out of their inscriptions, *Christmas*,[4] *Benison*,[5] or *Bealchier*.[6] One John Daune of York in 1459 owned a mazer *vocatam crumpledud*.[7]

The cup called *Benison* is easily understood when we read of Sir Thomas Ughtred's mazer inscribed *Benedictus Dominus in donis suis*[8] and the covered cup of Stephen le Scrope, archdeacon of Richmond, with the legend *Benedictus qui venit in nomine Domini*.[9] Each had a second inscribed cup, Ughtred with *Be mery and welcom* and Scrope with *Cujus finis bonus totum ipsum bonum*. A mazer of about 1430 has the legend *Ju caritate perfecta confirmet nos trenitas sancta*.[10] Cups with French inscriptions are rarer; William Walworth, a priest, had one in 1401 inscribed *Bien soit que Dieu voet*[11] and Richard II one—evidently a New Year's gift—with *a bonn estreyn*.[12]

The growing use of English may be illustrated from the longer inscriptions found on bronze vessels. A bell-metal jug of about 1380 from a manor-house in Norfolk[13] is inscribed *Goddis grace be in this place amen. Stond uttir from the fyre and lat ou lust come here.*

---

[1] Nicolas, *Test. Vet.* 203.

[2] *Arch.* l. 501; inventory of 1402. Compare Richard Rolle's cult of the Holy Name.

[3] 1397. *Arch. Journ.* liv (1897), 275.

[4] Colt Hoare, *Sarum*, 99.   [5] Nichols, 112.   [6] Ibid. 129.

[7] Hope in *Arch.* l (1887), 133.   [8] *Test. Ebor.* 244.

[9] Ibid. 387.   [10] Hope in *Arch.* l (1887), 150.

[11] *Test. Ebor.* 279.

[12] Palgrave, iii. 335. He also owned one with the English inscription 'Wyth Goddes help'. Ibid. 332.

[13] Now in the Victoria and Albert Museum, 217.1879.

Another bronze jug, with the arms and badge of Richard II,[1] bears the legend

> *He that wyl not spare when he may he*
> *schal not spend when he wold.*
> *Deme the best in every dowt*
> *til the trowthe be tryed out.*

Mazers of the same date often had similar inscriptions. One belonging to Walter de Bruge, canon of York, who died in 1396, had on the cover

> *Ho so ys lengyst alyue*
> *Tak this cope withowtyn stryfe.*[2]

A mazer of about 1420[3] has an inscription of the same kind:

> *hold yowre tung and sey þe best*
> *And let yowre neghboure sitte in rest*
> *Hoe so lyustþ god to plese*
> *Let hys neybore lyue in ese.*

They distil the wholesome wisdom of the hall fireside as clearly as the samplers of the eighteenth century do the genteel morality of the parlour.

Literature influenced English decoration in the latter part of the fourteenth century in other ways than the use of inscriptions. The literary subjects which had begun to come into vogue in the thirteenth century were further developed. A wooden casket[4] of about 1356 is carved with the scene from the Arthurian legend in which Tristram keeps tryst with Yseult beneath the tree; a few years later the same subject reappears on misericords at Chester and Lincoln, and on a cup belonging to Edward III in 1370.[5] The Knight of the Swan[6] and the *Lai d'Aristote*[7] are illustrated on misericords,

---

[1] Now in the British Museum. It travelled far, and turned up in the metal paid by the defeated Ashanti at Kumasi in 1896.

[2] *Test. Ebor.* 209. Cf. a mazer with an inscription on its silver rim:
> *In the name of the trinite*
> *fille the kup and drink to me.*
>
> *Arch. Journ.* ii (1846), 195.

[3] In the British Museum; see Hope in *Arch.* l (1887), 149.

[4] In the Victoria and Albert Museum.   [5] Palgrave, iii. 264.

[6] At Exeter and Chichester.

[7] Alexander's Flight occurs at Lincoln, Chester, Gloucester, Beverley (St. Mary's), Wells, and Darlington.

and the *Roman de Renard* appears on the misericords of Cockersand priory about 1340[1] and Bristol abbey some hundred years later. Bruin is sent to summon Reynard to the court of King Lion, Bruin is caught in a cleft stick and Tybert the Cat is caught in the gin; Isengrin and Bruin dance with delight to hear of Reynard's condemnation, and watch the gallows being erected for his execution.

So, too, the illustration of secular manuscripts progressed, if slowly. An exceptional manuscript of the *Bible historiale*[2] written in the second quarter of the fourteenth century shows a fresh hand at work, with little traditional skill but a kind of rustic vigour. The crude and lively line-drawings, faintly tinted, are at the beginning of a long series of characteristically English book-illustrations.

The *Canterbury Tales* were probably written in great part between 1387 and 1388; they received far less illustration than might have been expected. The fact depended on a lack of tradition; the genre of story-telling in English was too new to have achieved a place among the manuscripts that were illustrated, though it is perfectly clear that a school of illuminators who could paint the marginal decorations of the Luttrell Psalter about 1340 could well have illustrated the *Canterbury Tales* fifty years later.[3] One manuscript,[4] however, shows Chaucer reading his poems to a noble company, seated in a shady grove; the whole is rather French than English in feeling, though the miniature looks as if it had been painted by an Englishman.

Another manuscript, of the anonymous *Pearl*,[5] has four miniatures: one of the author sleeping in a meadow by a flowery mound; one of him standing by a river; one of him seeing a vision of a lady; and one kneeling by the water with a town in the background. They are undistinguished in execution and seem to be the work of an amateur dauber rather than of a skilled artist, but they are new illustrations of a romantic theme.

---

[1] Now at Lancaster.   [2] Holkham MS. 666.

[3] It is worth noting that all the decorative schemes described by Chaucer are based on French prototypes. See Joan Evans, 'Chaucer and Decorative Art', *Review of English Studies*, vi (Oct. 1930).

[4] Corpus Christi College, Cambridge.   [5] B.M. Cotton Nero A x.

The best manuscript of Richard Rolle's[1] poems has illustrations rather of the same kind; such a one as the picture of the author with the name of Jesus upon his breast has its own simple charm. *The boke of hunting that is cleped Maystere of game*[2] was illustrated with little pictures of huntable beasts, and the metrical life of St. Edmund the Martyr by John Lydgate[3] received adequate illustration in the copy presented to Henry VI on his visit to the abbey of Bury St. Edmunds in 1433. On the whole, however, the English illuminators fought shy of more romantic compositions. So late as 1445 the book of poems and romances in French[4] given to Margaret of Anjou by John Talbot, earl of Salisbury, who escorted her to England for her marriage, was a composite production. The miniatures illustrating the romances are French work; the volume may well have been first produced in Paris. But an English hand has added the miniatures that make it appropriate to the occasion—a genealogical tree, portraits of Margaret and her husband receiving the volume, and a stiff little border of daisies on the title-page.

It is therefore not surprising that models were lacking for pictorial tapestry, when the craft became rather precariously established in London in the fourteenth century. The ordinances of the trade of Tapicers date from 1331,[5] and the men named as members of the company bear English names,[6] but by 1362 they seem overshadowed by a 'trade of Alien Weavers'. By 1370[7] there are two guilds, 'the mystery of the Flemish Weavers' and that of the weavers of Brabant. In 1374, however, four tapicers with English names were prosecuting Katharine Dutchwoman for mixing linen and wool in a coster 'wrought upon the loom after the manner of arras'. The comparatively few pieces of tapestry that are recorded as having been made in London are all relatively small and simple heraldic pieces, such as the halling of blue with

---

[1] B.M. Cotton Faustina B 6, part 2.　　[2] Bodleian Douce MS. 335.
[3] B.M. Harley MS. 2278.　　[4] B.M. Royal MS. 15 E VI.
[5] Riley, 178.
[6] Walter de Stebenhuthe (Stepney), Richard Merk, Richard Frere, Nicholas atte Forde, John de Bromholm, and Nicholas de Suthereye.
[7] The Flemings met in the churchyard of St. Laurence Pountney and the Brabanters in the churchyard of St. Mary Somerset.

red roses and coats of arms, 'lately made in London', recorded in the 1392 will of Richard earl of Arundel[1] and the twelve cushions and five bankers with the arms of England and France which John Stoute made for Henry VI in 1425.[2]

Most of the large tapestries mentioned in English inventories are described as being of Arras work. The will of the Black Prince mentions his *Sale d'Arras du pas de Saladyn.* Many were gifts from France and Burgundy. In 1393 the duke of Burgundy gave the duke of Lancaster tapestries of King Clovis, Pharaoh, and Moses, *d'amis et amies,* and to Gloucester others with the life of the Virgin, and *Deduit et Plaisance ainsi qu'ils sont en gibier.* In 1394 he gave Richard II a Crucifixion, a Calvary, and a tapestry with the life of Saint Ursin, followed after agreement was made between them by a tapestry of Virtues and Vices accompanied by kings and emperors.[3] Royal gifts may also have been the source of many of the other tapestries recorded in England. Thomas duke of Gloucester, for example, in 1397 had at his castle of Pleshey arras with the histories of Charlemagne and Godfrey of Bouillon,[4] with the story of Love, with ladies in the Castle of Love, with Gamelin and Lancelot fighting, the siege perilous, *ove roles amy et amors* and with the story of *Geras filtz au Roy de ffryson.* The rest had religious subjects, such as St. George, the Nativity, the Presentation in the Temple, and the Purification of Our Lady, and the Sepulchre. Henry V owned tapestries of epic and religious subjects with French inscriptions: Charlemagne, St. George, the Three Kings of Cologne, the Salutation, Anthenor, Sir Perceval, Abraham and Isaac, the Five Joys of Our Lady, the Seven Ages of Man, the stories of Octavian king of Rome, and of King Pharamond: all subjects that find parallels among recorded tapestries of French or Flemish weaving. Two sets with the Chronicles of Jerusalem and the voyage of Godfrey of Bouillon[5] seem to belong to an earlier date. Two only seem to have been specially woven for the

---

[1] Nichols, 128.
[2] Devon, 393. I cannot accept as English the panel from Sir Hercules Read's collection (Royal Academy Exhibition 1924, no. 125).
[3] H. David, *Philippe le Hardi*, Dijon (1947).
[4] *Arch. Journ.* liv (1897), 275.   [5] Rymer, IV. iv. 105.

English market: one with the story of Bevis of Hampton[1] and one with that of St. Edward the King. Besides these tapestries of literary illustration he had others that reflect the lyrics and literature of courtly romance: arras tapestries with *la vie d'amours*, *l'arbre de jeunesse*, tournaments, a lady in a tent. Others, of which only the beginning of the inscription is recorded, clearly belong to the same group. *Vessi amour sovient, Dame cest Chapelet me donez, Vessi dames de noble afaire*; such *incipits* could only continue as courtly lyrics. The same feeling is evident in the decoration of a chest of about 1420, now at Queens' College, Cambridge: the front is painted with a man offering a woman a ring, while she in return holds out to him her heart.

Much more rarely religious art is a direct reflection of didactic literature.[2] The *Dit des Trois Morts et des Trois Vifs*, the story of three men who met three dreadful corpses, to find they were themselves, is illustrated in the later part of the Lisle Psalter about 1339. Thirty examples of it in wall painting are known to have existed in English churches;[3] twelve survive, of which those at Pickforth in Lincolnshire[4] and Widford near Burford are the best.

A window in the church of All Hallows, York,[5] has its fifteen panels each painted with one of the signs of the last fifteen days of the world as given in Richard Rolle's *Pricke of Conscience*, with explanatory inscriptions that do not exactly correspond with his text but are very close to it. Here we may guess at an illuminated manuscript as intermediary, but there is no evidence.

In 1426 Lydgate was in Paris, and saw the famous *Danse macabre* lately painted in the Cemetery of the Innocents; soon afterwards he translated the verses which accompanied the melancholy cavalcade, which showed Death leading men of every estate to their inevitable end.[6] In 1430 the cloister which Dean Thomas More

---

[1] Cf. the mazer, now at Harbledown hospital, with the story of Guy of Warwick on the print. W. St. John Hope in *Arch.* l (1887), 140.

[2] On the 'Christ of the Trades' see Appendix A.

[3] See E. Carleton Williams in *Journ. Brit. Arch. Ass.* 3rd ser. vii (1937), 31.

[4] See *Illustrated London News* (3 Jan. 1948), 24.

[5] Shaw, 33; Le Couteur, 53.

[6] See Dugdale, *St. Paul's*, 419; White, 350; Ellesmere MS., *Early English Text Society*, ed. White.

had lately built at St. Paul's[1] was adorned with paintings in imitation of the Paris ones, which had grown familiar to Englishmen during their occupation of the city. Jenkyn Carpenter gave the paintings in his capacity of executor to Richard Whittington, then lately dead.[2] Lydgate's verses were set under the paintings. Those for the Labourer may stand as an example:

> *I have wisshed after dethe ful ofte*
> *Al-be that I woude have fled hym nowe.*
> *I had levere to have leyne unsofte*
> *In wynde & reyne & have gon atte plowe*
> *With spade & pikeys and labored for my prowe.*
> *Dolve & diched & atte Carte goon:*
> *For I may say & telle playnli howe*
> *In this worlde here there is reste noon. . . .*

Yet even so it is sadly that the Labourer is led to the grave.

The troubled years of the middle of the fourteenth century are directly reflected in a dearth of illuminated manuscripts. The break, which can hardly have been complete, is none the less noticeable, and is far more clearly marked in England than in France. Evidently there were fewer trained miniature-painters in this country, and the loss of some of them in the plague years must have been more acutely felt. The standard of English manuscripts of the second half of the fourteenth century falls far below that of the French ateliers. It is perhaps significant that when King John of France was in London in 1359 he ordered a psalter from 'Maistre Jean Langlois, escrivain', but when he had seen it, did not buy it, but gave him instead a noble for his pains.[3]

Some curious and interesting illustrations of the Book of Genesis[4] probably date from about 1360; the expressive faces and bizarre choice of incidents show something of the vitality of the East Anglian tradition, but the trees are more in the French manner. The manuscript may come from the English dominions in France.

---

[1] Dugdale, 93; Weever, 378. It was in two stories.

[2] Another version was painted in the palace of Whitehall.

[3] Doüet d'Arcq, *Comptes de l'Argenterie des rois de France au XIVe siècle*, Paris (1851) 240.

[4] B.M. Egerton MS. 1894. See Paecht in *Journ. Warburg and Courtauld Institutes*, vi (1943), 51, who finds antique and Italian analogies.

Almost contemporary are a group of manuscripts that include the Fitzwarin Psalter[1] and two other books of devotions,[2] notable for the curiously massive architectural frames that surmount the page illustrations. Another version of the scheme appears in a group of manuscripts which were made for the Bohun family in the years round 1365[3] in which the pinnacles of contemporary work in wood and stone are used to form a cresting to the more important pages (Pl. 47). The pictured panels are framed in octagons and quatrefoils of sculpture; the backgrounds are of burnished and punctated gold. The figures are no longer dressed in the simple classical clothes of such manuscripts as the Lisle Psalter, but follow the latest fashion, with some loss of dignity and grace. The same tendency has caused David to be represented like the victor of a tournament bringing back the head of Goliath to a bevy of ladies in fashionable dress.[4] Some of the large initials have the inner field divided into four compartments each containing a small and rather restless figure composition painted in pale clear colours against a background of punctated gold.

The tradition of the Bohun manuscripts is continued in the great missal which Nicholas Litlyngton, abbot of Westminster from 1362 to 1386, gave to his abbey.[5] It was executed between 1383 and 1384 by Thomas Preston, a layman who was lodged, clothed, and fed by the abbey while he did the work. The most important illustration is a full-page Crucifixion:[6] an ambitious composition that tries to escape from the noble simplicity of tradition and succeeds only in dispersing the spectator's attention on subsidiary figures. It looks like the work of an English painter of the second rank who has come under Flemish or Dutch influences. These are

[1] Paris Bib. Nat. lat. 765.

[2] Bodleian MS. Misc. liturg. 198 and Cambridge, Fitzwilliam MS. 48, fol. 12 b. See Wormald in Journ. Warburg and Courtauld Institutes, vi (1943), 71.

[3] See James and Millar. To those there enumerated may be added BM. Egerton MS. 3277.

[4] Cf. Bodleian Lat. liturg. F 2, fol. 144 v, where the Dragon is slain by St. George dressed in a coat with immensely long pinked sleeves and a jewelled belt. It dates from soon after 1405.

[5] Millar, 28. M. R. James, A Descriptive Catalogue of MSS. in the Library of St. John's College, Cambridge, 8, relates to it a book of Statutes and Charters (MS. A 7) written soon after 1388. [6] Harrison, Treasures of Illumination, Pl. 21.

again apparent in a book of Hours[1] that may have been written for the marriage of Richard II and Anne of Bohemia, though it is wholly English in the admirable birds that decorate the borders.

Far finer than either of these manuscripts must have been a missal written and illuminated for the Carmelite House of the London Whitefriars before 1391. Only the miniatures now remain,[2] but the book has been most skilfully and ingeniously reconstituted by Dr. Margaret Rickert,[3] who recognizes certain foreign elements and thinks some foreign artists may have been employed. The page-size was unusually large, and though all the illustrations are contained in initials, they are none the less of considerable size. There are a few East Anglian survivals; one or two marginal grotesques, chiefly ostriches,[4] a group of the Trinity, with the Virgin and Child and two lay donors, with scrolls in the Tickhill manner,[5] and a few examples of the minute and closely set tiered compositions on which the East Anglian illuminators had been wont to exercise their skill.[6] The appearance of Gabriel in the Annunciation scene[7] as a feathered seraph recalls similar figures in East Anglian glass. One painter uses the delicately pricked gold grounds of the Lytlington missal.[8] Many of the miniatures, however, have a more pictorial quality than has hitherto been seen (Pl. 48 a).

By this time the stream of illuminated books was running in full spate. A surprising number of inferior books of Hours were produced in the reigns of Richard II and Henry IV;[9] a series less remarkable in itself than as forming the iconographic storehouse from which the artists of the late fifteenth century drew their models. Only a few stand out as being of exceptional quality. The lectionary which was written for John, Lord Lovel of Tichmersh,

---

[1] Bodleian MS. lat. liturg. fol. 3.

[2] B.M. Add. MS. 29704 and 29705.

[3] *Burl. Mag.* lxvii (1935), 99 and *Speculum*, xvi (1941).

[4] It may be remembered that the ostrich, chained, crowned, and holding a nail in its beak, was one of the devices of Anne of Bohemia. It appears on her dress in the Westminster effigy.   [5] 29704, fol. 35.

[6] e.g. 29704, fol. 16, Death and Coronation of the Virgin; 29704, fol. 17, St. Lawrence.   [7] 29704, fol. 2.

[8] 29704, fols. 8, 9, 19.   [9] E. Saunders, i. 108.

who died in 1408, as a gift to Salisbury cathedral[1] is remarkable as including a portrait of the scribe presenting it to his patron. Its illumination was directed by a Dominican, John Siferwas. Lovel's head is a fine piece of portraiture; the borders keep some of the pleasing variety of an earlier age; every detail is delightful, yet there is a certain want of consistency and plan that keeps the whole at the level of minor art.

The next manuscript painter in England known to us is a painter of Cologne,[2] who has been skilfully identified by Dr. Margaret Rickert.[3] His name is given in a book of devotions[4] in which a miniature is signed *Hermannus Scheerre me fecit* and a background is inscribed *Omnia leuia sun[t] aman[ti]* and *tout dus en une; qui bien ayme tart oblie.* The two clues make it possible to assign to him a whole group of contemporary manuscripts. The motto *omnia leuia sunt amanti* appears in the Bible of Richard II[5] (Pl. 48 *b*) which displays a pictorial technique like that of some miniatures of the Lytlington Missal. It is one of the few bibles that were illustrated throughout in the fourteenth century. Many of its illustrations, like those of the Carmelite Missal, are set in large initials, but some are rectangular pictures set in the text, like the illustrations of a secular romance. Another fine manuscript that can be identified as his work is the book of Hours[6] written between about 1399 and 1410 for John de Beaufort, earl of Somerset, and his wife Margaret de Holand. The borders curiously combine an architectural framing with the characteristic English marginal scroll-work; the compositions are pictorial and full of movement. One background is inscribed *Omnia leuia sunt amanti, Si quis amat non laborat: dedaer.* This second inscription

[1] B.M. Harley MS. 7026. Another manuscript illuminated under the same direction is the Sherborne Missal in the collection of the duke of Northumberland at Alnwick. It includes many pictures and some skilful portraits: the abbot, Robert Bruyning, is represented about a hundred times. The innumerable birds in the margins are nearly all labelled with their names.

[2] There were three German guilds in London in the fifteenth century; that of the Holy Blood of Wilsnach was organized by 1459. Cooté, 6.

[3] *Burl. Mag.* lxi (1935), 39.

[4] B.M. Add. 16998; the signature is on fol. 37, the inscription on fol. 67.

[5] B.M. Royal MS. I E X, fol. 229, together with some French and Low German inscriptions. Of the accompanying missal, Add. 297045, only the initials survive.

[6] B.M. Royal MS. 2 A XVIII. Millar, 35.

gives a clue to the Chichele Breviary[1] which has the inscription *Si quis amat non laborat quod Herman*. The Chester Beatty Hours, again, have the background inscription *si quis amat non laborat: omnia leuia sunt amanti*, and the Bedford Hours[2] two inscriptions *Herman your meke seruant* and *I am Herman your owne seruant*. Finally, Dr. Rickert has drawn attention to the wills of Peter of Cologne proved in London in 1407, in which his brother Herman of Cologne,[3] a Carmelite, is mentioned, and one 'Herman Lymnour' appears as a witness. Thus it has been possible to group a whole series of manuscripts together, and to name their painter; and since there was a Carmelite connexion it is by no means impossible that the splendid Carmelite Missal should be included in the group. The miniatures of one of its painters certainly show strong analogies with Herman's work.[4]

Foreign influence, if less markedly Rhenish, is also evident in the book of Hours written in the first quarter of the fifteenth century for Henry Beauchamp, earl of Warwick, and Cicely his wife.[5] There is little that is English about its predilection for such strong colours as a hot orange contrasted with a cold blue, or in its angels painted in blue, pink, and orange in the French court style; yet its decorative borders are entirely English. The same mixture of influences seem to be at work in the psalter of Humphrey duke of Gloucester,[6] dating from about 1415. The borders are English, but such miniatures as that which shows the duke kneeling before a Christ of Pity are evidently inspired by foreign models.

The normal English standard of the early fifteenth century is better represented by the Hours of Henry IV, of which the initials

---

[1] Lambeth Palace MS. 69.   [2] B.M. Add. MS. 42131.

[3] It may be recalled that in 1382 Richard II's embroiderer was John of Cologne. Tout, *Chapters in Admin. Hist.* iv. 390.

[4] See Kuhn, *Art. Bull.* xxii (1940), 138. He considers that the rest were painted by a Fleming temporarily resident in England. He adds to the list of Scheerre's work some (but not all) of the miniatures of the Sarum Hours, Bodleian lat. liturg. F 2.

[5] In the collection of Mr. C. W. Dyson Perrins, who has kindly allowed me to examine the manuscript. It was formerly MS. 59 in the Yates Thompson collection. It belonged to Elizabeth Woodville, whose signature appears on one page and is commonly known as 'The Hours of Elizabeth the Queen'.

[6] B.M. Royal MS. 2 B. 1.

are filled with crowded compositions in compartments that continue the East Anglian tradition with remarkable fidelity, or by such simple portraiture as that of the author presenting his English version of the *De regimine principum* to Henry V.[1]

The reign of Richard II is the most splendid in the history of English medieval painting on panel. The impetus for this development certainly came from abroad, but its sources seem to have been manifold. King John of France was accompanied, when he was a prisoner in England, by Girart d'Orléans, his favourite painter, to whom the portrait of him in the Louvre is often ascribed, and Froissart tells us that André Beauneveu did some work in England. At the same time the presence of John and Herman of Cologne in England establishes a link with the Rhenish school; and the great galleys of Genoa and Venice may well have brought minor works of Italian art, as well as silk brocades, in exchange for English wool. It is not necessary to talk of an 'International style' to explain the complex influences which can be seen in the art of the reign of Richard II.

The London painters mostly lived in Cripplegate; by 1389 St. Giles was the church of their guild.[2] Gilbert Prince of Litlington, the king's official painter, lived here until at the end of 1391[3] he was succeeded by his son or nephew Thomas Prince of Litlington, who continued to hold the office at least until 1402.[4] The recorded works of both men are for such things as banners and devices for tournaments, masquerades, and feasts; yet by analogy with the official painters of the French royal court it seems likely that they were accomplished artists who also painted panel pictures for their royal master, though none of these can now be identified.

One of the pictures of which the English origin is undoubted is the retable in Norwich cathedral (Pl. 51),[5] painted on oak boards set in a moulded frame of oak and divided into five panels. The frame is set with glass panels imitating enamel, and decorated with

---

[1] B.M. Arundel 38.
[2] Lethaby in *Walpole Soc.* i (1911–12), 71. The guild was the confraternity of Our Lady and St. Giles.　　　[3] Tout, iv. 390; Devon, 252.　　　[4] Devon, 291.
[5] Best described by W. St. John Hope in *Norfolk Archaeology*, xiii (1898), 295; Borenius and Tristram, 39.

leafage in gilt gesso. The back of the glass panels was painted with banners of arms, of which a few remain. These are of Despencer, for Henry Despencer, bishop of Norwich from 1370 to 1406; Hales, for Sir Stephen Hales, and Morieux for Sir Thomas Morieux, who both helped the bishop to suppress the rebellion of 1381; Kerdeston, Gernon, Howard, and Clifford, other Norfolk families who may well have taken part in the same campaign. For this reason Sir William St. John Hope suggested that it might have been a thank-offering for the suppression of the rebellion.

The five panels represent the Scourging of Christ, Christ bearing the Cross, the Crucifixion, Resurrection, and Ascension, painted in delicate colours on a gilt gesso background with sprays of oak and vine in relief. The whole offers a progression, rather than a break, from the East Anglian tradition of manuscript illumination. It may be compared with three panels in the Norwich church of St. Michael-at-Plea, that probably come from another retable by the same hand; they represent the Crucifixion and the Betrayal of Christ, and have gilt backgrounds with vine patterns. Two more panels were found on taking down a cottage in Huby's Yard, Norwich, and are now in the FitzWilliam Museum. Blomefield records a fifth panel of the Resurrection existing in his time at St. Michael-at-Plea, which would have completed the retable.

Thomas de Ocle is mentioned as a painter in the eleventh year of Richard II's reign, and Robert de Ocle in the reign of Henry IV.[1] This family of Norwich painters may well have produced the retables.[2]

The London pictures of the same time are no more easy to attribute to a painter or a school. The great panel of Richard II in Westminster abbey[3] has been cruelly restored; the diapered gilt ground and the gesso work of the crown, globe, and sceptre were

<hr>

[1] *Arch. Journ.* xlvii (1890), 76.
[2] *Burl. Mag.* xxvi (1913), 93; Borenius and Tristram, Pl. 74. A Crucifixion picture in the collection of the late Lord Lee of Fareham has also been brought into relation with the Norwich painters, though it seems to have a stronger tinge of Dutch or Flemish influence, and is painted in tempera on canvas and not in the English fashion on a primed oak panel. The background is not of gilt gesso, but of a dull blue.
[3] Borenius and Tristram, 26; Shaw in *Burl. Mag.* lxv (1934), 171.

all removed in 1866.[1] Yet it remains curiously impressive in its hierarchic impassivity; it seems a noble expression of Richard's doctrine of the Divine Right of Kings. Its exact date is not known: it probably dates from about 1388. In the eighteenth century Dart suggested that it commemorated St. Edward's Day in 1390, when the king kept the feast at Westminster in his royal robes.[2]

The Wilton Diptych (Pls. 50, 51) is without question the greatest picture of the age that is left to us. None has received more diverse interpretation.[3] On the face of it the picture is simple enough. The young Richard II kneels before the Virgin and Child; the king is accompanied by three patron saints, Edmund the King with his arrow, Edward the Confessor with his ring, and John the Baptist holding his lamb. Eleven angels wearing crowns of white roses are grouped round the Virgin; they wear collars formed of broom-pods and have the badge of a hart, lodged, gorged with a crown, and chained, embroidered on their blue dresses. One of them holds a tall staff from which flies the banner of St. George, *argent* a cross *gules*. The Holy Child, on whose halo the crown of thorns is incised, holds out His hands as if to take the banner and give it to Richard, whose hands are open ready to receive it. The king wears a collar of broom-pods and an ouch shaped like the hart badge of the angels; his dress of gold tissue is brocaded with medallions of the hart lodged within collars of broom-pods. The back of the diptych is painted in a coarser style with the arms of Edward the Confessor impaling those of France and England quarterly, surmounted by a mantled helm with the royal lion, and with the hart badge in a grassy field.

Lord Conway and Mr. Everard Green suggested[4] that it was an offering made at the altar of Our Lady of Pew at Westminster at the time of Richard's coronation. In their view Edmund and Edward point to the boy king as their successor; St. John the

[1] A photograph of the picture in its original state is in the library of the Victoria and Albert Museum, but is not sharp enough for reproduction.

[2] *Westmonasterium*, i. 51.

[3] The arguments have been most recently summarized by Professor Bodkin in *The Wilton Diptych*, 1947 (Gallery Books).

[4] *The Times*, 26 June, 1929: *Burl. Mag.* lv (1929), 209. See also Borenius and Tristram, 27; Borenius, *English Primitives*, 11; W. G. Constable in *Burl. Mag.* lv (1929), 42.

Baptist is there because Richard succeeded to the throne on his vigil and took him as his patron. Richard was in his eleventh year at the time, hence the eleven angels who accompany the Virgin. It should be added that in my own view St. Edward and St. Edmund are there not only as the English royal saints, but also to represent the young king's grandfather and father, Edward III and the Black Prince, of whom they are portraits. If it is not a coronation piece, it may commemorate the moment in 1389 when Richard assumed complete power by a kind of re-coronation in St. Stephen's chapel, with a renewal of homage.

The only serious objection to this date is the heraldic evidence.[1] The impaling of the shields of England and Edward the Confessor was made, according to the author of the *Annales Ricardi Secundi*, in 1397 or 1398, and the collars of broom-pods worn by Richard and the attendant angels seem to represent the collar of the *Ordre de la Cosse de Geneste* presented to Richard by Charles VI of France as a wedding gift in 1395 or 1396. On the other hand, the portrait of the king represents him as a beardless boy, and not, as does his bronze effigy made in 1395, with a mature countenance and a forked beard. While the shield on the reverse of the diptych may easily have been painted at a later date, the collars of broom-pods offer a real difficulty, though it is possible that as a Plantagenet Richard might wear such a collar on his own account. This possibility is confirmed by its use on the brocade of his dress round his personal badge of the White Hart.

The approximation of St. Edmund and St. Edward to the physical types of the Black Prince and Edward III,[2] and the evident portraiture of the young king, suggest that it must have been painted in England. There is nothing, indeed, but its superlative quality to suggest that it was by any other than an English

---

[1] First pointed out by Miss M. V. Clarke in *Burl. Mag.* (June 1931); reprinted in her *Fourteenth Century Studies*, 272. I do not accept her theory of a connexion with the Order of the Cross.

[2] Edward III's appearance is known to us from his tomb statue, an evident portrait. The Black Prince's shows him helmeted, but with the long straight nose and high cheekbones of the picture. His effigy as a weeper on his father's tomb and a badge in the British Museum which shows him kneeling before the Trinity portray him with a moustache and beard like those of St. Edmund.

artist. No French painter would be likely to set three figures in a row as the three saints are set, though an artist of the school of Stephen Lochner might do it, and the English artist who painted the Presentation in the Temple in St. Stephen's chapel did do it. No Cologne painter, however, would be likely to paint with that lucid clarity that illumines the Wilton Diptych; there is a total lack of Rhenish *morbidezza*. The whole idea of the diptych is French; such compositions of a great man and his patron saint kneeling before the Virgin were far from unusual in the royal chapels of France at the time.[1] It may well be that the Wilton Diptych was painted by an Englishman not unfamiliar with French painting, but we have as yet no evidence which will clinch the matter.

Another picture, much less fine in quality, has been claimed to represent Edward III, the Black Prince, and Richard II, under the guise of the Magi;[2] its two older kings certainly resemble the Edmund and Edward of the Wilton Diptych. The youngest king would seem to be about the age of Richard II in the diptych, and wears a collar of rays that seems an allusion to his badge of the rising sun.

Altar pictures on panel were by the end of the fourteenth century not uncommon in the chapels of nobles and rich prelates. In 1386, for example, Richard de Ravenser, archdeacon of Lincoln, had in his chapel 'j tabula lignea depicta cum diversis ymaginibus cum ij foliis includentibus tercium';[3] in 1397 there were among the goods of Thomas duke of Gloucester, seized at Pleshey, 'iij tablettes chescun de iij foils depeintez de diverses ymages'.[4] It is rare to find their subjects described, but the 1388 inventory of Westminster[5] describes two diptychs given to the church by Abbot Nicholas

---

[1] Professor Borenius, *English Primitives*, 11, compares it with the duc de Berry and St. John before the Virgin and Child in a manuscript in the Brussels Royal Library. Bodkin, Figs. 3 and 4. Cf. the post-mortem inventory of Philippe le Bon: 'Deux tableauz de bois, dont lun est à l'assemblance du Duc Philippe le Hardi, et l'autre Nostre Dame et pluseurs sains.' Laborde, *Les Ducs de Bourgogne*, ii. 165.

[2] *Illustrated London News* (15 August, 1936), 294.   [3] Pretyman, 11.

[4] *Arch. Journ.* liv (1897), 290. He also owned an embroidered diptych with the Crucifixion and the Coronation of the Virgin.

[5] Wickham Legg in *Arch.* lii (1888), 240.

Litlyngton, one with a Crucifixion with figures of the Virgin, Mary Magdalene, and St. John in one leaf, and the Virgin and Child between St. John the Baptist and St. Katherine on the other; and a second with the Salutation and the Nativity. The presence of St. John the Baptist and St. Katherine, who must have been the abbot's patron saints, makes a curious link with a diptych in the Museo Nazionale of Florence. It is usually regarded as French,[1] but does not fit in to any known series of French pictures. One leaf represents the Crucifixion, with St. John and the Holy Maries upholding the Virgin on one side, and St. John the Baptist and St. Katherine on the other. The second leaf (Pl. 52) represents the Adoration of the Magi. It is, I think, not impossible that it was painted in England for Abbot Nicholas Litlyngton.[2]

The members of the chapter of Westminster were, like their abbot, the patrons of painters. Among the paintings in the chapter-house are five arched compositions given by John of Northampton, a monk of the house between about 1372 and 1404.[3] They represent apocalyptic scenes, and are all directly derived from an illustrated manuscript of rather earlier date.[4] They must once have been of great beauty and a strange visionary intensity.

The number of pictures known to us from the early fifteenth century is curiously small compared with those of the reign of Richard II. We know that in 1412 Jean sans Peur, duke of Burgundy, gave Henry IV a picture, small enough to have its own travelling-case,[5] but its subject is not recorded. The next painting of any importance is of quite another level: it consists of two wings, perhaps once the doors of an aumbry in Ely cathedral.[6] The panels, which probably date from about 1425, are painted in distemper on a ground of gilt gesso patterned in relief. They

[1] Lemoisne, Fig. 20.

[2] It is interesting to surmise that there may have been some tie of blood or propinquity between the abbot and the two Litlington painters; all came from the Sussex village of Litlington.

[3] J. G. Noppen in *Burl. Mag.* lxi (1932), 146.

[4] Mr. Noppen suggests Trinity College MS. B 102 which has a Westminster connexion.

[5] Laborde, *Les Ducs de Bourgogne*, i. 45.

[6] Now in the collection of the Society of Antiquaries, Borenius and Tristram, Pl. 75.

represent scenes from the life of St. Etheldreda, the founder of Ely.[1] Even the references to pictures in wills are few.[2] The Dissolution inventories make mention of a considerable number of pictures,[3] but many of these may have been of the end of the fifteenth century or even later.

Yet about this time a portrait was expected to be so lifelike as to give real evidence as to the charms of the sitter. In 1442, when Beckington was trying to arrange a marriage between Henry VI and one of the daughters of the comte d'Armagnac, he sent instructions to his envoys, who included a painter: 'and at your first commyng thider, in al haste possible, that ye do portraie the iiij daughters in their kertelles simple, and their visages, lyk as you see their stature and their beauete and color of skynne and their countenances, with almaner of features, and these to be sent to the king in all haste for him to make his choice.'[4] None the less the oldest existing family portrait of an English gentleman, that of Edward Grimston,[5] was painted in 1446 by no English artist but by Petrus Christus, a Fleming.

The art of alabaster carving was in the fourteenth and fifteenth centuries characteristic of certain districts of England, notably Nottingham, Lincoln, and York, where the alabaster quarried in Staffordshire and Derbyshire was carved, and of the valley of the Meuse where alabaster was also found. In both countries the most important work lay in the field of monumental sculpture,[6] but England also developed a considerable trade in statues and reliefs

[1] Her marriage with Egfrid, prince of Northumbria; her parting from him; her superintending of the building of the first church at Ely; and the translation of her sister the abbess Sexburga in the presence of the bishop of Northumbria.

[2] e.g. Lady Ela Shardelowe, 1457: 'unam tabulam pictam stantem super altarem meum.' Tymms, 13.

[3] Pipewell abbey, Northants., had four 'tables of wood paynted' (Dugdale, v. 440); St. Martin's nunnery at Diss '11 olde small tables paynted wt. imagery' (ibid. iv. 542) and Peterborough five such tables (ibid. i. 316). The *Rites of Durham* (Fowler, 33) mention under the lantern 'a most curiouse and fine table with ij leves to open and clos againe all of ye noble Passion of our Lord Jesus Christ most richlye and curiously sett furth in most lyvelie colours all like ye burnishe gold, as he was tormented and as he honge on ye cross, which was a most lamentable sight to beholde'.

[4] T. Bekyngton, *Official Correspondence*, Rolls Series, ii. 183.

[5] Still in the possession of his descendant the earl of Verulam. The companion portrait of his wife is in the Berlin Museum.   [6] For England see below, p. 153.

for church use. The craft takes its place beside that of illumination (though on a lower artistic level) as one of the first to reach a commercial level of organization and production.

The earliest productions seem to have been images to set upon the altar in churches and private chapels. The earliest record is that of the images of the Trinity and the Virgin given to Durham by John Fossor, prior from 1341 to 1347.[1] By 1360 the usage was well established; an inventory of the possessions of the late Queen Isabella, made in that year, includes among the chapel stuff an alabaster figure of the Virgin and a broken one of St. Stephen.[2] A certain number of such images survive, for the most part headless; their number must once have been very great. At the Dissolution the small priory of Sandwell in Staffordshire had nine images,[3] St. Martin's nunnery at Dover two 'images of whyte Alleeblaster' in the chapel;[4] Pipewell abbey in Northamptonshire images of Our Lady of Pity[5] and St. Nicholas; Peterborough four images,[6] and the high altar at Durham alabaster statues of Our Lady between St. Cuthbert and St. Oswald, all richly gilded.[7] By 1382 such images were even sent to Italy. The licence exists by which the king ordered the customs officers at Southampton to allow Cosmato Gentilis, the pope's collector, to export three alabaster images of the large sort, of the Virgin, St. Peter, and St. Paul, and one smaller of the Trinity.[8]

Little images of the kind were often bestowed by will upon a church. The testament of Sir Thomas d'Arcy, drawn up in 1398, leaves instructions for his tomb at Henyngs and orders that twenty shillings be expended on an alabaster image of St. Anne for the altar of the Blessed Virgin in that church.[9]

Such images were destroyed by hundreds at the Reformation. In the little chapel of Flawford near Nottingham, however, pious hands buried three of them beneath the floor before the commissioners arrived, and a happy chance has brought them once

---

[1] Hope, 3.
[2] Palgrave, iii. 245.
[3] Dugdale, iv. 191.
[4] Ibid. iv. 542.
[5] Cf. will of John Raventhorp, chaplain, who in 1432 left to St. Saviour's, York 'ymaginem Pietatis de alabastis'. *Test. Ebor.* ii. 28.
[6] Ibid. i. 316.
[7] Fowler, *Rites of Durham*, 7.
[8] Rymer, *Foedera*, vii. 357.
[9] *Test. Vet.* i. 146.

more to light.[1] The figures are each about 3 feet high: a Virgin
(Pl. 53), St. Peter, with a little priestly donor at his foot, and a
bishop. They are remarkable less for their artistic excellence[2] than
as typical examples of sculpture such as most of the churches of
England must once have contained. Another Virgin of finer
quality and slightly later date, but headless, was found in the
churchyard of Broughton-in-Craven, Yorkshire, in 1863;[3] a third
is in Royston church.

A remarkably fine group of the Trinity,[4] probably dating from
the early years of the fifteenth century, is now at Boston (Pl. 54).
The dress of the donors who kneel at the feet of God show that
they were of the courtly class, and the statue was doubtless specially
ordered by them. It is an impressive piece of sculpture; the
monumental composition, the stylized hair like sun-rays of God
the Father, the noble hanging Christ, the souls of the righteous
held in a fold of God's mantle, are all greatly conceived and finely
carved. It is a measure of what we have lost.

St. Christopher was not uncommonly represented in churches
in the late fourteenth and fifteenth centuries, since it was believed
that anyone who looked upon his representation was safe from
violent death for that day. Most often he was shown in a crude
wall-painting, but occasionally he was represented by an alabaster
statuette.[5] Two are in the Victoria and Albert Museum; the earlier
has a little figure of its priestly donor at the base.

These sculptures, though they give the effect of being in the
round, are all flattened at the back to be set against a retable, upon
a screen, or in a niche. Alabaster, indeed, is not an ideal medium
for a free-standing figure, and most of the work of the alabaster
sculptors was in relief. Their chief work was on panels or 'tables'

---

[1] They are now in the Nottingham Museum. See Prior and Gardner, Fig. 60, 405;
Arch. Journ. lxi (1904), 225.

[2] The Virgin may profitably be compared with the contemporary French statue
from the Chapelle Saint-Jean near the Abbaye Royale d'Abbecourt. Gardner, *French
Med. Sculpt.*, Fig. 391.

[3] Hildburgh in *Burl. Mag.* lxxxi (1939), 63.

[4] The dove was probably once painted upon the cross.

[5] Occasionally, too, he was represented in larger sculpture, for example in the
stone statue on the tower of Terrington St. Clement, near King's Lynn, of about 1340.
Prior and Gardner, Fig. 380.

that were set in wooden frames to form retables and reredoses. The fact that both stone and wood were freely painted and gilded served to harmonize the two.

One of the first works of the kind of which we have documentary evidence is the great reredos of St. George's, Windsor, which was ordered from Peter Maceon of Nottingham in 1370 and completed in 1372.[1] It was so large that ten carts, each drawn by eight horses, were required to bring it from Nottingham to Windsor. Unfortunately the subjects of its panels are not recorded. In 1372 John, Lord Neville of Raby, gave Durham a new base for the shrine of St. Cuthbert, chiefly worked in alabaster, and in 1380 the great reredos with alabaster figures. Both of these were brought from London, packed in boxes, by sea.

The number of lesser retables or reredoses in the country was extremely large. The canons of Ripon, for example, had six alabaster retables in their church. Some were exported abroad at the time they were made, many at the Reformation; there is no branch of English medieval art which has to be studied over a wider field.

The dating of the alabaster tables is of unusual difficulty; stock types continued in use over long periods. The provisional dating established by Professor Prior in 1913[2] into two groups, before and after 1420, still holds good. The earliest group has flat backgrounds and inward-sloping rims; a typical example is the slab with the Adoration of the Magi at Long Melford.[3] The finest are the broken tables taken out of the walls of Kettlebaston church in Suffolk and now in the British Museum;[4] they seem to have originally formed a retable. A square slab from Beauchef abbey,[5] given by the Foljambes whose arms it bears, is carved with a rather stiff representation of the murder of Becket. It appears to date from about 1375. The subsequent series of slab-retables, which can best be studied in the Hildburgh collection in the Victoria and Albert Museum, must be treated as a whole, since it is rarely possible to date them exactly, and their final development falls

[1] Devon, 173.
[2] In *Illustrated Catalogue of the Exhibition of the Society of Antiquaries*, 26.
[3] Prior and Gardner, Fig. 539.   [4] Ibid., Fig. 541.   [5] Ibid., Fig. 554.

outside this period. They usually cover a well-known cycle, such as the Passion or the life of the Virgin. An exceptional series of about 1440 represents the signs that go before the Judgement,[1] like the 'Prick of Conscience' window at York.[2] Another group represents the martyrdoms of saints; another the saints and angels of the *Te Deum*.[3] Their more commercial production is indicated by the fact that no donors are represented, even by conventional figures. Exceptionally, an unusually fine Passion series in the Hildburgh collection shows a figure in knightly dress helping to take down the body of Our Lord from the Cross; it can hardly represent anyone but the donor (Pl. 55). This slab is well enough preserved to show the colouring with which all the alabaster reliefs were once adorned. The background is diapered in gold; the cross is red; the haloes are painted with patterns in gilt, and the dresses were once coloured, with details picked out in gold. A panel with a Trinity in the same collection has God the Father's robes in red, His throne dark blue, and the Cross dark blue with decoration in red and gold. Such painting must once both have supplemented the rather summary modelling of the reliefs and also have diminished the sugary texture of the stone.

The brief reign of Henry V may have been glorious in the military annals of England, but it was remarkably sterile in the history of English art. Except for a small amount of ecclesiastical building,[4] there is little to record. Conus Melver, his goldsmith, in 1419 made him a silver image of the Virgin for St. George's chapel, Windsor;[5] the name has a German or Flemish ring. One of the king's few existing possessions is the portable altar he gave to Chartres cathedral in 1420, of which the rim is adorned with shells and daisies; the shell of St. James and the daisy of Margaret that figure on its rim suggest that it was originally made for someone else. It appears to be the work of a Burgundian smith. The chantry chapel at Westminster that commemorates Henry V[6]

---

[1] Prior and Gardner, Fig. 567.

[2] See P. Nelson in *Trans. Hist. Soc. Lancs. and Cheshire*, lxx (1918), 67.

[3] This group seems to have a Norfolk connexion. In it may be included a panel with nine female saints which Blomefield saw in St. Peter Mancroft, ii. 635.

[4] See above, p. 78.   [5] Devon, 357, 358.

[6] See below, p. 180.

and was ordered in his will is curiously undistinguished in its magnificence; it tries to reach French standards and only succeeds in being provincial. The dumpy proportion and heavy drapery found at Exeter cathedral in the statues added to the west front about 1380 are exploited with more technical skill but with equally unimpressive effect. Of all the statues, that of the Confessor alone has real dignity; the rest look like commercial alabaster figurines magnified and coarsened. Compared with the rather earlier French sculpture of Claus Sluter and the rather later work of Jacques Morel—both engaged on similar commemorative work— the sculptures of Henry V's chantry show that the victor in a war is more often than not artistically vanquished.

Henry VI was only nine months old when his reign began. The leading men of his youth divided the patronage of the arts between them: Humphrey of Gloucester, with his classical and Italianate literary tastes; John of Bedford, with his strong Burgundian and Luxembourg connexions; Cardinal Beaufort, the legitimatized son of John of Gaunt, who besides countless journeys to France had been on pilgrimage to Jerusalem and on crusade to Bohemia; and Richard earl of Warwick, a completely English Englishman.

The king's coronation in 1429 was marked by extremely moral pageants of Generosity, Grace, and Mercy; the subtlety at the banquet, that showed him between St. Edward and St. Louis, had a 'balade' that was an admonition to prayer. Even the jelly was 'wryten and noted with Te Deum Laudamus'. He grew up, as Fuller says, 'fitter for a coul than a crown', and his reign was one of disaster for England and of eclipse for her arts. Even his splendid foundations of Eton and King's College could not be accomplished in his own time, for his generosity had not practical competence behind it.

The decline is evident in such work as the stall canopies at Norwich that date from about 1430.[1] They are ugly as few works of Gothic art are ugly. The cusps end in stupid moon-faces; the crockets are limp, flat, and mechanical; the very curve of the arch has lost its grace. A similar decline is evident in sculpture. The

---

[1] S. Gardner, 182.

statues of the Erpingham gate at Norwich are stunted and the tabernacle work over-elaborate in its leafage; a growing commercialism stultifies the alabaster reliefs. The finances of the realm were so low that in 1433 the great officers of the Crown voluntarily reduced their salaries.

Only men of exceptional wealth were in a position to order objects of luxury. The abbot of Bury could, in 1430, contract for a silver-gilt pastoral staff, with the Assumption on one side of the head and the Salutation on the other, twelve apostles round the stem and St. Edmund under a tabernacle in the crook.[1] Humphrey of Gloucester, in 1438, could give manuscripts to Oxford and altar frontals and tabernacles of silver gilt to St. Albans,[2] and a cup with diagonal bands of foliage and rich cresting to Christ's College, Cambridge;[3] but these were probably already in his possession. Even Henry VI's marriage to Margaret of Anjou in 1445 was the signal, not for a peace but only for a truce with France, and by 1453 all the English possessions overseas but Calais and the Channel Islands had been lost. That year the king went out of his mind; the duke of York, as regent, tried to pacify the north, but when the king recovered early in 1455 his measures were largely undone and he raised an army to march against London. The curtain had gone up on the tragedy of Civil War.

[1] Way in *Bury and West Suffolk Arch. Inst. Trans.* (1850), 1. The smith was John Horwell of London.

[2] H. T. Riley, *John of Amundesham, Annales Mon. S. Albani*, ii (1871), 187.

[3] It may not be English.

VI

THE HOUSES OF THE GREAT

THE reign of Henry III marked a new standard of civilization in domestic architecture; but the civilization was in the main derived from France and the standard was not maintained by his successors. Yet the fact that it had once existed in England still had its influence, and men whose minds were not preoccupied with warfare could still find time to remember the elegancies of Westminster and Clarendon. While Edward I and his barons developed the concentric castle, as a purely military building that made few concessions to beauty and none to decoration, his prelates and abbots, who were less closely bound by feudal duty, were gradually developing a domestic architecture of their own. It was much less firmly dominated by the necessities of defence, and far more strongly inspired by the aesthetic requirements of pure architecture. Moreover, a bishop or an abbot was likely to employ a master mason already known to him for his church-building, and already accustomed to enriching his work with sculptured stone. One of the debts of England to her medieval churchmen is the strengthening of her tradition of beauty in the building of dwelling-houses.

The idea that a bishop should be nobly housed was an old one; the bishops took their place beside the barons in the political life of the country, and lived like the baronage. About 1370 the bishop of Ely had no less than ten castles, manor-houses, and palaces attached to the see: palaces at Ely, London, and Downham; castles at Wisbech and Doddington, and manor-houses at Bishop's Hatfield, Much Hadham, Somersham, Balsham, and Ditton.[1] In the fourteenth century even the abbots, to whom Benedictine tradition had earlier granted a life no more luxurious than that of their brethren, were provided with more living-space. Their monasteries had become richer and more deeply involved in feudal

[1] Bentham, 163.

business, and by analogy they too came to live like feudal barons. Each abbot had a hall, chapel, and great chamber for his state apartments, and a set of living-rooms for his private use; the general plan can still be traced at Castleacre and at Westminster.

The most characteristic feature of such residences in the fourteenth century was a great gatehouse,[1] sometimes a defensive building, sometimes a noble entrance with a set of state apartments over the arch.[2] About 1309 a great gateway was added to the abbey of Peterborough, but Bishop Lindsey made more than a work of defence. Both sides were adorned by sculptured figures; on the north an abbot and a prior, on the south the apostles. The great gatehouse of the Augustinian priory of Butley in Suffolk, built by Prior William de Geytone between 1311 and 1332, was originally surmounted by a range of fine rooms. To the north were three richly traceried windows surmounted on the outside by a triple canopied niche, with a group of the Annunciation and a statue of the founder. To the south were three windows surmounted by a rose, and a splendid armorial panel commemorating the priory's benefactors (Pl. 35 b).

Still more splendid is the abbey gateway at Bury St. Edmunds (Pl. 56), built soon after 1327.[3] Here for the first time we have a building of defensive form enriched all over with the niches and arcadings of the Decorated style. In its architecture it is half fortress and half church. The niches immediately over the gate are said to have held statues of St. Edmund and the two archers who killed him; the upper range had a figure of Christ in the centre; and the twelve niches in the angle turrets probably held statues of the apostles.

[1] Many cathedral closes had been fortified in the last quarter of the thirteenth century, and these enceintes naturally had defensive gateways: Norwich 1276, Lincoln, York, and St. Paul's 1285, Exeter and Wells 1286, Lichfield 1299, Canterbury 1309. (A. Hamilton Thompson, *Mil. Arch.* 298.) The palace at Wells, built in the reign of Henry III, was in 1340 defended by a circuit of walls with a strong gatehouse, that is clearly conceived as part of the defensive work. Similarly the castle at Saltwood, built by Archbishop Courtenay about 1390, has a gatehouse with an entrance set between two embattled circular towers that is clearly a fortification.

[2] e.g. the abbot's apartments in the western gateway of Furness abbey, *c.* 1300.

[3] Among the shields of arms that adorn it are those of Edward II, John of Eltham, Thomas of Brotherton, and Henry of Lancaster.

At Thornton abbey, a house of Austin Canons in Lincolnshire,[1] the magnificent gatehouse erected soon after 1382 by Abbot Thomas de Gretham is developed as a great residential block containing the abbot's state apartments.[2] It is built of brick (Pl. 57), one of the first English buildings so constructed that is known to us.[3] The outer face has five stone tabernacles between its four turrets, of which the centre ones still contain statues of St. John the Baptist and St. Augustine, the patrons of the Austin Canons, on either side of the Coronation of the Virgin. The arcade over the gate is cusped as richly as a tomb; the cornices are delicately sculptured; yet a defensive purpose is still evident in more than the sculptured figures of men with swords, shields, and pole-axes that once decorated the turrets and battlements. There are no windows on this outer side; the walls and turrets are pierced with arrow slits; and a *chemin de ronde* goes beneath the tabernacles. The fortifications were completed in 1382, the year after the Peasants' Revolt and the murder of Archbishop Simon of Sudbury: a time when any rich churchman might well have taken his precautions.

The inner face (Pl. 59) is designed as a house, with a projecting central portion. The vaults of the entrance arch are elegantly cusped, but the system by which the inner side arches command the single arch giving outwards continues to suggest defence. For all their ball-flower mouldings and their sculptured corbels, these points of vantage could provide shelter from which a body of men-at-arms could command the entrance. The first floor contains a splendid great chamber, with a corbelled-out oriel over the gate. Its completely secular character is stressed by the sculptured corbel stones of the roof; one of them represents a woman petting a poodle.[4] The upper floor also contains a great room, with a traceried window.[5]

[1] It was a daughter-house of Kirkham, which also has a fine gatehouse.

[2] Plan in Tipping, *English Homes*, ii. 270, Fig. 392.

[3] It is later than Little Wenham Hall (see p. 130), which is built of imported Flemish bricks laid with occasional courses of stone and flints between.

[4] Prior and Gardner, Fig. 456.

[5] The *Porta Abbatiae* of Ely, built under the supervision of the master mason John Meppushall in 1396, is a good deal less impressive than Thornton, though less apt for

By now the actual houses of bishops were being built on a grander scale. St. Hugh had added a magnificent hall to the palace at Lincoln; Bishop Burnell, between 1274 and 1292, had built one no less magnificent at Wells; it had five aisled bays, with a great chamber behind the dais. The palace of Walter de Langton, bishop of Lichfield from 1297 to 1321, now totally destroyed, was reputed to be the most magnificent in England. The hall of the palace was painted in courtly fashion with the coronation, wars, and funeral of his patron Edward I.[1]

The characteristic of the fourteenth-century episcopal palace was that it had two great halls of almost equal importance; one was doubtless for the bishop, his ecclesiastical household, and especially distinguished laymen, and the second for the secular retinues of himself and his visitors. This plan was followed in the most important ecclesiastical residence built at this time of which any ruins remain: the palace at St. David's built by Bishop Henry Gower, who held the see between 1328 and 1347. The two halls, chapel, and state apartments are irregularly grouped round a quadrangle. He was a great builder, and also erected Swansea castle and the manor-house of Lamphey.[2] In all his houses a new type of architecture is employed, with ogee-headed doorways, polychrome masonry, and decorative parapets corbelled out and pierced by wide pointed arches, which mask the high-pitched roofs behind. It was probably the remoteness of these buildings from the ordinary highways of architectural taste that caused them to have so little influence.

The palace of the bishops of Chichester at Amberley was partly constructed by Bishop Robert de Stratford between 1337 and 1362, and completed and in part rebuilt by Bishop William Reed in 1377. Like St. David's it had two great halls, the more important of which had a parlour behind the dais with a solar over. The buildings were grouped round two courtyards, one of which was further divided by a wall. The palace at Southwell,[3] which had

defence. The window over the arch is traceried but there is little other decoration. See Harvey in *Journ. Brit. Arch. Ass.* vi (1941), 45.

[1] Turner, *Domestic Architecture*, ii. 48.

[2] See A. Hamilton Thompson, *Mil. Arch.* 238.

[3] The surviving remains include a corbelled-out turret in an angle that recalls a Burgundian *échauguette*.

been handsomely built about 1360, had a second great hall added to it a little later; its main buildings were ranged round a quadrangle, with hall and chapel to the north, state apartments to the east, living quarters to the south, and domestic offices to the west. In 1439 the hall and state apartments were enriched with traceried windows, sculptured fire-places, and ornamental chimney-shafts. Elsewhere we must judge of episcopal buildings by such fragments as the priory kitchen at Durham, which dates from 1366. It is roofed with a surprisingly elegant vault resting on eight intersecting flattened arches, with a louvre in the hexagonal space in the middle. At Westminster, again, the hall of Abbot Lytlington's house remains,[1] with a fine roof and screen probably by Hugh Herland, who made the roof of Westminster Hall.

Besides such palaces as these, a number of ecclesiastical dwellings of lesser rank survive in whole or in part. Salmstone, near Margate, was built in the reign of Edward II as the country residence of the abbot of St. Augustine's, Canterbury. The chapel and hall stand side by side and are much alike in outward appearance. The hall was originally divided into two floors; the great chamber on the first floor has windows of two trefoil-headed lights, carved head-corbels, a sculptured chimney-piece, and a fine oaken roof.

At Sutton Courtenay, an abbey manor-house, the timber roof of the hall rests on carved corbels and there is a long, low, side window.[2] Muchelney abbey in Somerset still has remains of its hall and of the abbots' lodging, with traceried and transomed square-headed windows and an embattled cornice. The style was set that in the reign of Edward IV was to be followed in the magnificent deanery at Wells. It was such houses that came to influence the plan and decoration of the houses of the gentry, as did the palaces of the bishops those of the great nobles.

'The changed significance of the castle is one of the main facts

---

[1] Lethaby, *Westminster Abbey Re-examined*, 143.
[2] The fourteenth-century timbered hall of Great Malvern priory was destroyed a hundred years ago, but is known from an engraving. Turner, ii. 34. Place House, Tisbury, built by the nuns of Shaftesbury, is hardly more than a farm; its most magnificent feature is its tithe barn.

which distinguish the history of the fourteenth century from that of its predecessors.'[1] The monarchy was doing all that it could to suppress militant feudalism; changes in the art of war, involving the use of masses of men-at-arms, were transforming the military function of the castle; and an increase in the amenities of civilization was bringing a new and purely aesthetic element into its architecture.

Warfare was ceasing to be a matter of castle sieges, and was becoming more and more a matter of battles in the open field. The reduction not of individual strongholds, but of fortified towns, had become the chief object of campaigns.[2] For such warfare mercenary troops in considerable numbers were more valuable than small bands of feudatories; and the retainers of great lords, who lived in the purlieus of his castle, ate his meat and were clothed, armed, and housed by him, were in fact mercenary troops.

The first Act against the maintenance of retainers was passed in 1327; the first against livery in 1377.[3] By 1388 it was ordained that no man should wear the badge of any nobleman unless he were retained by him for life, in peace as in war, under sealed indentures; and no valet or archer was to wear the badge unless he were a menial servant, engaged by the year.[4] Yet such measures were taken in vain; as late as 1451 William Paston could write: 'That is the way of your countrymen, to spend all the goods they have on men and liveries, and horses and harness, and so bear it out for a while, and at last they are but beggars.'[5]

Such armies, and the castles designed to house them, might constitute a menace to the State; and attempts were made by the monarchy not merely to limit the number of retainers but also to control the building and the situation of castles. The royal control meant that no castle could be erected without the king's 'licence to crenellate'. These licences make it possible to date

---

[1] F. M. Stenton, *The Development of the Castle*, 25.
[2] See A. Hamilton Thompson, *Mil. Arch.* 291.
[3] See W. Douglas Simpson in *Antiq. Journ.* xxvi (1946) 157.
[4] See *Retrospective Review*, 1827, 302.
[5] *Paston Letters*, no. 211.

almost all fourteenth- or fifteenth-century castles with some exactitude. Their number further serves to show the pace of castle building in any reign.[1] Forty-four such licences were issued by Edward I, and fifty-eight by Edward II, a very large number for a reign of less than twenty years. The rate was maintained by 180 in the more than fifty years of Edward III, but the fifty-two castles licensed in Richard II's reign of some twenty-three years show a slight drop. After his time the troubled state of the country brought the rate of building still lower and the tendency may have been encouraged by royal policy. Henry IV, in a little less than fourteen years, issued only ten licences to crenellate; Henry V, in over nine years, only one. The long reign of Henry VI from 1423 to 1461 saw the issue of only five licences.

The outward form of the castle continued to be dictated by the traditional needs of defence. Fire-arms seem to have been used by Hainault mercenaries against Scotland as early as 1327,[2] but it was long before the fear of them influenced the design of castles. From the middle of the thirteenth century the English castle had been a courtyard enclosure screened by curtain walls: a single bailey without a keep.[3] The walls were flanked at intervals by towers, two of which formed a gatehouse.[4]

These gatehouses could not, for defensive reasons, receive the same decorative elaboration as did the gateways of the English abbeys. That at Boarstall, dating from 1312, is typical; the hexagonal flanking towers are pierced only by cross-shaped arrow slits and are heavily embattled.[5] The secular gatehouse could hardly be developed to hold the great hall and the lord's apartments that were now demanded, and all kinds of expedients were adopted to fit them within the scheme. At Dacre castle, begun in 1307, a massive square tower to accommodate the larger rooms forms one

[1] Stubbs, iii. 555. A valuable list of licences to crenellate will be found in Parker, vol. ii.   [2] Ramsay, i. 194.

[3] See A. Hamilton Thompson, *Mil. Arch.* 304. He cites Richmond and Ludlow in their earliest form, Carew and Manorbier.

[4] Westenhanger castle in Kent, built by John de Kiriel in 1342, with seven towers and a gatehouse, is a rather late example of the type.

[5] A large window over the gateway, and small ones beside it, were added in the sixteenth century.

corner of the structure; at Dudley, built by Sir John de Somery, who held it from 1300 to 1321, one of the corner towers has an increased importance and contains the lord's apartments.[1] In the north, at Belsay and Chipchase, the tradition of the pele tower was modified to provide more living-space. At Belsay,[2] built about 1320, the great hall—'the inevitable, and indeed, the only essential feature of the English mediaeval house'[3]—is set on the first floor, with a chamber and an oratory to the west. A vaulted room below probably served as a kitchen; a chamber above as a solar. A building alongside provides four floors of plainer and smaller apartments.

In southern England a quadrangular plan was developed out of the scheme of the single bailey. At Maxstoke castle in Warwickshire, built in 1346 by Sir William de Clinton, later earl of Huntingdon, the hall, chapel, kitchen, seigneurial and retainers' quarters are set against the interior of the curtain wall to form a courtyard in a scheme already in use in France.[4] The gatehouse is developed as a quadrangular tower;[5] octagonal towers defend the corners, and the whole is surrounded by a moat. The entrance is finely vaulted and is defended by guard-rooms on either side. The hall, now destroyed, had a chapel at the south end with a great traceried west window.

A similar plan was followed at Beverston in Gloucestershire, rebuilt by Thomas, Lord Berkeley between 1356 and 1361, with four towers, a barbican, and a moat. The great hall has vanished; the surviving tower has a chapel on the first floor and an oratory above, with squints to make the altar visible from the adjoining bedrooms and solar.[6] Here we begin to be able to relate the building of castles with the economic conditions of later feudalism; Berkeley's great-grandson told Leland that Beverston had been built with the ransoms of Poitiers prisoners. In 1376, again, John,

[1] See W. Douglas Simpson in *Arch. Journ.* xcvi (1939), 142.
[2] The best account, with a plan, will be found in W. Douglas Simpson's article in *Arch. Ael.* xvii. 175. He finds in it a close analogy with Chipchase.
[3] Clapham and Godfrey, 69.
[4] Cf. the château de Bury near Blois.
[5] Cf. that at Mackworth, Derbyshire, *c.* 1350.
[6] Cf. the chapel at Compton castle, Devon, early fifteenth century.

Lord Neville of Raby was charged with having taken up the claims of Crown creditors at a discount, and then having obtained payment for himself in full.[1] Three years later he obtained licence to crenellate his castle of Raby, no doubt rebuilt with the proceeds.[2] Here, again, the buildings are round a central courtyard entered by a gatehouse, with massive towers at the corners, one of which contains the splendid kitchen. An outer enceinte was originally defended by a second gatehouse.

Dartington Hall in Devon originally had two quadrangles; little remains unchanged but the fine great hall, entered by an embattled porch. At Lumley castle, county Durham, a single quadrangle sufficed, since Ralph, Lord Lumley, who built it between 1389 and 1392, raised two stories over a basement all round it and defended it with towers at the corners. In consequence of this added height, the gatehouse, adorned with the sixteen shields of Lord Lumley's noble descent, is merged into the whole[3] (Pl. 58 b). Another variant of the plan occurs at Donnington in Berkshire, built in 1386. Here an oval takes the place of the quadrangle, with stair turrets in the external angles of the gatehouse, as at Maxstoke. This gatehouse is unusually large, and with the circular turrets, which have three marked string-courses and crenellated tops, and a fine Decorated window over the gateway, forms a whole of real architectural pretensions.

The most impressive example of the quadrangular plan, however, is the castle which Sir Edward Dalyngrigge built at Bodiam in Sussex in 1386[4] (Fig. 6). The curtain wall, fortified by a round tower at each corner and a square one in the middle of each wall, is here the exterior wall of the residence. Because of the width of the moat the rooms can have windows as large as if they looked on

---

[1] Ramsay, ii. 53.

[2] He died in 1388. It was finished by his son Ralph before his death in 1426.

[3] W. Douglas Simpson has shown evidence that Durham castle (1345–81), Bolton, Carlisle, and Warkworth were all by John Lewyn or Lewen (*Arch. Ael.* 4th Ser. xix (1941), 93), and J. Harvey considers that Lumley, Dunstanburgh, and Sheriff Hutton should also be attributed to him. *Journ. Brit. Arch. Ass.* vi (1941), 44.

[4] Plan in Curzon, 53; and see W. Douglas Simpson in *Antiq. Journ.* xxvi (1946), 157. Professor Hamilton Thompson compares it with the château de Villandraut, Gironde, built about 1250.

to a courtyard, and the whole castle brings the spaciousness of an unfortified house into a defensible place. The chapel is built in with the rest; the hall appears to have been L-shaped, with a round turret in the inner angle. The castle shows a considerable development of the living quarters. It had a great chamber, a solar, a room for the lord and lady with a bower leading out of it, and a donjon tower for a strong room and a last stand in case of need. Altogether apart from these, it had quarters for the lord's retainers with their own hall and kitchen. The main gate, the postern, and the cellar are well away from these and under the lord's direct control.[1] This entrance side has smaller windows and a more defensive intention, since here the moat is narrower; the only adornment is three stone shields of the owner's arms set over the entrance arch.

The entrance was originally over a timber bridge which led to a gatehouse (Pl. 60 *b*), fortified with machicoulis, an introduction from France. Its use, indeed, is characteristic of the castles that were built out of the spoils of the French wars: Bodiam, Cooling, Tattershall, Caister, Hurstmonceux, Hever, Leeds, Raglan, and Scotney.[2]

The first of these, Cooling castle[3] in Kent, built by John, Lord Cobham between 1374 and 1375,[4] follows Bodiam in its general plan.[5] The gatehouse remains, with a copper tablet shaped like a parchment deed let into its south face. The tablet is inscribed in enamelled letters

> *Knowyth that beth and schul be*
> *That I am mad in help of the cuntre*
> *In knowyng of whyche thing*
> *This is chartre and wytnessyng.*

[1] W. D. Simpson, loc. cit., compares the arrangements with those at Pierrefonds.

[2] See W. D. Simpson in *Journ. Brit. Arch. Ass.* xl (1935), 186.

[3] Also spelt Cowling and Couling.

[4] The master masons were Thomas Wrek, Henry Yevele, and Thomas Crump. The accounts which survive (*Arch. Cant.* ii (1859), 95) show that the construction began in 1374, though the licence to crenellate was not obtained until 1380–1. This is valuable, as showing that the licence was usually obtained when the castle was nearly finished.

[5] Cf. Shirburn castle, Oxon., 1377; Nunney, Somerset, 1373; Sheriff Hutton, Yorks., 1381; Scotney, 1380; Wingfield castle, Suffolk, 1384, and the royal palace at Sheen.

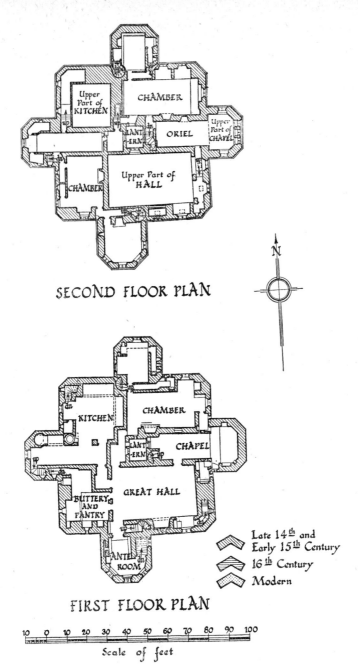

SECOND FLOOR PLAN

Upper
Part of
KITCHEN

CHAMBER

LANT
-ERN

ORIEL

Upper
Part of
CHAPEL

CHAMBER

Upper Part of
HALL

N

FIRST FLOOR PLAN

KITCHEN

CHAMBER

LANT
-ERN

CHAPEL

GREAT HALL

BUTTERY
AND
PANTRY

ANTE
ROOM

Late 14ᵗʰ and
Early 15ᵗʰ Century

16ᵗʰ Century

Modern

10   0   10 20 30 40 50 60 70 80 90 100
Scale of feet

FIG. 4. *Plan of Warkworth Castle, The Keep, c. 1377–90*

An enamelled seal hangs by cords of metal below. The castle was indeed built after French and Spanish vessels had landed and ravaged this part of Kent, and the tablet records the patriotic intentions of its builder.

It has already been said that 'tower' castles of the earlier type continued to be built on the Scottish border: an instance of about 1385 is Langley castle in Northumberland, which has four floors each with one large room and four small ones in the corner towers.

Even in the midlands at Warwick castle, Guy's and Caesar's towers, both built by Thomas Beauchamp the second towards the close of the fourteenth century, are magnificent tower-residences that rival the donjons of France. Guy's tower is twelve-sided and measures 128 feet to the top of its machicolated parapet; its five floors are all vaulted; and each contains a large central room and two smaller ones, reached by two winding stairs. Caesar's tower is a quatrefoil, with the inner lobe flattened; it too contains five floors and two vaulted staircases.

The whole idea of the tower-castle was renewed on a greater scale as the curtain walls of the quadrangular castles became solid wings of buildings. As improved water fortifications made it possible for their windows to look outwards, they once more began to approximate, especially in the smaller instances, to the outward-looking tower-castles. The approximation becomes evident in Queenborough castle in Sheppey,[1] erected between 1361 and 1377 with William of Wykeham as supervisor (Fig. 5).[2] Here a circular building was planned round a small central court; it was defended by six towers, each with an independent stair. At Wardour castle, built by John, Lord Lovel of Tichmersh in 1393, the plan is developed as a regular hexagon with two square entrance towers three stories high. The whole surrounds a hexagonal courtyard. The great hall is set on the first floor over the entrance passage, with a solar to the west and the kitchen to the south.

[1] Plan in Clapham and Godfrey, Fig. 108. It was the castle of a new town and was named after Queen Philippa.

[2] J. Harvey considers that Henry Yevele was master mason. *Journ. Brit. Arch. Ass.* vi (1941), 42; *Yevele*, 26.

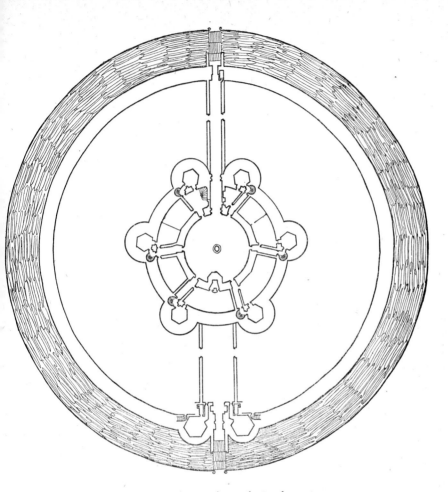

FIG. 5. *Plan of Queenborough Castle, 1361–77*

At Warkworth,[1] built probably between 1377 and 1390 (Fig. 4), the courtyard is reduced to a central light shaft. The castle is otherwise a solid block: a large square with canted angles, with a great bay projecting in the middle of each side. Within this an ingenious asymmetrical plan fits in a great hall, buttery, kitchens, chapel, and great chambers, with a few bedrooms tucked away in odd corners and reached by little stairways within the walls. Like many ingenious plans, it does not provide enough light for many of the rooms; not only is the central light-well too small, but for reasons of defence there are no large external windows near the ground. At the end of the fifteenth century a new and lighter great hall and kitchen were built alongside. Here, as at Dudley, the central tower-castle forms the lord's residence, and the mercenaries were housed in older domestic buildings alongside.

The next landmark in the history of the English castle is that built at Caister in Norfolk by Sir John Fastolf[2] with the ransom of the duc d'Alençon whom he captured at Verneuil in 1424. It is worth remembering that Sir John was not only a soldier and a great landlord but also a merchant; he invested his money at 5 per cent. with London merchants *ad mercandizandum* and established a flourishing cloth industry, largely run by Flemings, in his Wiltshire manor of Castle Combe.[3] Caister reflects the double activities of its master: it is neither quite castle nor quite manor. Originally it was 300 feet square, with a tower at each corner; it depended on a moat for its main defence. The surviving round tower originally had five stories of handsome rooms, with arcaded fireplaces. The castle had both winter and summer halls. The curious spindly tower is finished with machicoulis and immense gargoyles; it looks as if the other towers had been of lesser importance. The whole plan and style recall such castles as Kempen in the Rhineland; it is another reflection of Germanic influence.

[1] See Gotch, *Growth of the English House*, 83; Simpson in *Arch. Ael.* 4th Ser. xv (1938), 115 and xix (1941), 93; A. Hamilton Thompson, 328. Gotch is inclined to date it rather later, about 1435 and 1440; Mr. Douglas Simpson, who has studied it in greater detail, thinks it the work of the first earl of Northumberland between 1377 and 1390.

[2] The story quoted by Floyer in *Arch. Journ.* lxx (1913), 126 is not tenable; W. Douglas Simpson at Society of Antiquaries, 2 Dec., 1948.

[3] Scrope, 201; Cunningham, 110.

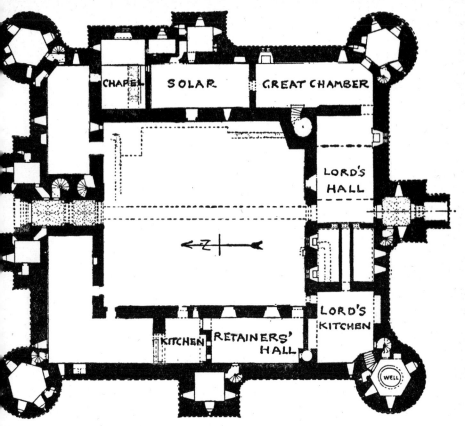

CHAPEL SOLAR GREAT CHAMBER

LORD'S
HALL

LORD'S
KITCHEN

KITCHEN RETAINERS'
HALL

WELL

FIG. 6. *Plan of Bodiam Castle, 1386*

The most striking thing about Caister castle is that it is built of brick. Building accounts among the Paston manuscripts show that the work was in hand, under the supervision of Master William Granere, as early as 1432.[1] The brick was made locally; the ashlar was imported from France. This fact establishes it as the first brick castle in England of which we have any knowledge. It was, however, soon succeeded by others. By 1436 at least seven German masons and brickmakers were employed in England. In 1439 Sir John Montgomery was granted licence to crenellate Faulkborne Hall in Essex either in stone or brick; the fragment of his east front that survives is in brick. Bricks were used for stairs and dungeon at Windsor in 1439–40, and in 1447 William Veysey, brickmaker, was appointed to the king's service.[2]

By this time the second great English brick castle, that of Hurstmonceux in Sussex, was well under way (Pl. 60 a).[3] It was built by Roger Fiennes, who received the licence to crenellate it in 1440. He was treasurer of the household to Henry VI, and in that capacity must almost certainly have known William Veysey, the king's brickmaster; it is a tempting surmise that Veysey may have worked here, turning the local clay into rosy-red bricks and having them set in English bond. In 1436, however, John Stase, John Rowelond, and James Bavord, all of Malines, were employed here, and may well have been Flemish brickmakers.

In general plan[4] Hurstmonceux follows the scheme of Bodiam on a much larger scale, with octagonal instead of circular towers. It is all of brick except for the mouldings and dressed work, which are of stone. It had four courts, one large and three small. The hall had a central hearth; three rooms lay at its eastern end, one 40 feet long, with a chapel beyond. A grand flight of stairs beyond the hall led to an apartment above the chambers. Grose, who visited it before it was gutted in 1777, found the chambers on the first floor 'sufficient to lodge a garrison'; they were linked by a labyrinth

[1] See W. D. Simpson in *Arch. Journ.* xciv (1942), 110. It must be remembered that brick had been used for the gatehouse of Thornton abbey soon after 1382. See p. 115.

[2] Tipping, ii. 169.

[3] Work was still going on in 1453.

[4] Only the outside is in any way medieval, and this has been considerably if skilfully restored.

of secret staircases. In his time the glass in every window was painted with the alant or wolfdog badge of Sir Roger Fiennes.

A third great brick castle, Tattershall in Lincolnshire,[1] is almost contemporary with Hurstmonceux. It was begun in 1434 by Ralph Cromwell, treasurer of the king, under the supervision of Thomas Croxby, and seems to have been finished about ten years later. Only the great residential tower survives (Pl. 62), denuded of the high conical roofs and the finials on the four angle towers[2] that originally crowned it. When these existed, its heavy string-courses, its corbelled machicolations, and its massive battlements must have completed its likeness with such a French castle as Saumur, as known to us from the miniatures of the *Très riches Heures* of the duc de Berry. But the likeness is not complete; Tattershall has arched windows with simple tracery, Saumur rectangular windows with mullions and transoms; Tattershall had large dependencies containing the great hall and the retainers' halls and quarters, while Saumur was self-contained: and, finally, Tattershall is of brick and Saumur of stone.

It is built with as much loving care for detail as any building of dressed ashlar. Each floor has its rooms connected by a long, high, narrow passage; this is elaborately vaulted in brick, with armorial bosses of carved stone. The rooms, which have handsome fire-places, are lit by wide windows, and by rather low-pitched oriels with vaulted ceilings of brick. The plain walls are evidently intended to be hidden by ornamental hangings. Even in their present denuded state the rooms give a remarkable impression of spaciousness, dignity, and fine proportion; they were planned to be the home of highly civilized people of noble birth.

The Tattershall brickmaker, Bawdwin Dorneman, was probably a German, and what French influence there is may have reached England at second hand from east Prussia.[3] When Tattershall was finished, with its second moat to enclose the pleasaunces and fish-ponds, it must have stood as a magnificent example of the late

---

[1] See Curzon and Tipping; W. D. Simpson in *Journ. Brit. Arch. Ass.* xli (1935), 77. It rises not many miles from the brick gatehouse of Thornton abbey.

[2] See the eighteenth-century engraving reproduced in Curzon and Tipping, Pl. 7.

[3] See W. D. Simpson, loc. cit.

English medieval castle, complete with its domestic chapel, its collegiate church and college, its almshouses, market cross, mill, and village.[1]

The time had come when the actual tower scheme could be modified. Compton castle in Devon, built at the very end of the reign of Henry VI, is planned as an H with towers at the corners. A vast amount of machicolation serves both to defend it and to give massiveness to the architectural whole; but a new plan had been found that was to be fully developed in the two ensuing centuries as an unfortified and purely domestic house.

The manor-house was not merely a smaller dwelling than the castle, but it fulfilled a different function. It might or might not be fortified, but it was the administrative centre not of a great fief but of a single manor. It housed the immediate servants of its owner, not a great retinue; it was often of no greater architectural importance than a magnified farm.

The contract made between Sir John Bishopsden of Lapworth and his two masons in 1314[2] for the building of his manor-house provides for a block only 40 feet in length and 18 in width within the walls, with gables on the end walls and a door in the middle connected with a drawbridge over the moat. The ground floor was to be divided into a base chamber and a chamber; above it was an upper chamber with two fire-places, and two garderobes. This seems to provide for no more than a kitchen, a hall, and a chamber.

The manors of the beginning of the fourteenth century still keep the tradition of the earlier pele towers. Little Wenham Hall in Suffolk, for example, has a square tower to the east with a vaulted undercroft, a chapel on the main floor and a chamber above, all served by a newel staircase in a projecting turret. Alongside this, touching it at the stair, a broader and lower block holds a vaulted storeroom and kitchen, and a great hall with

---

[1] Buckden palace, built by Bishop Rotherham of Lincoln soon after 1472, remains as a smaller version of Tattershall that still shows more of the general layout than its great prototype. See W. D. Simpson in *Journ. Brit. Arch. Ass.* 3rd series, ii (1937), 121. Other variations on the same theme are known to have existed. Little is left of Heron Hall in Essex, begun by Sir John Tyrrell before his death in 1437, but the tower at Middleton, built by the Lord Scales who was murdered in 1460, still survives.

[2] Turner, ii. 5.

traceried windows and a timber roof. The whole is not designed primarily for defence, yet the tower is defensible. The chief note of novelty is struck in its material: it is built of Flemish brick with occasional courses of stone and flint.

Markenfield Hall, in Yorkshire, built in 1310 by John de Markenfield, the King's Remembrancer,[1] is another L-shaped house, but here the two blocks are closely integrated (Pl. 62 a). The first floor has the chapel in the angle over an undercroft,[2] the hall fills one limb of the L and the chamber the other; east of the hall, which has a central hearth, is a solar with a fire-place. The hall has traceried windows; it was originally reached by an external staircase. What fortifications there were consisted in an enceinte away from the house.

Another early-fourteenth-century country house survives at Woodcroft near Peterborough. This is closer to the castle plan in being of quadrangular form; it originally had a tower at each corner and a gateway, with a chapel over, in the centre of one front. The hall has three tall windows with transoms and shouldered archheads.[3] Woodlands manor, at Mere in Wiltshire (Pl. 62 b), probably built by Thomas Doddington about 1380, has a hall with a fine open timber roof entered through a porch. The chapel, which is in another block, is on two floors, with an outside staircase for the tenants' use. Woodlands remains a remarkably perfect example of an unfortified manor-house of a modest kind, in which the Perpendicular style is domesticated.

In the next stage the manor was planned round two quadrangles. An early instance is the old manor at Little Hempston in Devon, which seems to have been built about 1360 as the house of a knight, probably Sir John Stretch. It has two courtyards, a base court for the farm-buildings, and an inner court for the hall and offices. The hall, which has a central hearth and louvre, fills two stories, but does not break the line of the long, low house round the quadrangle.

Lord Cromwell, besides building his great brick castle of Tattershall, also built a stone manor at South Wingfield a few years

[1] Tout, *Place of Ed. II*, 348.   [2] For other instances see Turner, ii. 79.
[3] Cf. Norborough Manor, not far away.

later, probably in 1441.[1] It is planned in two asymmetrical quadrangles,[2] the first a base court with the servants' quarters and stables, the second containing the seigneurial apartments: the private rooms, with two bay windows, to the west, the great hall and its oriel (Pl. 63) to the south, with the great chamber at the entrance end, and the chapel, now destroyed, to the east. The house court is defended by a gatehouse to the base court; a strong tower, four stories high, at the south-west corner of the enclosure, only to be entered from an outer door, served as a last defensive post in case of need. Since the house occupies a strong position on an almost isolated hill, it has no outer fortifications, but a deep dry moat on the weak side.

The significance of South Wingfield manor lies not only in its coherent scheme but also in its sculptured decoration. Such parts as the great hall and the state apartments have battlements decorated with carved quatrefoils with shields of arms in the crenellations, rich rosettes on the archmoulds, and traceried windows as elaborate as those of a church. The same trend is evident in the house known as King Ina's palace at South Petherton, which was built by Sir Giles Daubeny in the reign of Henry VI. The gables are surmounted by crouching monsters in stone; the drainheads are lions' masks, and the traceried windows rise from panels of heraldic sculpture.[3] A decorative scheme in stone has been worked out on a domestic scale.

Some of the other houses of the time are notable for their construction in other materials than stone. Kent and Sussex are still rich in such timber-framed houses as Wardes at Otham near Maidstone, built by a yeoman or small squire about 1390. The central hall, which has no chimney, rises from the ground to the roof, with a kitchen at one end and a parlour at the other, both with bedrooms over. The upper floor overhangs on the corbels of the ground-floor roof, and forms with the slightly recessed wall of the hall a façade of varying relief.

[1] Professor Hamilton Thompson compares the stonework with the great hall and chambers at Tutbury usually attributed to John of Gaunt. *Mil. Arch.* 336.

[2] Plan in Gotch, 69.

[3] These may be compared with those, apparently re-used, in the old rectory, Chewstoke, Somerset.

In the west, too, there are many houses that illustrate the various local systems of timber framing.[1] Tretower court, a fortified manor in Brecon,[2] is a quadrangular structure with its outside of stone, almost windowless, and its inner court largely of wood. The western range, dating from the years about 1400, includes a fine banqueting hall, with an open-timbered roof. The upper floor, which communicated by a gallery with the gatehouse and courtyard, contains chambers with open roofs of similar construction, with the gable pierced with trefoils and quatrefoils. Nearer London, Crowherst Place in Surrey, built by John Gainsford soon after 1423,[3] still has a courtyard enclosed by a moat. Here appear the rich open-timbered hall roof and the window frames of carved wood that are one of the chief glories of the style.

The finest of all these timbered houses is that built by Sir John Norreys at Ockwells near Bray;[4] it was not quite finished when he died in 1465 (Pl. 64). The chapel, which has been destroyed, was probably of stone; the rest is wholly of rosy brick framed in oak. There was once a great court of offices entered through an archway, with a barn and other farm-buildings to the east. The house proper was entered to the west by a passage that had the hall screens to the right and the buttery to the left. It leads to a tiny quadrangle round which the living quarters are arranged, with the kitchens to the south.

At Ockwells the hall is remarkable for its screens (Pl. 67) and for the complex richness of the roof at the dais end. The windows display a splendid series of shields of arms set against a background of diagonal stripes, bannerwise. They belong to the patrons, friends, and relatives of Sir John Norreys; some display the distaff that was his badge as master of the royal wardrobe.[5] The most striking feature of the exterior is the great increase in the size and number of the windows. There is no thought of defence; almost for the first time sunlight is allowed to pour into the house. The oaken window frames are cusped and traceried, and have in some

[1] See Tipping, ii. 221.   [2] See *Illustrated London News* (7 July 1934), 24.
[3] See Tipping, ii. 153.   [4] See ibid. ii. 163.
[5] On their identification see E. Green in *Arch.* lvi, pt. 2 (1899), 323. They must have been set up before 1461.

instances lines of shields between them like those carved in stone at South Petherton. The whole house is thought out in terms of its oak framing. Mr. Christopher Hussey writes of it:[1]

'The nameless architect of Ockwells planned his foundations on a simple mathematical basis of rectangles, with sides of various multiples of five and six. Each rectangle is formed by four of the columnar posts round which the house is built. Thus, the hall, without the width (approximately six inches) of the springing trusses, is forty feet long and twenty-four feet broad, divided into four bays, theoretically ten feet . . . wide. The South end wall above the screen contains, concealed by plaster, exactly in its centre, one of the supports of the south wing; the south-east and south-west corner posts of the hall form its fellows to east and west, and thus we get the spacing of the wing posts: twelve feet, except in the case of the easternmost bay, which is only ten feet deep, to fit in with the porch that adjoins it and is constructed on the hall dimension of ten feet. . . . Thus a simple mathematical relationship underlies not only the form of the hall, but of the whole building, a fact which contributes more largely than one realises to the pleasure we experience in looking at the structure, whether within or without.'

Such manors, indeed, were the fine flower of a joiner's craft that had been learned through centuries of barn-building. There is little essential to distinguish such a hall as Tretower from such a barn as that of the nuns of Shaftesbury at Place House, Tisbury (Pl. 65). Here, as in the domestic architecture built of stone, laymen were indebted to the Church, for almost all the known barns of the period with architectural pretensions were built to hold the tithes of the bishops and the harvests of the monastic lands.

By the reign of Edward II the great hall of the castle had ceased to be the common room of the lord and his mesnie. A smaller room for the lord's use was commonly added to the hall at the dais end; at Ightham Mote it was built early in the fourteenth century, with an oriel window to catch the sun. At Mettingham, begun in 1343, there was a wainscoted parlour at the end of the hall, with a chimney and a bay window giving on to a little court

[1] Quoted in Tipping, ii. 171.

bounded by the moat.[1] At Wardour the great hall, which is on the first floor, has a solar to the west. At Broughton it lies to the east. At Wingfield the great chamber lies at the entrance end of the hall; it has a magnificent traceried window looking into the court. The great oriel or bay window of the hall dais (Pl. 63) is here notable for its elegant sculpture and tracery. The scheme of a parlour adjacent to the great hall was general; the particular arrangement was dictated by the plan and the site. The new arrangement was deplored by Langland about 1377.[2]

> Elynge is the halle eche day in the wyke,
> There the lord ne the ladye lyketh noughte to sytte.
> Now hath each riche a reule to eten by hymselve
> In a pryvye parloure for pore menes sake
> Or in a chambre with a chymneye and leve the chief halle
> That was made for meles, . . .

Few of the more splendid royal halls of the time survive. In Edward II's hall at Caerphilly the windows have ogival hood moulds inside with ball-flower decoration rather in the ecclesiastical manner. Ludlow castle was enriched about 1330 when Roger Mortimer erected a great hall on the north side of the middle ward. It was very high, with two stories each of three chambers to the east, and a vast parlour to the west. Even in its decay it is most impressive. John of Gaunt's Palace of the Savoy was totally destroyed, with all its splendid contents, in the Peasants' Revolt of 1381, but considerable ruins of the great hall he built at Kenilworth about 1392 still remain.[3] It is 90 feet long and half as wide, raised above a vaulted undercroft and reached by a flight of steps. The great transomed side windows have notably rich tracery, which shows the development of a domestic style rather more angular than the tracery used in churches. The two fire-places were opposite each other, half-way down. There is an octagonal oriel at the east end of the dais and a fire-place in the south-west corner. On the west a tower gave access to the rooms to the south, which were John of Gaunt's living-quarters.

---

[1] Description of 1562: *Suff. Inst.* xi (1903), 315. The roof of the great hall was removed to the old Guild Hall at Yarmouth in 1544.

[2] *Piers Plowman*, B x. 94.   [3] Plans and drawings in Gotch, 96, 97.

The most magnificent royal hall is, of course, that of Westminster, of which the reconstruction was begun in 1393, with Henry Yevele and William Wynford as master masons and Hugh Herland as master carpenter. The sculptured figures of kings which adorned the end were by Master Walter Walton.[1] In the vast room with its long line of traceried side windows hooded by the splendid roof, in the Perpendicular tracery which fills the spandrels, in the angels that support the side-posts, and in the majesty of the whole, we see the fine flower of late Gothic, turned from glorifying God in church to glorifying human empire in a palace.

The halls of lesser men followed the royal models in varying degrees. At Haddon Hall[2] the main hall, probably built between 1300 and 1310, could be entered from both the courtyards of the house: an originality of the plan that may owe something to monastic prototypes. The hall was sheltered at the entrance by the fixed screens that are one of the characteristic features of the English halls of the time. A great chamber lay behind the dais with a solar over; there was originally a central hearth, but a chimney was added later. The great hall at Penshurst, built about 1341 by John de Poultney, four times lord mayor of London, is very wide and has a roof of carved oak and traceried windows. Behind the screens three linked doorways[3] lead to kitchen, buttery, and pantry. The central hearth remains, with a louvre to let out the smoke.

The plan was followed elsewhere on a much smaller scale.[4] At Marlow Urban in Buckinghamshire[5] the hall, which has square-headed traceried windows, has an open king-post roof; at Chapel farm, near Wigmore in Herefordshire, the roof exploits naturally curved beams to form a kind of tracery, in a way that recalls the roof of the great barn at Frocester in Gloucestershire.

Wanswell Court, near Berkeley in Gloucestershire, is the kind of house that Chaucer's franklin must have lived in; it was built

---

[1] Devon, 228, 263. [2] Plan in Gotch, 48.
[3] The doors were altered in the sixteenth century.
[4] Turner, ii. 280 and 282, illustrates a remarkable and indeed unique aisled hall at Nurstead court, near Gravesend, but this has since been remodelled.
[5] The house is now called the Old Parsonage.

by John Thorke about the middle of the fifteenth century. A modest porch leads straight into a hall of the full height; a kitchen lies at the back of the hall, a low parlour with a fire-place and a charming window at the end where the dais would have been, with a chamber above. The hall is nearly square,[1] with a fine collar-beam roof on stone corbels, carved with male and female heads and crouching figures. The consistency of the medieval plan is evident from the hall of the king to the hall of the franklin. We are reminded that in Chaucer's *Nun's Priest's Tale* even the poor widow's cottage has its hall and bower, though they were sooty because there was no chimney.

In the great houses at this time, however, the chimney-piece was beginning to take its place as one of the decorative features of the room. Tattershall is famous for its chimney-pieces of stone sculptured with the shields of Cromwell and his family alliances, his treasurer's purse, and his canting device of the wild gromwell (Pl. 66). Such carvings were but part of a domestic interior that was growing more and more luxurious. The walls were sometimes painted; Tamworth castle had frescoes on the hall wall of Sir Lancelot of the Lake and Sir Tarquin,[2] and Chaucer in the *Book of the Duchess*[3] describes a chamber painted with the *Roman de la Rose* with 'al the storie of Troye' depicted in the glass. The Great Chamber at Longthorpe Tower near Peterborough had its walls painted about 1340 with a whole series of religious and secular subjects: Apostles bearing scrolls of the Creed, a wheel of the Five Senses, the Three Living and the Three Dead, a Nativity and other biblical subjects, shields of arms and a great heraldic diaper and many birds. The variety of the subjects and their style are reminiscent of the Luttrell Psalter.[4] More often halls were hung with painted cloths. The 1360 inventory of things belonging to the late Queen Isabella[5] includes a dorsal and banker of worsted painted with the Nativity, and a hanging for the hall

---

[1] Turner, iii. 77, suggests that there was never a dais but only the parlour.
[2] Parker, i. 67.
[3] Skeat, i. 288. Another painted chamber is described in the *Knight's Tale*, i. 1975.
[4] Paper read by Mr. E. Clive Rouse to the Society of Antiquaries, Feb. 24, 1949.
[5] Palgrave, iii. 246.

painted with the Apocalypse. In 1376 Richard Gilbert, a gentleman living in Salisbury, had both his hall and his parlour hung with 'stained cloths', the first depicting the story of Solomon.[1] Alicia Langham of Snaylwell, who died in 1448, left to her son 'unum pannum depictum cum historia Roberti Regis Cesilie',[2] and John Baret of Bury in 1463 left to his nieces 'the steyned cloth of the Coronacion of Oure Lady' and another with the Seven Ages of Man.[3] In richer households the hangings were of tapestry; until lately the walls of the hall at South Wingfield manor still showed the hooks for hanging them. The inventory of Sir John Fastolf of Caister, a wealthy man who knew France well, includes no painted cloths but a number of pieces of arras, one with the Assumption of the Virgin, and others with such secular subjects as the Siege of Falaise, 'a gentlewoman harping by a castle', hunting and hawking scenes, shepherds, and the Nine Paladins.[4]

Apart from such wall decoration the rooms were sparsely furnished with a few benches and a few carved chests: a good chest of about 1400 in the Victoria and Albert Museum is carved with scenes of the Annunciation, the Nativity, the angels appearing to the Shepherds, the Adoration of the Magi, and the Coronation of the Virgin. An inventory of 1311 gives the hall furniture as two pots, three lavers, boards and trestles, but by 1397 it is increased by two dorsals, two bankers, two pottery vessels, a laver and a bowl of brass, a fixed table, two chairs, three benches, and three stools.[5] The subsidiary chambers usually held beds of some magnificence. The will of Margery de Aldeburgh, proved in 1391,[6] includes one of black and red stuff worked with red and white roses, one de opere Northfolch (presumably worsted) with foxes, one of blood-red embroidered with a unicorn and a tree, one of green and yellow with birds and rabbits, and another in the same colours with vine-leaves, one of red with a lion beneath a tree, and coats of arms, and one of white with coats of arms held by griffins.

[1] Colt Hoare, Sarum, 101.

[2] Tymms, 12. Such painted cloths are now extremely rare; a fragmentary one is in the collection of the Society of Antiquaries.   [3] Ibid. 22 and 33.

[4] Paston Letters, no. 336. On such tapestries see also p. 92.

[5] Turner, ii. 51.   [6] Test. Ebor. 149.

VII

FUNERAL EFFIGIES

EFFIGIES cut out of sheet latten and inlaid into stone tomb-slabs are recorded in England as early as 1208;[1] the earliest surviving one, that of Sir John Daubernon, is like the drawing of an effigy.[2] Though some thirteenth-century brasses, like his, commemorate knights, the great majority are of abbots or bishops; it was felt that the sculptured effigy befitted the dignity of the territorial magnate and the flat incised tomb the humility of the churchman.[3] With the fourteenth century, however, the use of incised brasses became widespread in every rank of society under the princely; it is computed that more than 100,000 brasses were laid down,[4] of which some 4,000 survive in whole or in part. About 500 are known or recorded for the first half of the fifteenth century, but by this time the brass was declining in social standing, and only five of these commemorate members of the nobility.

Brasses are found in every part of England, but the greater number come from the eastern side of the country, notably Norfolk, Suffolk, Essex, and Kent; it has been suggested that they were cut from plates brought from Flanders. The workmanship of all but a few is undoubtedly English, and occasionally the use of a cartoon for more than one brass can be established. For instance, on the brass of Lady Margaret Berkeley at Wotton-under-Edge the little dog with its collar of bells is almost identical, though in a reverse sense, with that on the brass of Lady (Isabel) Russell at Dyrham not far away. The figures show certain resemblances and may be compared with that of Lady Warwick at St. Mary's, Warwick; she was born a Berkeley, and the same brass cutter may well have been employed. People were not represented by portraits but by

---

[1] The earliest recorded in Germany is of 1231. On the whole subject I am greatly indebted to Macklin, *Brasses of England.*

[2] At Stoke d'Abernon, Surrey; illustrated Crossley, *English Church Monuments*, 250.

[3] Priests' brasses are commonly floriated crosses; out of fifteen cross brasses known, nine are of priests.   [4] Crossley, 247, sets the figures as high as 150,000.

types: the knight, the lady, the widow, the bishop, the priest, were remarkably constant in their facial representation and often in their dress. The knight's armour varies far more than his face. The figures have something of the same abstract dignity as those in stained glass.

A typical brass of the beginning of the fourteenth century is that of Sir Robert de Septvans, who died in 1306, at Chartham in Kent (Fig. 7). It shows him bareheaded, with a full surcoat over his coat of mail; his legs are crossed, and his feet rest upon a little lion. The whole is remarkably skilful and graceful in its composition; it is easy to see that such a brass befits even a knight. Another aristocratic brass is that of Sir John Creke and his wife Alyne at Westley Waterless in Cambridgeshire, which originally had a double ogival canopy (Fig. 8). It is notable as having an engraver's mark—the letter N reversed, in a circle with a mallet, a crescent and a star—stamped on the bottom of the lady's dress. A third knightly brass of notable elegance is that of Sir Hugh de Hastings in the church he built at Elsing in Norfolk shortly before his death in 1347.[1] This is the equivalent in brass of such a canopied tomb as that of Edmund Crouchback (Pl. 3). A gabled canopy is inlaid in the stone, with a roundel in the gable representing St. George and the dragon. In the cusp below angels hold the image of the soul of the departed; above the gable is the Coronation of the Virgin. At the side figures of knights bear the shields of Edward III, Thomas de Beauchamp, Henry, earl of Lancaster, Ralph, Lord Stafford, Almeric, Lord St. Amand, and three others, now missing. A brass of equally elaborate design was that of Louis de Beaumont, the crippled half-wit who was bishop of Durham and died in 1333. The matrix only remains, but the brass is known to us by the description in the *Rites of Durham*.[2] The bishop was portrayed in cope and mitre, holding his crosier, with censing angels on either side. The border contained images of the twelve apostles with a further border of 'pictures of his ancestors in their coat armour beinge of the bloud royall of france'. The pretentious inscription ended, *Consors sit sanctis Lodouicus in arce tonantis.*

[1] Blomefield, iv. 374, records that his portrait also occurred in the east window.
[2] Fowler, 14.

FIG. 7. *Brass of Sir Robert de Septvans, d. 1306. Chartham, Kent*

Hardly less elaborate brasses of this type were used to commemorate simple priests. Laurence de St. Maur, rector of Higham Ferrers, who died in 1337, has his brass not in a pavement slab but on an altar tomb. An elaborate canopy over his head includes representations of God receiving his soul, two angels, four evangelists, and four apostles. At the sides are the Annunciation, St. Stephen, St. Laurence, St. Maur, and St. Christopher. At his feet two dogs quarrel over a bone.[1]

At this time the development of the trade in alabaster effigies made these the fashionable tombs for knights and nobles. Brasses began to be used at another social level. The first known brass of a tradesman is that of Nicholas de Cumberdene, fishmonger, at Taplow; it dates from the middle of the fourteenth century and represents a cross rising from a dolphin embowed. Not long afterwards the first English inscription is found on a brass at Brightwell Baldwin in Oxfordshire.

> *Man com & se how schal alle dede be:*
> *Wen yow comes bad & bare:*
> *Noth hab ven ve away fare:*
> *All ys werines yt ve for care:*
> *Bot yt ve do for godysluf we haue nothyng yare.*
> *Hundur yis graue lys John ye smyth*
> *God yif hys soule hewen grit.*

The most magnificent brasses in England in the second half of the fourteenth century are all of foreign workmanship. Four of the merchant princes of England and the Hanseatic League are commemorated by huge brasses[2] that come from a common workshop. The merchants represented are Adam de Walsoken and his wife at King's Lynn, about 1349; Robert Braunche, who died in 1364,

---

[1] Macklin, 100. The Virgin of the Annunciation and the figure of St. Laurence are now missing. Such brasses may be compared with certain incised stone slabs in France, for example, that of Mathieu Cornet, abbé de Jumièges, d. 1310 (Bodleian Gaignières MS. 18353, fol. 27); Jean de Cerees, d. 1327, ibid. 18350, fol. 89; Jean de Blangy, bishop of Auxerre, d. 1344, ibid. 18350, fol. 98; and Regnault de la Chapelle, d. 1382, once in the Célestins of Paris, ibid. 18351, fol. 54. The incised stone slab is rare in England; those of James Samson, *c.* 1350, at Middleton, Essex, and of Alice, Lady Tyrrell, d. 1422, at East Horndon, Essex, may be noted.

[2] That of Robert Braunche is 8 ft. 10 in. long and 5 ft. 1 in. wide.

Fig. 8. *Brass of Sir John de Creke and Alyne his wife, c. 1325. Westley Waterless, Cambridgeshire*

and his two wives, in the same place, and Alan Fleming, who died in 1375, at Newark. The brass of a third Lynn merchant, Robert Attelath, is now lost, but is known from a rubbing (Fig. 9). Besides these, three priests have brasses of the same kind: Abbot Thomas Delamere, who died in 1360, at St. Albans; Simon de Wenslegh at Wensley in Yorkshire; and an unnamed priest at North Mimms in Hertfordshire.

In each case the brass is not cut out in silhouette and inlaid in the stone, English fashion, but is a rectangular plate engraved all over after the fashion of the continent. In each the diaper of the background is of trefoils with dragons;[1] in each the merchant's head rests on a cushion diapered in leaf pattern and supported by two angels. At the foot of each man a selvage man struggles with a lion, monster, or eagle; each lady has a lap-dog at her feet. Each figure has an elaborate and beautiful canopy with the eidolon of the soul carried by angels or resting in the hands of God, among angels censing or playing musical instruments. The side shafts have prophets and saints, except for one that has men and women mourners. Below the effigies each brass has a long narrow compartment with figures. That of Walsoken has a horseman carrying grist to the mill, two men carrying their master in a litter over a stream, hunting-scenes, and a fight with a poacher; Braunche a peacock feast. Mr. Macklin has well shown that east Prussia and probably Lübeck is indicated as their common origin. The brass of Albrecht Hovener at Stralsund closely resembles that of Robert Braunche.

The Teutonic Hanse was founded by that city and by Hamburg in 1266, and by 1271 they had an affiliated house at Lynn. Not long afterwards they had another branch at Hull, the natural trading-port of Newark. The merchants' patronage of a foreign atelier is thus explained without difficulty. The priests' brasses are less easily explained, but Hertfordshire was not far from London nor Yorkshire from Hull.

Besides these brasses with their affiliations with Lübeck, two survive that seem to be Flemish in origin. These are those of Ralph de Knevyngton, who died in 1370, at Aveley in Essex, and of

---

[1] The Walsoken brass adds satyrs, mermaids, animals, and butterflies.

FIG. 9. *Brass of Robert Attelath*
formerly at King's Lynn

Thomas de Topclyff who died in 1391, and his wife, in Topcliffe church in Yorkshire: this is a palimpsest brass with a Flemish inscription on the back. A third brass, that of Roger Thornton, who died in 1429, and his wife at All Saints', Newcastle-on-Tyne, appears to be German.

None the less, other merchants and other churchmen were content to have brasses of English workmanship. A finely drawn brass of a priest, about 1365, in Walton church, Hertfordshire, and the brass of Archbishop Thomas Cranley, who died in 1417, may serve as examples. A number of notably elaborate priests' brasses date from the first years of the fifteenth century (Fig. 10). Dugdale records[1] that to Thomas de Evre, dean of St. Paul's, who died in 1400. It was set in a marble tomb, and had a quintuple canopy over a representation of the Annunciation, with a border of the twelve apostles. A brass at Balsham, Cambridgeshire, of almost equal splendour, commemorates John Sleford, who was chaplain to Queen Philippa, master of the wardrobe to Edward III, and archdeacon of Wells. It is set inside the screen which he gave to the church before his death in 1401. The triple canopy is adorned with figures of the Trinity and shields of England, France, Hainault, Flanders, Ely, and Wells. The archdeacon wears a cope of which the orphreys are adorned with figures of saints, including St. Etheldreda and St. Wilfred. That of Henry de Codryngtoun, rector of Bottesford in Leicestershire, is little less elaborate.

A good example of a merchant's brass is that of Walter Pescod at Boston in Lincolnshire; it has a light canopy over the effigy and the apostles in niches as a border on either side. The inscriptions on such brasses had often a homespun quality all their own. One of 1400 in St. Mary-le-Bow[2] read:

> *Such as I am, such sall ye be;*
> *Grocer of London somtym was I:*
> *The Kings weigher mor than yeres twenty,*
> *Simon Street callyd in my plas*
> *And good Fellowshyp fayn wold tras:*
> *Therefor in heuen euerlastyng lif*
> *Iesu send me and Agnes my wyf.*

[1] Macklin, 45.   [2] Weever, 404.

FIG. 10. *Brass of William de Fulbourn,*
d. 1391. Fulbourn, Cambs.

Kerli Merli my words were tho,
And Deo gratias I added therto.
I passyd to God in the yere of Grase
A thousand four hundryd iust hit was.

Towards the end of the fourteenth century the fashion for brasses revived among knights and even among nobles who were no longer enriched by the spoils and ransoms of successful war. Sir John de Foxley, who died in 1378, ordered in his will that a brass should be made of him and his two wives, ornamented with their arms.[1] The brass of Sir Edward Cerne and his wife in Draycot church, Wiltshire, and that of Sir John Cassy, who died in 1400, and his wife Alice at Deerhurst, may stand as examples of knightly brasses: he wears the dress of a law officer; she has a little dog at her feet with his name, Terri, underneath.

Thomas, Lord Berkeley, when his wife Margaret died in 1392, set up a brass to her and himself in his church at Wotton-under-Edge that is no more elaborate than Sir John Cassy's. Alianor de Bohun, duchess of Gloucester, wife of the king's son William of Woodstock and one of the greatest heiresses in England, when she died in 1399 was commemorated only by a brass at Westminster[2] (Fig. 11). It has a graceful canopy with three cusped gables and pinnacles between; six shields of arms are hung on the side pillars. The figure is noble in its simplicity; the head rests on two cushions delicately patterned. It is a fine brass of an extremely English kind. The brass of Thomas Beauchamp, earl of Warwick, who died in 1401, is the last of this aristocratic series.[3] It is adorned with a very rich diaper of a pointillé kind over heraldic charges, much like that on the effigies of Richard II and his wife at Westminster.

The fifteenth century is remarkable for a series of brasses commemorating the wool-merchants who were then rising to wealth and importance. William Grevel, the greatest of them, who died in 1401, is commemorated in the church he built at Chipping Campden by a brass that describes him as *flos mercatorum tocius Anglie.* It is the first English brass to display a merchant's mark. Other

---

[1] *Arch. Journ.* xv (1858), 268.   [2] Dart, ii. 125.
[3] In St. Mary's, Warwick.

Fig. 11. *Brass of Alianor de Bohun, Duchess of Gloucester, d. 1399. Westminster*

woolmen's brasses are to be found in the Cotswolds at Northleach, Cirencester, Lechlade, and Chipping Norton. Another group is to be found in the grazing districts of Bedfordshire and Hertfordshire; a third group at Lynwode and Stamford in Lincolnshire. The two brasses of John de Lyndewode, father and son, 1419 and 1421, show them with their feet resting on woolpacks; the son's pack is stamped with his merchant's mark.

By this time almost all the inscriptions on brasses were in English; one of the latest in French is that of the chief cook to the French Queen Katherine,[1] and he may well have been a Frenchman. A few were still in Latin; Blomefield records a beautiful instance of the time of Henry V from the brass of Jane Heydown in Baconsthorpe church:

> O Jesu tolle a me quod feci
> Et remaneat mihi quod tu fecisti
> Ne pereat quod sanguine tuo redemisti.

The English inscriptions are far from stereotyped. Sometimes they alluded in punning fashion to the name of the man commemorated. The brass of a man called Palmer, in the church of Snodland, Kent,[2] was inscribed

> Palmers al our faders were
> I a Palmer livyd here
> And trauylled still, till worne wyth age
> I endyd this worlds pylgramage
> On the blyst assension day
> In the cherful month of May
> A thowsand wyth fowre hundred seuen
> And took my iorney hense to Heuen.

The humility of a flat tomb-slab was the mark of the earlier middle ages. It might bear an inscription or even an image of the dead incised in the stone or inlaid in it in brass, but it was a part of the floor and could be trodden underfoot. Soon, however, pride set the effigy above the path of men's feet; and with the elevation the image soon became an effigy in the round.

[1] Meistre John Hunger, 1435, All Saints, Hertford.
[2] Weever, 331.

FIG. 12. *Brass of a knight and lady of the Massingberd family, c. 1400. Gunby Church, Lincolnshire*

Knyghtes in her conisantes clad for the nones
All it semed seyntes y-sacred upon erthe;
And lovely ladies y-wrought leyen by her sydes
In many gay garmentes that weren gold beten.[1]

Such were the typical tombs of the fourteenth century: effigies
lying upon altar-tombs after a fashion that had once been used
only for saints or for men of religion who might one day be
canonized.

The line between saints and laymen, however, was no longer so
clearly drawn; we have seen[2] how the commemoration of Queen
Eleanor was on a scale that seems to be a prelude to canonization.
Her lovely bronze effigy sets a standard for the new century. It
finds a modest parallel in such stone effigies as that of a lady at
Aldworth in Berkshire,[3] which has beautiful flowing drapery that
may be compared with that of the queen. Its male equivalent is
such a statue as that of Sir John Laverock in Ash church, Kent;[4]
elegant alike in the graceful irregularity of the pose, the rich details
of the armour, and the delicate finish of the whole. Both must
date from the first decade of the fourteenth century, or near it.
Priestly effigies worthy to set beside them are that at Welwick in
Yorkshire, and that of Chancellor Swinfield in Hereford Lady
chapel.[5]

These effigies were of stone,[6] painted, and gilt. The colouring
of an oaken effigy[7] of a knight who died in 1311 and was buried
at Fersfield in Norfolk will give some idea of their original vivid-
ness. The coat of mail was gilt, the shield was painted with his
arms, the surcoat with his colours of ermine and gules. The pillow
on which his head rested was scarlet flowered with gold. The
details of belt, sword, and spurs were gilt and inlaid with painted
glass to imitate enamel. The tomb of John of Sheppey, bishop of

---

[1] *Pierce the Plowman's Crede*, ed. Skeat (1906), 8.   [2] p. 2.
[3] Prior and Gardner, Fig. 396, where it is suggested that it may be the work of the
Abingdon School. Cf. an effigy of a lady in Worcester Lady chapel.
[4] Stothard, 54.   [5] Prior and Gardner, Figs. 690 and 710.
[6] This is not the place to consider the question of the quarries used and the distribution; it is fully treated by Prior and Gardner.
[7] Gough, *Sep. Mon.* ii. 82. Oak effigies continued in use in the early years of the
fourteenth century, but the chief examples are of the preceding century.

Rochester, who died in 1360, was later walled up where it lay in his cathedral. When it was revealed some seventy-five years ago much of its original colour was still manifest. The flesh and hair are naturally tinted; the cope is a deep red, powdered with a pattern in gold; its lining is dark green. All the other vestments are painted in elaborate patterns.

Not long after 1330 the stone effigies were modified by the use of alabaster and soft stone in place of the harder stone used hitherto. The change had many repercussions; it served to divorce tomb sculpture from the greater architectural sculpture of churches, it fostered the commercial development of the trade, and encouraged a more detailed and delicate style of carving in the softer material.[1] The effigies, it would seem, were made at Hanbury and Tutbury, and later at Chellaston, not far from the quarries from which the alabaster blocks were cut.[2]

The earliest important effigy in alabaster is that of Edward II in Gloucester cathedral. A wooden figure with a copper gilt crown was originally placed upon his coffin, and when it was safe to do so the abbot replaced it by the shrine-tomb that is now one of the glories of the abbey (Pl. 73). The base is of Purbeck marble, the canopy of freestone, but the effigy is of a remarkably clear and luminous alabaster. It is carved with great mastery in Christ-like fashion; the subtle modelling of the brow and the bold treatment of the hair are extremely fine (Pl. 69). The king lies crowned, bearing the sceptre and orb of earthly dominion, but the effigy is of one who was to be honoured as a saint.

The subsequent effigies hardly reach this level. That at Westminster of John of Eltham, the second son of Edward II, who died in 1334, is none the less accomplished in its pose and in the treatment of the drapery. Two lovely angels here hold the helmeted head. The tomb of his nephew, William of Hatfield, who died ten years later and was buried at York, shows him as a civilian, with a cut-edged mantle; the pose has here something of the pathetic flatness of a corpse. These three effigies, all of men close of kin to Edward III, appear to have come from the same

[1] See Arthur Gardner: *Alabaster Tombs of the Gothic Period.*
[2] W. St. John Hope in *Arch.* lxi (1904), 233.

workshop, but we do not know who directed it. The Westminster tomb of the two young children of Edward III who died in 1340 have miniature alabaster effigies which are known to have been bought from John Orchard, *latoner* of London; it does not by any means follow that they were carved in his workshop, which seems rather to have specialized in effigies in metal.

The early fourteenth-century effigies of knights are notable for a romantic vigour of pose. An alabaster knight at Hanbury in Staffordshire[1] and another at Dorchester in Oxfordshire[2] are represented drawing their swords; seven at Aldworth near Oxford show a gradual rise and decline of animation. A curious romantic tomb is that of Sir Oliver de Ingham, at Ingham in Norfolk; he had been seneschal of Gascony in 1326 and died in 1343. He is represented lying upon a bed of pebbles, originally coloured blue-grey, wearing a cyclas of his arms, paly per fess *or* and *vert* a cross moline *gules*, over grey and black armour, with his feet resting on a white lion. Another effigy from the same workshop is that of Sir Roger de Kerdeston in Reepham church, Norfolk (Pl. 68); wearing fine armour, a rich surcoat, and heavy jewelled belt, he lies on a rocky bed as if washed up on a shore. The wall behind him was painted with a hunting-scene in a wood.[3]

No woman's tomb is as romantic as this; but in that at Much Marcle of Blanche, daughter of Roger Mortimer, who died in 1347, and in that of a lady at Ledbury near by (Pl. 77 a), a kind of romantic realism is shown in the fall of the train of the dress over the edge of the tomb; it is as if they had been laid sleeping upon the carved chests.

Another kind of realism is evident in the tomb of Queen Philippa, the work in her lifetime of Hennequin de Liége, a pupil of Pepin de Huy, a Fleming.[4] The effigy is obviously, and indeed unkindly, a portrait; the tomb is remarkable for the increased use of bronze, which is employed not only for the effigy and its

[1] Prior and Gardner, Fig. 725.   [2] Ibid., Fig. 726.
[3] To judge by his church at Ewerby, Lincs., he was a distinguished patron of architecture.
[4] He was paid for it in Jan. 1366–7. It was finished by John Orchard, who provided the angels. Devon, 189, 199.

canopy but also for the arcading on the sides of the black marble tomb-chest. The canopied scheme was also followed on the tomb of Edward III, with a rather archaic bronze effigy, bronze weepers, and splendid heraldic shields of enamelled bronze.

The tomb of Queen Philippa was perhaps too foreign to have much influence, and the English workers in alabaster continued to work out their own types. Their production, to judge from what remains, must have been extraordinarily abundant; unfortunately it was not equally distinguished. Almost all the effigies are typical rather than individual; this quality is sometimes recognized in wills, when the testator mentions some well-known monument which is to serve as the model for his tomb.[1] Such an effigy as that of Sir Humphrey Littlebury, who died in 1360, and was buried at Holbeach in Lincolnshire, is a fine example of the knightly type.[2] That of Sir Richard Willoughby, chief justice of the King's Bench to Edward III,[3] may stand for the legal type; that of Thomas Quatermain of North Weston and his wife, at Thame, for the rich yeoman. The tomb of a London merchant, Richard Lions, who was beheaded by Wat Tyler in 1381, is described by Stowe:[4] 'his picture on his grave-stone verie faire and large, is with his haire rounded by his eares and curled. A little beard forked, a gowne girt to him downe to his feet, of branched Damaske, wrought with the likeness of flowers, a large pursse on his right side, hanging in a belt from his left shoulder, a plain whoode about his neck.'[5] The Westminster tomb of Cardinal Langham, made by Henry Yevele and Stephen Lote, may stand for the episcopal type.

The next landmark is the bronze effigy of the Black Prince, set up at Canterbury in accordance with the provisions of his will (Pl. 70). We do not know the name of the sculptor; his work has a stiff hieratic dignity. The details of the armour are worked out

---

[1] Sir Walter Manny, for instance, in 1371, directed that a tomb of alabaster should be made for him, with his image as a knight, and his arms, like that of Sir John Beauchamp in St. Paul's. *Test. Vet.* i. 86.

[2] Crossley, 15.   [3] At Willoughby church, Notts.; Stothard, 78.

[4] The whole series should be studied in Crossley, in Prior and Gardner, and in Gardner's *Alabaster Tombs*.

[5] A good surviving tomb of this time is that of John Oteswich in St. Helen's, Bishopsgate. Prior and Gardner, Fig. 785.

with exquisite precision; the face, though in some measure a portrait, is curiously lifeless.[1] Here the long French inscription mourns the passing of life and its pleasures.

> . . . *En terre avoy grant richesse,*
> *Dont je y fys grand noblesse,*
> *Terre, mesons, et grand treshor,*
> *Draps, chivalx, argent et or.*
> *Mes ores su je povres et cheitifs,*
> *Profond en la terre gys.*
> *Ma grand beauté est tout alée*
> *Ma char est tout gastée.*
> *Moult est etroite ma meson . . .*

It ends with a plea for prayer, and a prayer in return:

> *Tout cil qi pur moi prieront*
> *Ou a Dieu m'acorderont*
> *Dieu les mette en son paradys*
> *Ou nul ne poet estre chetifs.*[2]

An indenture of 1394[3] engages Nicholas Broker and Godfrey Prest, citizens and coppersmiths, to make effigies of Richard II and Anne of Bohemia, in bronze gilt.[4] The king is represented holding his wife's right hand;[5] they lie under a canopy of bronze. The images in themselves do not show any very great advance on that of the Black Prince, but are noteworthy for the extraordinarily delicate pointillé work of the diaper of heraldic devices with which the robes are powdered. Richard's head, however, is a fine and unflattering piece of portraiture, and the robes have an easier flow than those of Edward III.

[1] Crossley, 28, notes that the bronze effigies were made from a 'patron' in wood, but that of the Black Prince looks as if it had been cast from clay.

[2] The whole text was prescribed by the will of the Black Prince (Nichols, 67). It is derived from a French translation of the *Clericalis Disciplina* of Petrus Alphonsus, the *Castoiement d'un Père à son fils*. See Macklin, 64; A. Hilker and W. Söderjelm, 'Petri Alfonsi Disciplina', *Acta Societatis Scientiarum Fennicae*, Helsinki (1922), xlix, 136, 1. 3533 and 157, col. *a*. In the book a philosopher sees the inscription upon a monument.

[3] Bradley and Neale, ii. 107.

[4] The tomb itself was made by the masons Henry Yevele and Stephen Lote. Devon, 258. They had already worked together on the tomb of Cardinal Langham.

[5] Cf. the contemporary alabaster tomb of a knight and lady at Elford, Staffs. Prior and Gardner, Fig. 779.

In 1408 Jeanne de Navarre, the second wife of Henry IV, engaged three London men, Thomas Colyn, Thomas Holewell, and Thomas Poppehove, to make an alabaster tomb for her first husband, the duke of Brittany, which was then shipped out to France.[1] It was destroyed at the Revolution, but earlier drawings[2] show it to have been of the usual knightly type with the crested helm under the head,[3] closely resembling that of an unknown knight at Swine, Yorks.[4] It is altogether eclipsed in importance by Henry IV's own effigy at Canterbury, set up about 1405 (Pl. 71). This is one of the finest of the English alabasters: a portrait, yet a portrait of a king. The effect of the whole is spoilt by the much lesser size of his queen, a touch of realism found in other monuments of the period: yet his statue, taken alone, forms a noble ending to the long series of English royal alabaster effigies that begins with Edward II. The effigy of bronze that Henry V ordered for his mother's tomb in the Royal College of Leicester in 1413,[5] and his own silver image, have both disappeared; the series of funeral images in metal ends in our period with the great bronze effigy of Richard, earl of Warwick. This was cast by William Austin, citizen and brass founder of London, and polished and gilded by Bartholomew Lambspring, Dutchman and goldsmith; the tomb chest was made by a marbler of Corfe according to a drawing supplied to him. The whole seems to have been supervised by a marbler, John Essex, who perhaps made the model from which the bronze image was cast. It is clearly a portrait, with a rather blunt nose, a long upper lip, a furrowed brow, and an oddly shaped ear: details, perhaps, in which we may trace the advice of Roger Webbe, warden of the London Company of Barber Surgeons, who was called in to help the sculptor. The hands, too, are exquisitely veined, and are the more

---

[1] Rymer, viii. 510.

[2] One is illustrated in Crossley, 27. See also Bodleian MS. Gaignières 18346, fol. 102.

[3] The use came in about 1340; it reflected a funeral custom. See, for example, will of Sir Nicholas de Lovaine, 1375 (*Test. Vet.* i. 98), 'I will ... that my helmet be placed at the head of my corpse'.

[4] Prior and Gardner, Fig. 518.

[5] It was bought from William Godezer, citizen and coppersmith of London. Devon, 321.

striking in contrast with the smooth conventional surfaces of the plate-armour which encases the body.

Many alabaster effigies of the first half of the fifteenth century survive, but they show few changes from what had gone before; the trade had become in the main commercialized (Pl. 72 *a*). The finest of them is that of Ralph Greene and his lady in Lowick church, Northamptonshire; they have niche heads in the French manner over their heads. The contract for the tomb, dated 1419, still exists,[1] by which Thomas Prentys and Robert Sutton of Chellaston agree to deliver an 'image contrefait à un esquier en armes en toutz pointz et contrefait à une dame gisant en sa surcote ouverte'.

The only great change in such imagery reflects the pre-occupation of the fifteenth century with the idea of death. The tomb of Bishop Fleming in Lincoln cathedral, set up about 1430, has the corpse decaying in its shroud laid beneath the upper stone on which he lies in pomp.[2] The same scheme is followed in the tomb of Archbishop Chichele at Canterbury about 1440; and in that of Thomas Beckington, bishop of Wells and one of the early English humanists (Pl. 72 *b*).[3] The will of Isabel, countess of Warwick, drawn up in 1439[4] directs that she is to be buried at Tewkesbury, and her hair ornaments with the balas rubies to be sold and delivered to that house 'so that they grutched not with my burial there'. She further directs:

'And I will that my statue be made, all naked,[5] with my hair cast backwards, according to the design and model which Thomas Porchalion has for that purpose, with Mary Magdalen laying her hand across, and St John the Evangelist on the right side, and St Anthony on the left; at my feet a scutcheon, impaling my arms with those of the Earl my husband, supported by two griffins, but on the sides thereof the statues

[1] Hartshorne, *Effigies of Northamptonshire*, 312.

[2] The scheme is found in France as early as 1393 in the tomb of Guillaume de Harcigny at Laon.

[3] It was also followed on the lost tomb of Dean Heywood at Lichfield. Lord Winchelsea's Album, fol. 7.

[4] *Test. Vet.* i. 239.

[5] Cf. the half-naked knight on an effigy at Lichfield drawn by Sir William Dugdale in 1640-1. Lord Winchelsea's Album, fol. 7 *v*.

of poor men and women in their poor array, with their beads in their hands.'[1]

It was the custom at medieval funerals for the family mourners to be supplemented by bedesmen and bedeswomen who were given mourning cloaks and hoods, walked in the procession, and were under an obligation to pray for the dead person's soul for some time afterwards. The 1426 will of Thomas Beaufort, duke of Exeter, prescribes that he is to be buried in his wife's grave at Bury St. Edmunds, with as many torches as there are years to his age, and as many poor men and poor women clothed in white.[2] They were, however, less often represented on the sides of tomb-chests than the members of the dead person's family.[3]

Such weepers, of whom the earliest English instance[4] seems to be those on the tomb of Lady Fitzalan in Chichester cathedral, dating from 1275, became a feature of noble tombs in the years after 1290.[5] Those on Edmund Crouchback's tomb were arranged in pairs facing each other,[6] in elegant swaying poses; they much resemble the statues on the Eleanor crosses. The tomb of Edward II has lost its weepers; that on Edward III has six stiff little doll-like figures left that shields of arms beneath once identified as the king's sons and daughters. The weepers on the tomb of Queen Philippa, once as many as thirty, are now reduced to two; these also had shields of their arms beneath to identify them.[7]

John of Eltham's tomb at Westminster is the earliest to have alabaster weepers; their painted shields were set in quatrefoils

---

[1] The tomb no longer exists. It showed her clothed, but in a simple smock, not in state robes. Shroud brasses, which express the same feeling in a simpler form, were also made. Macklin, 210.

[2] Nichols, 246. Cf. the will of Philippa, duchess of York, ibid. 224.

[3] See Crossley, 127 et seqq.

[4] They are found a decade or more earlier in France.

[5] Archbishop Peckham, d. 1292, at Canterbury, has bishops for weepers; on the tomb of Baron Fitzalan, d. 1301, at Bedale, Yorks., the end panel, now reset, shows him on his death-bed with an angel receiving his soul; Henry de Lacy, earl of Lincoln at St. Paul's, d. 1310, had weepers who appear to be the surpliced canons of the church to whom he had been a great benefactor. Dugdale, 57.

[6] Cf. two monuments at Lincoln, c. 1380, and others of c. 1375 at Colne priory and Barthomley, Cheshire. Prior and Gardner, Fig. 447.

[7] See Gough, ii. 123.

beneath them. They show great variety in pose; evidently the artist designed them to contrast with the quiet figure lying above.

The tomb of Richard II, made in 1394, differed from that of Edward III chiefly in having saints and angels round it instead of weepers. Angels were simultaneously taken over by the Chellaston alabaster workers; they appear on the Arderne tomb at Elford holding shields before them with both hands. The tomb of one of the Hiltons at Swine in Yorkshire, dating from about 1410, has the shields each upheld by two angels; that of Sir Ralph Vernon, who died in 1451, and his wife Benedicta at Tong in Shropshire, has statues of the apostles alternating with the angels bearing shields.[1] On the tomb of Sir Ralph Grey at Chillingham statues of saints occupy the chief niches, and the angels holding shields appear on the lesser ones between. On other tombs an impression of equal magnificence is obtained by setting the shield in a cusped panel; the most splendid instance is perhaps the tomb of the Black Prince.

[1] A difference in scale rather spoils the effect.

VIII

CANOPIED TOMBS

THE history of the Christian tomb is always linked with the history of the Christian shrine. The form of commemoration that is awarded to the saint in one generation is usually extended, with some modification, to the ordinary man in the next.

The century between 1275 and 1375 was notable for the construction of new shrines and shrine-bases in many of the English cathedrals. At Lincoln a stone base was set up to support the châsse of St. Hugh's body, a church-like reliquary in silver gilt.[1] At Oxford a new base was built for the shrine of St. Frideswide in 1289,[2] with a heavy cusped arcade rising from a base like an altar-tomb. At St. Albans the saint's shrine was given a new basis in 1305, an altar-like structure surmounted by a richly carved gabled arcade which rises to a heavy cornice.[3] Much was done to glorify St. Erkenwald's shrine in St. Paul's cathedral between 1319 and 1339;[4] at Ely, St. Etheldreda was given a new shrine about 1330;[5] and at Lincoln, the shrine of St. Hugh's Head was newly set out about 1350. Finally, in 1370 the bones of the Venerable Bede were translated to a place in the galilee at Durham and enshrined in a monument with statues of female saints in an ogival arcade round the base, a Crucifixion group in the end gable, and a scaled roof with a leafy cresting.[6] In 1372 Lord Neville of Raby gave the new base of marble and alabaster, brought from London by sea, for the shrine of St. Cuthbert.[7]

All these shrine bases are known to us in a truncated form that gives a false impression of the original whole. We may imagine the gilded shrines, resting above them at the time of great feasts of the

---

[1] 1536 inventory; Dugdale, *Monasticon*, vi. 3, 1278.

[2] Illustrated Crossley, *English Church Monuments*, 51.

[3] The fragments were rediscovered when the abbey was restored in 1880; illustrated Crossley, 62.   [4] Dugdale, *St. Paul's*, 15, 74, 339.

[5] Crossley, 64. It may be compared with the choir screen at Exeter.

[6] Fowler, *Rites of Durham*, 45; Dugdale's album (Lord Winchelsea's collection), fol. 101.   [7] *Hist. Dunelm. Script.* iii. 135.

Church, but we are apt to forget the wooden covers that normally crowned them. The book of the *Rites of Durham*[1] describes how on feast-days the cover was carried up on a pulley, with bells on the rope so that they 'did make such a good sound yt. it did stirr all ye peoples harts that was within ye Church to repaire unto it'. The cover 'was all gilded over and on either side was painted fower lively Images curious to ye behoulders and on the East End was painted the picture of our Saviour sitting on a Rainbowe to give Judgment . . . and on the West End of it was ye picture of Our Lady and Our Saviour on her knee. And on the topp of ye cover from end to end was most fine carved work cutt owte with Dragons and other beasts moste artificially wrought. . . .' Thus surmounted, even on ordinary days the shrines must have had the spiry quality that they now lack.

Their analogy with contemporary and rather later tombs is evident. The scheme of the arcade rising from a base was already to be found in such tombs as that of Bishop Giles Bridport at Salisbury;[2] this even has a roof like that of a wooden shrine-cover. The two-storied scheme occurs in the contemporary tomb of Archbishop Walter Gray at York, which is undoubtedly inspired by the idea of a shrine.[3] The most splendid tombs of the age show a modification of the shrine scheme into one of the most beautiful ever devised for a tomb. The monument of Edmund Crouch-back, earl of Lancaster, in Westminster Abbey (Pl. 3) has the base, which here, unlike bases of the shrines, is the tomb, surmounted by three arches of unequal height, to form an open canopy over the effigy that lies upon the tomb.[4] They have no shrine to support, and the gables of the two lesser arches are directly crowned by pinnacles. The central gable, however, has four stands on either face which once held gilded figures of angels holding candlesticks.[5] At the head of the effigy two saints hold up the eidolon of the departed soul.[6] Without blasphemous imitation the tomb of a

---

[1] Fowler, 4.   [2] Crossley, 49; he died in 1264.

[3] Crossley, 48; he died in 1255.

[4] The scheme is found in a simple form with three equal arches and gables on the tomb of Bishop Aqua Blanca, *c.* 1268, in Hereford cathedral.

[5] Similar stands appear on the tomb of Aymer de Valence, earl of Pembroke, d. 1324.   [6] See Stothard, 46.

private person has been given the dignity and splendour befitting the shrine of a saint.

This canopy scheme is the most interesting and characteristic of the early fourteenth century.[1] In the free-standing form used for the tomb of Edmund Crouchback at Westminster, it is known in at least seven examples of the first half of the fourteenth century, of which the tomb of Bishop William of Louth, who died in 1298, in Ely cathedral[2] is one of the finest; unfortunately the tomb-chest and effigy have been destroyed. The tomb of Roger de Mortival, bishop of Salisbury, who died in 1330, has a roof after the manner of a shrine-cover,[3] surmounted by a kind of skeleton spire with flying buttresses, that here takes the place of the metallic spire of a shrine. The tomb is also notable for the crockets of the gable, each formed as a little angel, and for the remarkably heavy central finial. Archbishop Stratford lies at Canterbury under a free-standing canopy which has two tiers of light tabernacle work at the top, rising from a bowed cornice which has its own array of pinnacles. The splendid monument of Aymer de Valence, earl of Pembroke, at Westminster, dating from 1324, is closely modelled on Edmund Crouchback's, but lacks the side arches and gables. The Westminster tomb of John of Eltham, the son of Edward II who died in 1334, originally had a light and elegant canopy with three equal arches, the central gable and pinnacles being higher than the rest; this was destroyed in 1760.[4] The tomb of John of Gaunt and his wife, set up in old St. Paul's in 1374, is known to us from an engraving by

---

[1] In its developed form it seems to be an English creation. A French example of the type is that of Thibault de Chalon, abbot of Cormery, d. 1331 (Bodleian MS. Gaignières 18359, fol. 165), which had a pierced gable and a richly cusped and recusped arch, not unlike the tomb of Aveline at Westminster. That of Cardinal Jean Cholet in the abbey of Saint Lucien de Beauvais was surmounted by a roofed canopy with light gables and heavy pinnacles (ibid. 18354, fol. 14). The tomb of Jean d'Artois, comte d'Eu, d. 1386, at Eu likewise had a gable canopy with a richly cusped arch and angel pinnacles (ibid. 18346, fol. 57). All of these, however, were later than their English parallels.

[2] Crossley, 60. Cf. the tomb of Archbishop William Greenfield, d. 1315, at York.   [3] Ibid. 61.

[4] Crossley, 57. Cf. the tomb of Prior Alexander of Sutton, d. 1320, in Oxford cathedral, and the lost tomb of Bishop Blith at Lichfield, of which a drawing by Dugdale is in Lord Winchelsea's collection. Other lost canopies are those of the tombs of Lady Montacute, c. 1340, at Oxford, and Ralph Greene, d. 1419, at Lowick.

Hollar.[1] Here the Perpendicular feeling for horizontal line was expressed in a more quadrilateral scheme; the pinnacles have become no more than a spiky cresting, the gables no more than a sparse surface decoration. Within a century a splendid type of tomb has passed through all the stages of development and has here reached decay. John of Gaunt's will[2] includes directions for his funeral of a curious detailed symbolism: there are to be ten great candles for the Ten Commandments against which he has sinned, and seven more for the Seven Works of Mercy in which he has been negligent and for the Seven Deadly Sins. Further, there are to be five for the Five Wounds of Christ,[3] and for the five senses that he has too fondly indulged, and three for the Trinity that may yet bring him salvation. None of this symbolism, however, seems to be reflected in his permanent tomb. A canopy of another kind was used for the tomb of Edward II in Gloucester cathedral, set up after the fall of Mortimer in 1330 (Pl. 73). Here the deeply recessed arcades of the base are the foundation for a two-storied canopy of the most complex kind that shows a further elaboration of the kind of tiered canopy work that had been worked out some twenty years earlier in the Bishop's throne at Exeter (Pl. 13).[4] Here, however, the intention was to erect a monument not only to a king but also to a saint. The royal house still lacked a saintly protector; the cult of Edward the Confessor, much though it owed to the encouragement of Edward II, seemed to be national rather than dynastic. A rival had to be found, too, to Thomas of Lancaster, a cousin of Edward II who had been beheaded by his order; miracles had been recorded at his tomb by 1323, and a hanap of

---

[1] Dugdale, 60, reproduced in Harvey, *Yevele*, Fig. 51.

[2] Nicholas, 145.

[3] He also left many bequests of 5 marks to religious houses in honour of the Five Wounds.

[4] The question of how far the existing canopy is original is hard to solve. It is of a different stone from the base, but the plan seems to be homogeneous. Sandford in 1707 gave a plate of it that differs in some respects from the present canopy; we can only guess at the accuracy of his plates by comparing that of the tomb of Edward III on p. 177 with the monument, and here the canopy is only represented with fair accuracy. Gough, ii. 92, says: 'The elegant canopy as appears by an inscription on it, is modern, not strictly copied from the old one.' Oriel College, Oxford, is known to have restored the tomb in 1737, 1789, 1798, and 1876.

mazer with a print representing him as a saint was sold in London in 1338.[1] Edward II's murder was his chief claim to sanctity, but for a time sufficed; over a hundred silk and gold brocades were offered at the shrine, and the money oblations paid for the great vault of the choir and the stalls on the prior's side.[2] Edward III in 1341 gave a gold ship to the tomb in fulfilment of a vow made when in peril of shipwreck;[3] his son Edward of York gave a cross-shaped reliquary with a fragment of the true Cross; and many other jewels were dedicated. Attempts to secure a formal canonization were made; in 1395 Richard II paid for a book of the miracles of Edward II to be conveyed to Florence and given to the pope,[4] and two years later sent an embassy to Rome to endeavour to negotiate the canonization. As late as the last quarter of the fifteenth century the dying agony of the king was represented on two roof-bosses in the north transept of St. Augustine's, Bristol.[5]

Edward II's favourite, Hugh Despencer, who had married the eldest coheiress of Gloucester and had used the inheritance to make himself the autocrat of south Wales, met an end hardly less dreadful than that of his master. His remains were later collected and buried at Tewkesbury at the back of the sedilia in a splendid tomb with some forty niches for statues. His son, another Hugh, who died childless in 1349, has a spiry canopy over his tomb that is a lesser version of Edward II's. His widow then married Sir Guy de Brian, and when he died he too lay under a canopy of three stories of arcading. Apart from these, the canopy of the Gloucester tomb was not imitated in England.[6]

Instead there arose a fashion for a great wooden tester hanging over the tomb: a fashion that must have arisen by analogy with

[1] Riley, *Memorials*, 203.
[2] *Chron. of Gloucester Abbey*, Rolls Series (1863), 48.
[3] The stone stand for it projects in front of the tomb.
[4] Devon, 259.
[5] See C. J. P. Cave, *The Roof-bosses of Bristol Cathedral* (1935), 13.
[6] It seems to have furnished a model for the tomb of Pope John XXII at Avignon, made by Jean Lavenier of Paris in 1345. It is worth noting that two Englishmen were working at Avignon at the time: Hugues Wilfred 'dit l'Anglais' as assistant mason on the Tour des Fourières of the Palais des Papes, and 'l'anglais Thomas Daristot' as an assistant painter. Labande, *Le Palais des Papes*, Marseilles (1925), i. 42.

the baldaquins that were carried over the heads of royal and princely persons in state processions. A great tester still hangs over the effigy of the Black Prince, painted on its inner face with the Trinity to whom he owed a special devotion (Pl. 74). His son Richard II has a similar tester over his tomb painted with the Coronation of the Virgin and the Majesty, with angels holding the royal arms.[1] Henry IV lies at Canterbury under a tester painted with his motto, and his queen's, on an ermine ground. As late as 1452 a wooden tester supported by slender shafts was set up over the tomb of Archbishop John Kempe at Canterbury.

Before this, however, the canopied tomb had developed into two types of monument: the chantry chapel, which will be considered later, and the tomb niche. This differed from the canopied tomb in being set against the wall instead of being free-standing; consequently it was much more widely used and is to be found of every degree of importance.

The canopied wall-niche with rich decoration seems at first to have been the prerogative of the builder or chief benefactor of a church. Stephen Alard, admiral of the Cinque Ports, thus lies at Winchelsea under a triple canopy; his two relatives who are buried near by have simpler and lower canopies.[2] The normal decoration of such canopies is cusping, crocketing, and foliage; some, however, have figure sculpture. The tomb of Sir Edward of Maley, who died in 1314, at Barnton, Yorkshire, has the gable of the canopy filled with angels holding the eidolon of the soul of the dead man in a sheet, from which it rises to be received by God the Father.[3] An empty canopy in Exeter cathedral has the gable filled by a mandorla with Christ in glory; the side pinnacles are formed of three tiers of canopied niches holding statues. A remarkably fine recess on the north side of the nave at Belchamp Walter in Essex, perhaps the tomb of Sir John Boutetort, has a richly cusped cinque-foiled arch. The cusps hold shields with foliage round them, and

---

[1] Devon, 262; Dart, ii. 44.

[2] They may be compared with those over the tomb of Archbishop Guillaume de Flavecourt, d. 1306, at Rouen.

[3] Similar figures that top the chapter doorway at Rochester (S. Gardner, 130) suggest that this may have been a memorial.

other shields hang on the side buttresses.[1] Its importance suggests
that he was a benefactor of the church. The cenotaph of the *con-
dottiere* Sir John Hawkwood at Sible Hedingham has an ogival
canopy with hawks of various kinds in the spandrels, and lesser
animals below.[2]

The framing of a panel of wall by the canopy made it possible
to include it in the scheme. The tomb of John Gower in St.
Saviour's, Southwark,[3] was surmounted by a triple canopy. Inside
the alcove the walls were once painted with figures of Charity,
Mercy, and Pity. Charity had a scroll inscribed:

> *En toy qui est fitz de dieu le pere*
> *Sauvez soit que gist souz cest piere.*

On Mercy's scroll was written:

> *O bon Jesu fait ta mercie*
> *A lalme dont le corps gist icy;*

while Pity bore the prayer:

> *Pour la Pite Jesu regarde*
> *Et met cest alme en sauve garde.*

The increasing feeling for horizontal line brought about a
modification of the arch and gable canopy fairly early in the fourteenth century;[4] even so, it was hardly a novelty since the roof-
line of such free-standing tombs as Archbishop Greenfield's had
already introduced a horizontal behind the gable. At Hereford
the tomb of William, Lord Graunson, who died in 1325, is completely rectangular in its main lines (Pl. 75). The effigy lies in an
oblong niche of which the line is only modified by a light cusping
at the top. Above this an arcade of six arches rises to a cornice and
a crested balustrade of quatrefoils. The arches are filled by a fine

---

[1] Cf. the canopy with the gables filled by shields on the tomb of Simon Burley,
d. 1388, in old St. Paul's. Dugdale, *St. Paul's* (1818), 69.

[2] Gough, ii. 153.

[3] He died in 1408. For the paintings see Berthelet's edition of the *Confessio Amantis*,
1532.

[4] See the Exeter tombs of Bishop Thomas de Bitton, d. 1307, and his successor,
Walter Stapeldon, d. 1326.

group of the Coronation of the Virgin, and by statues of four bishop saints.[1]

A similar emphasis on horizontal line is evident in the canopy of the Westminster tomb of Lewis Robsart, Lord Bourchier, who served as standard-bearer at Agincourt and died in 1431.[2] Here the low-pitched arch is surmounted by two rows of arcading divided by plain architraves painted with shields of arms and surmounted by a frieze carved with badges and an embattled cornice. A lion on one side of the tomb and an eagle on the other hold banners of his arms. The whole once glowed with colour: the stone groundwork was blue, powdered with golden Catherine-wheels: the details were picked out in gold, the painted shields were held by angels with golden wings, and every shield was emblazoned.

A more general fashion was to allow the gable to break through the horizontal line of the cornice in a scheme which combined simplicity and elegance. It is found on the tomb of Sir Roger de Kerdeston, who died in 1337,[3] on the tomb of John Wingfield at Wingfield in Suffolk, about 1355,[4] and on that of Sir William de la Pole, who died in 1367, in the church of Holy Trinity, Hull.[5] The last two show an embattled moulding to the cornice which was to become of great importance on other monuments.[6] In the west a heavy embattled cornice combined with a decoration of shields of arms came into fashion about the middle of the century. It is best shown on the monument to Blanche, Lady Grandisson, who died in 1347, in Much Marcle church, Herefordshire; and in a smaller monument that appears to be by the same hand at Ledbury (Pl. 77 a).[7]

The tomb of Bartholomew, Lord Burghersh, who died in 1356,

---

[1] It may be compared with the Harrington tomb in Cartmel priory which is only a little later in date (Crossley, 67). This has a group of the Coronation of the Virgin above the main cornice. A French parallel is afforded by the tomb of the founder, Enguerrand de Marigny, d. 1315, at Ecouis. It had a flat-topped canopy with statues of Christ showing His wounds, the Virgin and St. John, and Enguerrand and his wife.

[2] Crossley, 41.   [3] See above, p. 154, Pl. 68.
[4] Crossley, 66.   [5] Ibid. 66.
[6] e.g. a good tomb niche of about 1390 at Shalford, Essex.
[7] See p. 154.

in Lincoln cathedral, illustrates a further stage in the development of the canopy. The triple arcade has no shafts; the gables that rise from it are no more than lines of cusping set against the background. The inside of the niche is treated as a sham vault, with a cusped arcade at the back to echo that in front and give the appearance of a free-standing canopy.

The end of the series in our period is the tomb of Thomas, Lord Berkeley, who died in 1461 and is buried in St. Mark's, Bristol (Pl. 76). The arch still keeps its ogival line and its multiple cuspings; it runs up into an elongated finial that breaks through cornice and cresting. Yet the whole monument, in its rather heavy richness, its rather stereotyped magnificence, is typical of the England of the latter half of the fifteenth century.

Meanwhile, a new influence was at work in the process of the approximation of the tomb of a Christian sinner to the shrine; and in this case, to the shrine of the Body of Our Lord. When Margery Kempe visited the great church at King's Lynn on a Good Friday, somewhere about 1420, she saw 'priests kneeling on their knees and other worshipful men with torches burning in their hands before the sepulchre, devoutly representing the lamentable death and doleful burying of Our Lord Jesus Christ after the good custom of Holy Church'.[1] The *Rites of Durham*[2] give a fuller account of the Good Friday ceremony. 'After the Passion was sung two of the eldest monkes did take a goodly large crucifix all of gold . . . lyinge uppon a ueluett cushon.' They held it up, and the monks came barefoot one by one and kissed it.

'The service beinge ended the two monkes did carrye it to the sepulcre with great reuerence, which sepulchre was sett up in the morninge on the north side of the quire nigh to the high altar . . . and there did lay it in the said sepulchre with great deuotion with another picture of our sauiour Christ, in whose breast they did enclose with great reverence the most holy and blessed sacrament of the altar, senceinge it and prayinge unto it uppon their knees a great space.'

On Easter Day, between three and four in the morning, at the time of the Resurrection, two of the oldest monks came to this sepulchre, which was covered with red velvet embroidered with gold, censed

[1] W. Butler Bowden, *Book of Margery Kempe*, 210.   [2] II.

it, and took out of it 'a marvellous beautifull Image of Our Sauiour representinge the resurrection with a crosse in his hand in the breast whereof was enclosed in bright Christall the holy sacrament of the altar'. This was carried to the high altar to the singing of *Christus resurgens*, and then carried in procession round the choir, and finally brought back to stand upon the high altar until Ascension Day.[1]

Few churches could boast such an image to hold the consecrated Host, though Coldingham priory bought one in 1370,[2] Cardinal Beaufort left one of silver gilt, representing Christ rising, to Wells cathedral,[3] and Humphrey de Bohun left one to the Austin Friars of London.[4] In most churches, however, the rite was carried out with a simple pyx.

The normal sepulchre structure was, as at Durham, a temporary affair of wood[5] covered with rich embroidery.[6] In some churches, however, a permanent stone niche was built on the north side of the choir; the earliest seem to date from the thirteenth century.[7] Examples may be found in most counties of England. Sometimes another form was adopted; at Dorchester in Oxfordshire the reticulated window at the end of the north aisle has as the sculpture of its chief boss Christ rising from the tomb, with the soldiers sleeping below; it seems evident that here the altar beneath served as an Easter sepulchre.

With the fourteenth century some of the sepulchre niches came to receive more elaborate treatment, especially in eastern England. A notably fine example is that in Lincoln cathedral which is merged into the arcades of the sedilia at the end nearest to the high altar. The tomb-chest is carved with three sleeping soldiers; the risen Christ was presumably represented by a portable image that only appeared at the Paschal season.[8] Two smaller examples,

---

[1] On the history of this rite see Heales in *Arch.* xlii (1869), 264.

[2] Heales, 270.   [3] Dugdale, ii. 280 n. 1.

[4] Nichols, 47: 'Une sepultre ove tabernacles et finols et ove pierres pur mettre einz le corps nostre seigneur.'

[5] Wooden ones still survive at Cowthorpe, Yorks., and Snitterfield, Warwickshire.

[6] John of Gaunt in his will of 1397 leaves to his wife all his 'drap enbroudes pur la Sepulchre'. Nichols, 154.   [7] Young, ii. 510.

[8] It may be compared with that at Northwold. Blomefield, i. 517.

evidently from the same workshop, may be seen at Navenby in Lincolnshire and Hawton in Nottinghamshire (Pl. 78). They are richly sculptured, with a triple gabled arcade rising from a kind of tomb-chest from which a figure of Christ is represented as rising. A little aumbry in the wall no doubt served to house the consecrated Host. At Hawton the whole is crowned by figures of the apostles watching the Ascension; at Navenby by the Three Maries and the angel at the tomb. A third sepulchre from the same shop is that at Heckington,[1] that has the same elements rather differently arranged. The tomb-chest, which is almost identical with that at Hawton, is surmounted by a central niche to receive the Host, with the figure of Christ rising from the gable above it, and the Three Maries and the angel in arcades on either side.

John Chandler of Brasted in Kent, in his will of 1431,[2] directs that he is to be buried 'ubi sepulchrum dominicum tempore paschali stare consuetum est'. At Hawton, a century earlier, the sepulchre was set up alongside the tomb of Sir Robert de Compton, who presumably gave it to the church; he died in 1330.[3] A similar and even closer approximation between an Easter sepulchre and a tomb may be seen at Irnham, also in Lincolnshire, where the tomb of Sir Geoffrey Luttrell (for whom the Luttrell Psalter was written) is combined with an Easter sepulchre of great splendour (Pl. 77 b). In two other instances, at least, a tomb seems also to have served as an Easter sepulchre. Sir William Dugdale's drawing of the sepulchre at Lincoln[4] describes it, on evidence now lost to us, as the tomb of one Robert Blewett; and in my own view the position and plan of the famous Percy tomb at Beverley indicates that it served a double purpose.

The Percy tomb seems to have been erected by Idoine, wife of Henry, Lord Percy;[5] it stands to the north of the high altar, at right angles to the screen behind the altar, to which it is joined by an enclosed spiral stair (Pl. 79). The Lady Idoine did not die until

---

[1] Prior and Gardner, Fig. 53.   [2] Bonnell, in *P.M.L.A.* xxxi. 682.

[3] He seems also to have given the richly carved sedilia that obviously came from the same workshop.   [4] In Lord Winchelsea's album.

[5] The tomb has long been called that of Lady Eleanor Percy, who died in 1328; it bears, however, the arms of France and England quarterly as adopted by Edward III in 1339. The ascription to Lady Idoine is due to Sir Alfred Clapham.

1365, but the monument may well have been set up some time before her death, when the screen of which it forms a part was erected, and have served as an Easter sepulchre before it served as a tomb. The tomb-chest is flat, with no effigy; it could serve either as an altar-table on which a portable altar could be set, or as the basis on which an Easter sepulchre of wood could be set up or any image-monstrance be displayed. The monument is built like a canopied tomb between a pier of the chancel and the enclosed spiral staircase that leads to the screen. The upper line of the gable is straight, but the lower is heavily bowed, so that the group which forms the finial stands out in front of the gable which forms a background to it. The cusps of the arch have enchanting sculptures of Lady Idoine and her husband holding shields of their arms (Pl. 33); the corbels are carved with symbolic beasts.[1] The iconography of the sculpture reflects the double purpose of the monument: the finial group represents God receiving a human soul, and the pinnacles are crowned by figures of angels holding the instruments of the Passion (Frontispiece). The whole is one of the most beautiful creations of the English middle ages, not merely in its delightful detail, but also in the proportion and elegance of the whole. It is, too, a characteristically English monument; for it was only in England[2] that the Easter sepulchre took the place of the Entombment groups that were elsewhere erected to form the setting of the drama of Good Friday and Easter Day.

[1] Illustrated in Prior and Gardner, Fig. 16.

[2] A sixteenth-century Easter sepulchre with the three soldiers sleeping, and a figure of Christ in relief inside the tomb-chest, may be found in Utrecht cathedral. It had large figures at the sides, and combines the English Easter sepulchre with the French Entombment group.

IX

CHANTRIES AND COLLEGES

THE idea that the sufferings of a soul in purgatory could be shortened by the prayers of those on earth is at least as old as the institution of All Souls' Day by Abbot Odilo of Cluny in the eleventh century.[1] Such prayers were for long of a general kind, for all the members of a religious order, or for all the faithful departed; but, perhaps by analogy with the *obit* of a deceased monk, they came in time to be endowed for the soul of a single person. By a curious instance of human self-centredness, they were usually endowed by the person who was to benefit by them. It was only in fulfilment of a promise by Henry IV to Pope Gregory XII that Henry V in 1415, founding three religious houses[2] in expiation of the deaths of Richard II and Archbishop Scrope, bound their members to pray for the man whose throne his father had usurped.

> *Five hundred poor I have in yearly pay,*
> *Who twice a day their wither'd hands hold up*
> *Toward heaven, to pardon blood; and I have built*
> *Two chantries, where the sad and solemn priests*
> *Sing still for Richard's soul.*

A distinction is here rightly drawn between the simple prayer for a soul, that might be offered by priest and layman alike, and the saying of a mass by a priest for the repose of a soul. The first, the simple prayer, early left its mark on epitaphs. They might themselves end with a prayer, as did the long rhymed epitaph on the tomb of William of Valence, who died in 1296[3] and was buried at Westminster:

> *O clemens Christe celos intret precor iste*
> *Nil videat triste, qui pretulit omnibus hisce.*

[1] The fragment of an Anglo-Saxon cross of the middle of the ninth century, found near Dewsbury church, Yorks., and now in the British Museum, is inscribed 'Pray for the soul'.

[2] Carthusians near the palace of Sheen, Brigittines at Sion, and a third house (not completed) of Celestines. Waugh, i. 212.

[3] Weever, 479.

The vernacular inscriptions are yet more direct and touching. John, Lord Cobham, the builder of Cooling castle, had upon his tomb:

> De terre fust fait et fourme
> Et in terre (suis) retourne
> Cobham founder de ceste place
> Le Saint Trinyte mercy de mesme.[1]

Soon the direct prayer was changed into a plea to the passers-by to pray for those who lay at their feet; the change seems to coincide with the shift to English as the language of epitaphs. William Chichele, the brother of the archbishop, lies at Higham Ferrers with his wife Beatrice under the legend:[2]

> Such as ye be such wer we
> Such as we bee such shall ye be
> Lerneth to deye that is the lawe
> That this lif now to wol drawe.
> Sorroe or gladnesse nought letten age
> But on he cometh to lord and page.
> Wherefor for us that ben goo
> Preyeth as other shall for you doo
> That god of his benignyte
> On us have mercy and pite
> And nought remember our wykkedness
> Sith he us bought of hys goodnesse.
>
> > Amen.

The demand for the help of those yet living grew ever simpler and more direct:

> Here lies William Banknot and Anne his wyff
> Swete Iesew grant to them and vs euerlastyng lyff.
> Pray yow hertely for cherite,
> Say a Pater Noster and an Aue.[3]

Soon the plea for prayer took the first place in the epitaph:

> Pray for the sowle of Ione Keriell,
> Ye friends all that forth ypasse;
> In endlesse lyff perpetuall
> That god it grant mercy and grase. . . .[4]

[1] Weever, 328.   [2] Macklin, 165.   [3] Weever, 324.   [4] Ibid. 265.

Exceptionally, something might be offered in return. The inscription on the tomb of John Warren, earl of Surrey, who died in 1304 and was buried at Lewes, begins,

> *Vous qe passez ov bouche close*
> *Pries pur cely ke cy repose . . .*

and ends

> *Ky pur sa alme priera*
> *Trois mill iours de pardon avera.*[1]

Certain gifts to the church, or to the public, were felt to carry with them a claim on the prayers of those who benefited. A cross at Ednam in Lincolnshire, already destroyed in Stukeley's time, had borne the inscription: *Priez pur lalme Raule fiz rob(ert)* ✠ *Priez pur almes des tuts.*[2]

A brass of about 1400 at Holme-by-the-Sea in Norfolk[3] was inscribed:

> *Herry Notyngham and hys wyff lyne her*
> *Yat maden this Chyrche Stepull and Quer;*
> *Too Vestyments and Bells yei madden alsoo,*
> *Christ hem sav therfor for woo,*
> *And to bring her soules to blis of hevyn*
> *Seyth Pater and Ave wyth myld Stephyn.*

It was a short step from this to the endowment of a chantry in connexion with the gift to a town, as, for example, the endowments for the saying of mass in the chapels of certain bridges.[4]

Already we have passed over the line that divides the prayers of the living from organized masses said for the dead. The monastic custom of *obits* for dead brethren and benefactors came to involve an enormous number of soul-masses; by the middle of the thirteenth century the monks of Durham were under the obligation of saying more than 7,000 soul-masses every year.[5] Fourteenth-

---

[1] Gough, ii. 80.   [2] Stukeley, i. Pl. 11.

[3] Gough, ii. 215; Weever, 822.

[4] Wakefield bridge, Yorks., dating from 1360, still has a chapel not later than 1398. Edmund of Langley founded a chantry in it: see Cook, 44, where the whole question of bridge chantries is well discussed.

[5] Ibid. 80. It is noteworthy that Lincoln cathedral about 1342 and St. Albans about 1400 instituted collective chantries for all minor benefactors. Ibid. 113; Batsford and Fry, 8.

century wills provide for an incredible number of soul-masses; Joan, Lady Cobham, in 1369, made provision for 7,000;[1] Edward, earl of March, in the following year left money to nineteen Benedictine abbeys and three Augustinian houses for masses for a year after his death.[2]

Besides these, since a limit was evidently set to the number of masses that monk-priests could say, it became the custom for a wealthy man to endow a chantry, usually in a non-monastic church: that is to say, to ensure a regular payment to a priest who should say a mass for his soul, if possible daily.[3]

One of the first chantries known to Dugdale dated from the reign of Henry II, and provided for the endowment of one priest in St. Paul's.[4] Other early instances are those of Bishop Hugh of Wells at Lincoln cathedral, founded about 1235, and Bishop Stavenby at Lichfield some three years later. It will be remembered that Edward I endowed a whole group of chantries for his queen.[5] These doubtless helped to canalize a movement for such endowments.

Chantries received a new importance in the fourteenth century. England was already over-abundantly supplied with small monasteries and spiritual advisers were unlikely to counsel the foundation of further religious houses on a small scale. The endowment of a chantry, however, assured the prayers and masses that hitherto had been secured to the founders of religious houses; it involved far less expense than the adequate endowment of a monastery, and was especially suited to those who lived in a town or on a manor for whom the parish or friars' church was the natural focus of religious practice.

All the Orders who reached a new importance in the England of the fourteenth century welcomed and fostered the chantry movement. The Augustinians especially favoured it; witness the Bruce choir at Guisborough and the Berkeley choir at Bristol. The small Augustinian houses, of which many had been founded early

[1] *Test. Vet.* i. 81.
[2] Nichols, 104. He had already founded a chantry at Wigmore.
[3] See K. L. Wood-Legh in *Trans. R. Hist. Soc.* xxviii (1946), 47, and Cook.
[4] Dugdale, 18.   [5] Above, p. 4. See Cook, 6.

in the thirteenth century as part of the organization of a great estate, kept up a close link with the families of their founders, and nothing was more natural than that they should undertake additional masses for the founder's family, especially as all the members of the Order were priests.[1] Both Orders of Mendicants, who were apt to stress the terrors of Purgatory, received many chantry endowments. The Dominican noviciate house at King's Langley was founded by Edward II chiefly as a chantry foundation, first for his Plantagenet ancestors; and then, after Piers Gaveston had been buried there in 1313, for his favourite.[2] Humphrey de Bohun, earl of Essex, in his will made in 1361,[3] treats the Austin Friars of London, whose church he rebuilt in 1354, as chantry priests. By 1436 space was so limited in the great church of the Blackfriars in London that Lord Fanhope had his chantry chapel built in the churchyard. The calendar of London wills shows nearly 200 bequests to friars for chantries and soul-masses between 1324 and 1400.[4] A document of 1431[5] shows that the London Charterhouse may be regarded not only as a monastery of contemplatives but also as a community of chantry priests, for every founder of a cell stipulated that its occupant should pray for his soul.

The city of London was the great chantry centre;[6] more soul-masses were sung in St. Paul's than in any church in the country. There was no parish in the city to which chantries were not attached; nearly 350 were founded there in the course of the fourteenth century. The chantry priests far outnumbered the parish priests, and the hospital of St. Augustine Papey was founded about 1440 by four London priests to be a refuge for their old age.

Since the fulfilment of his duties was a matter for the priest's own conscience, abuses sometimes crept in. In 1345 the mayor and

---

[1] e.g. the will of Philippa, countess of March, drawn up in 1378 (Nichols, 98), directs that she is to be buried at Bisham abbey, the Augustinian house founded by her father forty years before. She leaves money for her tomb, and her chapel furniture, and a sum for building to the abbey, and legacies to the prior, sub-prior, and canons for prayers.

[2] Jarrett, 5. Gaveston's commemoration was dropped in the time of Edward III.

[3] Nichols, 45.

[4] Cook, 30. Isabella of France, for example, was buried in the Greyfriars beside her lover in the habit of the Poor Clares.

[5] Cited ibid. 27.   [6] See ibid. 39.

aldermen of London formally complained to the dean and chapter of St. Paul's that while any number of chantries had been founded in that church, very few chaplains came daily to sing mass.[1] A further complication lay in endowments that had become inadequate; in 1348, for example, Sir Thomas Chedworth endowed a chantry at Bettisham in Cambridgeshire, for two secular priests; but by 1351, after the Black Death, the revenues had so much declined that they sufficed only for one.[2] In 1362 Archbishop Islip fixed the salary of the chantry priests attached to Westminster at five marks a year; and in 1380 this had to be raised to seven.[3] For a man of learning an endowed chantry provided a way of life that did not make too many demands upon his time; Langland, we may remember, was a chantry priest. The whole institution not unnaturally incurred the enmity of the Lollards; William Emayn in 1430 declared 'Hit is not lawful to any prest which ministreth the Sacrament or singeth for a soule in church collage or other place to take ony salary for his labour'.[4]

When chantries were endowed at an established altar, they did not necessitate any new construction. They came, however, to be more and more closely connected with the actual tomb of the person commemorated. Where there was no effigy and a daily mass was not asked for, it is likely that masses may sometimes have been said at a portable altar laid upon the actual tomb or even upon the tomb itself; the slab of the tomb of Edmund of Langley at King's Langley bears the consecration crosses of an altar. It is certain that endowments for more frequent masses soon brought about the enlargement of the tomb canopy to form the screen of a tiny chapel with its own altar.[5]

By the middle of the fourteenth century a chantry was often founded in the lifetime of the donor, sometimes with the obliga-

---

[1] Riley, 224.   [2] Cunningham, *Growth of English Ind.* 332.

[3] Cook, 55, gives a useful account of the legal administration of chantries.

[4] Somerset Record Society, *Register of John Stafford, Bishop of Bath and Wells,* 1423–43, i. 78.

[5] An intermediate stage is represented by Roger de Waltham, canon of St. Paul's, who died in 1326, leaving houses and shops to endow a chantry, and also rich furniture for a chapel. An exceptional chantry chapel is that built at Tewkesbury in 1397 in honour of the founder of the abbey, who died in 1107.

tion that a daily mass should be said *pro bono statu* until masses for his soul were begun after his death. So the Black Prince founded two chantries at Canterbury in 1363 in gratitude for the dispensation which allowed him to wed the Fair Maid of Kent. A miniature church was made for this in the crypt, where a Perpendicular veil was laid over the Norman structure.[1] By his will he left his missal with his badges to the chapel.

Edward, Lord Despencer, by his will of 1375, desired to be buried in the abbey of Tewkesbury, near to the bodies of his ancestors, and left to the abbey a rich set of vestments, two gilt chalices, and a gilt hanap and ewer for use at Corpus Christi which had been given him by the king of France.[2] In return the abbey allowed his widow to build a miniature chapel of the Trinity, to balance the chapel just erected by Abbot Parker in honour of the founder. It is an airy structure; above a niched base two great unglazed windows rise on either side to a crested cornice. It is a chapel and not a tomb; the effigy kneels under a spiry canopy upon the roof.[3] It had a wall-painting above the altar representing the Trinity and the Coronation of the Virgin; Despencer and his wife were shown kneeling in adoration beneath.

The chantry chapel of William of Wykeham in Winchester cathedral (Pl. 80) is yet more loftily planned. It altogether fills one arcade of the aisle, with three lofty arches cusped but not traceried, of which the ogival gables rise to the balustrade. A transom-cornice runs across at a fairly low level, with the two tiers of Perpendicular tracery beneath. The tomb has at its foot the images of the three chantry priests who had to say mass in the chapel thrice daily.

The chantry chapel which was erected at Tewkesbury in 1422 above the tomb of the earl of Worcester by his widow Isabel Despencer, who was later buried there[4] by his side (Pl. 84), is a

---

[1] The sculptures include the white hind lodged, ducally collared and chained, as a badge of the Fair Maid of Kent. See C. P. J. Cave in *Arch.* lxxxiv (1935), 61.

[2] *Test. Vet.* i. 99.

[3] The colouring has lately been admirably restored by Mr. R. P. Howgrave-Graham. For a coloured illustration, see *Illustrated London News* (27 May, 1939), 1.

[4] In 1423 she married Richard Beauchamp, earl of Warwick, and the chapel is often called the Warwick chantry.

lighter and more ornate development of the Wykeham scheme, with only two supports between cornice and transom, and the cornice bayed to form a series of tabernacle heads.[1] The vault is a miniature fan-vault with pendants: an early non-structural experiment that was later to bear fruit on a larger scale.

A much simpler scheme is followed in the tomb of Michael de la Pole, earl of Suffolk, who died in 1415, at West Wingfield.[2] An arch that divides the chancel from the aisle serves as a canopy; its mouldings are powdered with the de la Pole shields and devices. On the chancel side three stone seats are built against the tomb, to serve as stalls for the three chantry priests. A more elaborate version of the scheme serves at York Minster for the chantry of Archbishop Bowet, which he founded in 1413 for two chaplains who were to pray for him, his master Henry IV, Henry, bishop of Winchester, and Richard Pittes, archdeacon of Cleveland.[3] A canopy here spans the arch: the altar lies outside it and at right angles to it.[4]

At Wells the chapel of Bishop Bubwith, who died in 1424, is of another form. It lies as usual between two pillars of the nave, but is bayed out to form a hexagon, thus affording a good deal more room inside. The strong rectilinear lines of the screens give an impression of solidity, though in fact they are light and open.

The first great royal chantry chapel was that built at Westminster in accordance with the will of Henry V, which endowed three masses to be sung there daily. The will declared that it was to be a raised relic-chapel with two stairways, with an altar to be dedicated to the Virgin and all saints. The tomb lay directly east of the shrine of Edward the Confessor, round which the tombs of his royal descendants were grouped. The chapel was built over a screen or bridge flying between two piers that have been turned into stairways, with iron gates to protect the tomb without shutting it off from the shrine. It served to house relics which had formerly been

[1] The canopy originally had elaborate pinnacles, but they were badly damaged in the fire of 1829.
[2] Cf. that of Sir William Wilcote, d. 1411, and his wife (later Lady Blackett) at Northleigh, Oxon.
[3] Browne, i. 209; Raine, 274.
[4] The lower arcade affords an early instance of an almost triangular-headed arch.

shown on the site of the tomb. Its altar has a tabernacled reredos with the Virgin and St. George for England, St. Denis for France, and the royal saints St. Edmund and Edward the Confessor.[1] On the ambulatory side Henry's coronation and a battle scene are represented; the frieze and cornice are studded with his badges.[2]

The next important royal chantry is that of Humphrey, duke of Gloucester, which was erected at St. Albans in his lifetime under the abbatiate of John Stoke, between 1440 and 1451.[3] It was served by two priests. It is of the bridge-canopy type, with a super-structure that completely fills the arch into which it is fitted. The whole is far nobler in scheme than is Henry V's chantry, and, indeed, brings to chantry architecture something of the dignity of architecture on a greater scale.[4] In few buildings is heraldry more splendidly married to the severe geometry of the Perpendicular style.

Duke Humphrey's great enemy, Cardinal Beaufort, the legiti-matized son of John of Gaunt and the ablest man of his house, lies under a splendid chantry arch at Winchester (Pl. 81). It represents a compromise between the arch-scheme of Archbishop Bowet's chantry and the screen-chapel type; the central part is an open arch that permits the tomb to be seen from the aisles, but it is flanked by lesser arches that have transom-cornices and fairly solid screens. The whole edifice is crowned by a forest of niches and pinnacles. The effigy is an addition of 200 years later; originally the tomb itself probably served as altar. The chantry of his successor, Bishop Waynflete, was planned as a pendant; here the screen runs across the central arch.[5]

The series of English chantries—a series unique in the history of European art—closes, so far as our period is concerned, with the great chapel built at Warwick in accordance with the will of

---

[1] The whole seems to have been planned by John of Thirsk, the architect of the nave.
[2] See W. St. John Hope in *Arch.* xlv (1913–14), 129 et seq.
[3] T. D. Kendrick in *Antiq. Journ.* xxvi (1946), 1.
[4] The north front originally had 34 statuettes, now lost. The south has 17 statues of kings. Kendrick, loc. cit., has pointed out the interesting fact that Duke Humphrey, a humanist with many intellectual relations with Italy, uses the Gardens of Adonis as a badge.
[5] The Scrope chapel at York, built about 1450, has altogether disappeared.

Richard Beauchamp, earl of Warwick.[1] It stands to the east of the south transept of St. Mary's, as a separate structure,[2] with its only entrance from the church. His will, made in 1435, declares:[3]

'I will that when it liketh to God that my soul depart out of this world, my body be buried within the collegiate church of Our Lady of Warwick, where I will that in such place as I have desired, which is well known, there be made a chapel of Our Lady built in fair and goodly fashion; within the middle of which chapel I will that my tomb be made. . . . Also I will that there be said every day, so long as the world lasts, in the aforesaid chapel . . . three masses.'

Of all the seven executors of this will only three were involved in the construction of the chapel: Thomas Huggeford, the earl's right-hand man in all his affairs, Nicholas Rody, his steward, and William Berkswell, priest and dean of St. Mary's. They did their work faithfully and well.

The Purbeck marble tomb is in the tradition of those of the family of Edward III, with bronze weepers cast by William Austin of London[4] (Pl. 83). These show a great advance, and are not unworthy to stand beside the weepers of the Dijon tradition. The shields beneath them show that they represent particular members of the Warwick family. Between them stand little bronze angels holding scrolls inscribed *Sit deo laus et gloria, defunctis misericordia*. . . . The effigy is protected by a bronze herse, over which an em-broidered pall could be thrown at festival seasons. A long in-scription in English begins:

'Prieth devoutly for the Sowel whom God assoille of one of the moost Worshipful Knightes in his days of monhode and conning Richard Beauchamp late Earl of Warrewik, lord Despencer of Ber-gavenny and of mony other grete lordships, whos body resteth here under this tumbe in a ful feire vout of stone set on the bare rooch' . . .

It goes on to give the main events of his life and to declare the steps

---

[1] See Stothard, 94, Chatwin in *Arch.* lxxvii (1928), 313; Le Couteur, 19; Crossley, 148; Cook, 155; Prior and Gardner, Fig. 412. The accounts were published by Dugdale, *Antiquities of Warwickshire*.

[2] Cf. the Percy chapel built at Tynemouth priory, Northumberland, by Henry Percy, before 1455. I am not sure, however, how far this is a chantry chapel and how far a chapel of St. Oswin.

[3] *Test. Vet.* i. 23.   [4] Illustrated in Prior and Gardner, Fig. 491.

taken for the building of the chapel and the tomb; and is, in fact, in part a justification of the executors in the carrying out of their duty.

The executors commissioned John Prudde of Westminster, a famous glazier, to fill the windows with 'the best, cleanest and strongest glass of beyond the seas that may be had in England, and of the finest colours', with instructions that he was to use as little white, green, or black glass as he might, and to submit his cartoons for approval. Originally the east window had figures of Earl Richard, his two wives, and his children, beneath representations of St. Alban, St. Thomas of Canterbury, St. John of Bridlington, and St. Winifred—the English saints to whose shrines the earl bequeathed an image of himself in gold. The background was diapered with oak leaves and with his badge of the bear. The mullions of the window are carved with tabernacles enshrining statues of God the Father, female saints, angels in their nine orders, and others holding shields and the arms of the earl and the two countesses (Pl. 83). The centre of the reredos was occupied by a group of the Annunciation; the theme of the Virgin's glory was echoed in a carving of her as Queen of Heaven on the central boss of the vaulting, whence she gazes down on the praying effigy of Warwick. Angels everywhere, in sculpture, glass, and painting, sing her praises. At the west end of the church a painting was made in 1449 by John Brentwood, citizen and stainer of London, of the Last Judgement; traces under the subsequent repainting show that it represented Christ seated upon a rainbow with angels holding instruments of the Passion on either side.[1] Alongside the main chapel stands a little building no bigger than a chantry chapel, that doubtless served for the saying of the daily low mass for Richard Beauchamp's soul.

It has been said that the houses of Augustinian canons came to be associated with many chantries, and it has been suggested that the chantry priests' performance of their duties unsupervised was not always conscientious. It was a natural consequence that men who could afford it and wished to endow several chantry priests should do so as a small community of secular canons.[2]

A number of collegiate churches were founded at the end of the

[1] Chatwin, 331.   [2] See A. Hamilton Thompson in *Arch. Journ.* lxxiv (1917), 139.

thirteenth century and the beginning of the fourteenth;[1] it is not easy to say how closely these foundations were associated with obligations to say soul-masses. The little community of a master and four secular priests attached to the Virgin's altar in the church of St. Margaret at Stanstead in Hertfordshire by Sir William de Goldington in 1315 certainly looks as if it were a chantry foundation. It is significant, too, that various older foundations were re-endowed on a collegiate basis at this time, notably St. Stephen's chapel which Edward III endowed as a college of twelve secular canons, thirteen vicars, four clerks, six choristers, a verger, and a keeper of the chapel. Similarly, the collegiate church of St. Thomas of Glasney in Devon, that had been founded by the bishop of Exeter in 1264 with a provost, twelve canons, and thirteen vicars, was in 1275 given an increased endowment with new obligations for soul-masses.[2] In 1331, again, Henry, duke of Lancaster endowed the collegiate church of Our Lady of Lancaster to serve as a mausoleum for his house.

Another early certain chantry college is that at Cotterstock in Northamptonshire[3] which was founded about 1336 by John Gifford, canon of York, with a provost, twelve chaplains, and two clerks. The choir built for them dwarfs the older parish church to which it is attached: they were under an obligation to sing a daily mass in choir for Edward III and his family, and John Gifford and his kin. Similar foundations were naturally made by wealthy prelates. Bishop Grandisson of Exeter re-endowed the church of Ottery St. Mary in 1337 as a chantry college of canons, with a master of grammar for the choir-boys; it was attached to his family rather than to his see, and his brother, a layman, has a fine tomb there and shared in the masses. At Stratford-on-Avon the chapel of St. Thomas of Canterbury in the parish church, which had been built

---

[1] Foundations in the thirteenth century were Bishop Auckland, for a dean and nine prebendaries, by Anthony Beck, bishop of Durham, 1292; Wingham, Kent, by John Peckham, archbishop of Canterbury, before 1294; Attleborough, Norfolk, by Sir William Mortimer, d. 1297; St. Elizabeth's, Winchester, for a provost, 6 priests, 6 clerks, and 6 choristers, by John de Pontoys, bishop of Winchester, c. 1300.

[2] It was rebuilt in 1379; nothing remains. Similarly the collegiate church of Crediton was rebuilt between 1409 and 1415.

[3] *Notitia Monastica*, sub. 'Northants'; Cook, 52.

by John Stratford, archbishop of Canterbury, was on his death in
1348 transformed into a chantry college of five priests, bound to
pray for the souls of the kings of England, the bishops of Winchester, and the founder.[1] A number of other collegiate chantry
foundations of the time are recorded, but have left no trace.[2]

Such chantry colleges were soon thought to complete a great
estate as naturally as a small Augustinian house had done in the
thirteenth century. The castles of Wingfield, Warkworth, Caister,[3] Greystock,[4] Maxstoke,[5] and Mettingham,[6] all had such colleges established near them; little now survives.

The Civil Wars only served to add to their number. In 1406
Roger Ive, a Lancastrian priest, obtained a charter to build a
collegiate church with eight chaplains to sing mass for those killed
in the battle of Shrewsbury, with a college house, a small school,
and an almshouse attached. The Perpendicular church survives
with the significant name of Battlefield: a fine and stately aisleless
edifice, with a good balustrade of quatrefoils and elegant pinnacles.[7]
Another fine Lancastrian college was that founded by Ralph
Neville, earl of Westmorland, on his Raby estate at Staindrop, for
a master, six priests, six clerks, six poor gentlemen, six poor officers,
and other bedesmen. His monument shows him between his two
wives, all wearing the Lancastrian collars of S's; at the feet of each
of the figures are two little chantry priests with their missals.[8]

One of the most complete examples left to us of the architectural
ensemble of such a college is that at Edington in Wiltshire. The
parish church there originally belonged to the nuns of Romsey, but
in 1351 they surrendered it to the bishop of Winchester, who had

[1] Cook, 53.
[2] Archbishop Courtenay's college at Maidstone has been rebuilt but for the gateway; the tomb of its master, Thomas Wotton, d. 1417, is now in All Saints' church.
[3] Sir John Fastolf also endowed the college of St. John Baptist near Yarmouth.
Weever, 863. See *Norfolk Arch.* ii (1887), 225.
[4] *Test. Vet.* i. 230 shows it established by 1434.
[5] It was already well established by 1460. *Test. Vet.* i. 295.
[6] See *Arch. Journ.* vi (1849), 62.
[7] What is left of the fine glass, including many portraits, is now in Prees
church. See Bodleian Ashmole MS. 854, and B.M. Add. MS. 21236. The church
was dedicated to the Magdalen as the battle was on the eve of her feast.
[8] Stothard, 68.

been born in the parish, for transformation into a collegiate foundation. The splendid church[1] was dedicated in 1361; it was served first by a dean and twelve secular chaplains and then by a community of Bonshommes. The dignified and simple house that served as their residence still exists, with no ornament but its embattled cornice like that of the church. Edington was a chantry college, but the founder's tomb, with a tiny chantry chapel, stands not at Edington but in the nave of Winchester.

John, Lord Cobham in 1362 founded a perpetual chantry of five chaplains under a master in the existing church at Cobham, which is still remarkable for the six canopied brasses to members of his family that remain. The chaplains were housed in little dwellings set round a quadrangle, in the Carthusian manner.[2] At Manchester Chetham's hospital, founded in 1653, took over with little change the buildings of a college of chantry priests founded in 1422 by Thomas Delawarr. The hall still has its oaken screens, divided into three panelled parts; the simple cloister still survives with hardly any change (Pl. 84 *b*).[3] St. William's College at York, founded in 1461 by Bishop Neville of Exeter and his brother Richard, earl of Warwick, to house the chantry priests of the cathedral, is quadrangular in plan, but far more domestic in style.

The dissolution of the alien priories provided a further incentive to the foundation of colleges of chantry priests. At Arundel, which had been served by five alien monks,[4] a college of thirteen chaplains, assisted by fifteen clerks, was established to pray for the house of Arundel; the tomb of Thomas FitzAlan, earl of Arundel, who died in 1406, shows them as weepers round the tomb.

The college of chantry priests at Fotheringhay, on the other hand, was enriched by property derived from the alien priories.[5] It succeeded a castle chapel, founded by Edmund of Langley, and was licensed in 1412. It was intended to serve as a mausoleum for

---

[1] See above, p. 70.

[2] Plan in Harvey, *Yevele*, Fig. 29, by Sir Alfred Clapham. Much of the houses still survives in the present almshouses.

[3] The dormitory now serves as Chetham's Library.

[4] Nichols, 120.

[5] Cox in *Arch. Journ.* lxi (1904), 241; A. Hamilton Thompson in ibid. lxxv (1918), 243.

the house of York, just as Leicester did for the house of Lancaster. Edward of York, who fell at Agincourt in 1415, was buried in the unfinished church; the nave, which alone remains, dates from 1434.[1] The college had a master, twelve chaplains or fellows, eight clerks, and thirteen choristers. Exceptionally, its master and fellows were elected by a majority of the fellows when a vacancy arose. Five masses were said every day, six on Saturday and Sunday, and more on particular feasts. The college was supplemented by an almshouse, intended especially for men who had been tenants on the Lancaster estates. It is a regrettable fact that as early as 1438 and 1442 the Visitations show that the statutes were already ill kept.

A great chantry college was founded at Tattershall by Lord Cromwell as an appendage of his splendid castle. It was begun about 1440, when he founded a college of seven chantry priests and six choristers, and transferred to it the endowments of the rectory. It was accompanied by an almshouse for thirteen almsmen and thirteen almswomen. The church was not finished when he made his will in 1454, and work was still going on in 1459.[2] The founder and the two nieces to whom he left his estates were commemorated by canopied brasses set side by side. The glory and the colour have gone from Tattershall; but the noble and austere skeleton of the church remains, that with its uncusped windows and its dependence on the repetition of simple units for its effect belongs in spirit to the succeeding age.

The real importance of the colleges of chantry priests lies in their application of the Augustinian system of life in common to communities not following a definite Rule. The principle was soon extended. At Wells the hostel for the chantry priests was accompanied by a whole set of buildings for the vicars of the cathedral, whom Bishop Ralph of Shrewsbury in 1346 incorporated into a college. They were housed in forty sets of chambers of uniform

---

[1] For the contract, see Coulton, *Art and the Reformation*, 459. Some of the stalls from the choir survive; seven in the neighbouring church of Tansor, two at Benefield, and ten at Hemington.

[2] The glass and screen are later: what is left of the glass is now for the most part in St. Martin's, Stamford Baron, to which it was removed in 1757.

size and design,[1] comprising a living-room with a bedroom over it, a yard at the back, and a little garden in front. There was a common hall, with its kitchen, store-chamber, buttery, and bake-house; the hall[2] had a painting of the vicars kneeling before their benefactor with a scroll inscribed:

> Per vicos positi villae pater alme rogamus
> Ut simul uniti, te dante, domis maneamus.

The bishop holds another scroll:

> Vestra petunt merita quod sint concessa petita
> Ut maneatis ita loca fecimus hic stabilita.

Two fine Annunciation figures of painted oak remain from the original decoration of the hall. It was not without reason that Bishop Ralph felt able to ask every vicar to say an Ave and a Paternoster for him every time he went out or came in. The community was soon the possessor of plate for the hall; John Lombard, for example, left it in 1361 a mazer with the inscription, 'Let ye wynd blowe'.[3] The chapel is a little later in date; it is very simple, with a good wooden roof and a canopied niche on either side of the altar-window. The college quarters were finally completed when Bishop Beckington built the great gateway, closed nightly by a chain, to connect the vicar's close with the cathedral (Pl. 85 a).

Wells was not the only cathedral to have some of its priests incorporated as a college; at St. Paul's, for instance, Richard II in 1385 established the petty canons as a college of twelve, to meet and dine together in hall, under the obligation to pray for his soul after death and Anne of Bohemia's, and their ancestors and all faithful departed.[4]

We have seen that in such chantry foundations as Fotheringhay and Tattershall the college of priests was accompanied by an alms-house of bedesmen that perpetuated the funeral prayers of the poor just as the college of priests perpetuated the funeral masses.[5] At

---

[1] See Pettigrew in *Journ. Brit. Arch. Ass.* xiii (1857), 36. The chambers are now represented by the twenty-six surviving houses.

[2] Modified in the time of Elizabeth.

[3] Hope in *Arch.* l (1887), 182.   [4] Weever, 373.

[5] These were sometimes quite small, as for instance the hospital for four or six poor men under a chantry priest founded by William Heron, Lord Say, at the church of Buckstead by his will of 1404. *Test. Vet.* i. 163.

Elsing Spittle near Cripplegate, William Elsing, citizen and mercer of London, founded a college of a warden, four secular priests, and two clerks, attached to a hospital for a hundred poor men and women, among whom blind, paralytic, and disabled priests were to have the first claim to admittance.[1] Cardinal Beaufort in 1446 planned to add an almshouse of Noble Poverty to the ancient hospital of St. Cross at Winchester. It was to consist of two priests, three nursing sisters, and thirty-five brethren who were to be noblemen or gentlemen of the cardinal's household. Owing to the Wars of the Roses it was never completed, but some of the brethren's houses and the cardinal's splendid gateway remain.[2]

Gradually such chantry colleges came to be associated not only with almshouses but also with schools. It is significant that Richard Whittington, mercer and lord mayor of London, when he founded his chantry college of St. Spirit and St. Mary in 1410, with a hospital of God's House for thirteen poor men attached,[3] laid down that the four fellows of the foundation should be masters of arts. John Kempe, archbishop of Canterbury, when he converted the parish church of Wye into a college of secular priests to pray for the souls of his parents[4] combined it with a grammar school. At Ewelme the hospital built and endowed in 1437 by William de la Pole, duke of Suffolk, and his wife Alice[5] combines a bedehouse for twelve poor men under a master and a free school under 'a well disposed man apt and able to teach and inform children in the faculty of grammar'. A similar triple community was founded by Archbishop Chichele at his birthplace of Higham Ferrers[6] in 1422, with a college of eight chantry priests, four clerks, and six choristers, a bedehouse and a grammar school. The amount of building involved in such a foundation was considerable; at Higham Ferrers we may still see the fine chantry chapel added to

---

[1] *Not. Mon.* sub 'Middlesex'. In 1340 the college was refounded with a prior and five regular canons.

[2] In 1486 the foundation was reduced to one chaplain and two brethren.

[3] His beneficent work is still carried on under his Mercer's Company at Whittington College, Tottenham, which provides a home for ladies in reduced circumstances.

[4] Weever, 229.　　　　　　　　　　　　　　[5] See Cook, 176.

[6] A grammar school seems already to have been in existence. See Armytage Smith, i. 103.

the parish church (Pl. 86 *a*), the gateway to the college surmounted by three canopied niches, and the hall of the bedehouse (Pl. 86 *b*), with its noble traceried window at the west end. The hall has a large fire-place; its windows once held glass with the arms of Chichele, Canterbury, and England.

It was, however, in the universities of Oxford and Cambridge that the chantry foundations reached their true flowering and passed into a wider field of service. The earliest hostel for scholars who were not members of a religious order at Oxford was Merton, which seems to have been envisaged as early as 1262.[1] It not only established the idea of a corporate fraternity dedicated to learning, but also established the material form of such a house, with its chapel and its hall as the centres of the life of the community. The word 'college' was first applied to a university hall of residence in 1324, in the royal licence which permitted Adam de Brome to found the 'college of Scholars' that still serves learning as Oriel College. Every member of a college was, and is, under obligation to pray for its founder, and it is only in the present century that the obligation to attend chapel for this purpose has been relaxed.

The fourteenth century witnessed the foundation of five colleges at Oxford[2] and seven at Cambridge;[3] and these were followed in the first half of the fifteenth century by three at Oxford[4] and three at Cambridge.[5] Many elements went to their making: the monastic hostel and the chantry college were combined in their

[1] A distinction must be drawn between a college such as Merton, which was a self-contained community, and a hall, such as St. Peter's Hall, which was merely a hostel for students whose first loyalty was to the Benedictine houses of which they were members.

[2] Exeter College, 1314–16, by the bishop of Exeter; Oriel, 1324, by Adam de Brome; Queen's, 1341, by Robert de Eglesfield; Canterbury, 1361, by Archbishop Simon Islip; New College, 1379, by William of Wykeham.

[3] King's Hall, before 1316, by Edward II; Michaelhouse, 1324, by Hervey de Stanton; University or Clare Hall, 1326, by Elizabeth de Burgh; Pembroke, 1347, by Marie de Valence, countess of Pembroke; Gonville, 1349, and Trinity Hall, 1350, by William Bateman, bishop of Norwich; and Corpus Christi, 1352, by the Cambridge Guild of Corpus Christi.

[4] Lincoln, 1429, by Bishop Richard Fleming; All Souls, 1438, by Archbishop Chichele; Magdalen, 1448, by William of Waynflete, bishop of Winchester.

[5] Godshouse, 1439, by William Byngham; King's, 1441, by Henry VI; Queens', 1448, by Margaret of Anjou.

constitution; the Augustinian's lodgings, the noble's hall, buttery, and gatehouse, and the chantry chapel in their buildings. To these they added a common room, found earlier at Cambridge than at Oxford, and a library, that owe something to monastic usage but yet bear the stamp of the college. The quadrangular courts that now seem the peculiar characteristic of a college were not so when they were built, for in the middle ages such courts were common to monastery, almshouse, and manor.

Very little remains of the earliest collegiate constructions; they were no more elaborate than those of contemporary almshouses. The first library at Exeter College was a rustic construction with a thatched roof.[1] Queen's College, Oxford, founded in 1341, was the first to have studies partitioned off, in the corners of the sleeping-chambers which were shared by two or more fellows. Canterbury Hall, founded in 1361, had the quadrangle open on one side in the fashion that was later to become characteristic of Cambridge; the upper floors of its buildings were timber-framed. At Cambridge we know little of the early buildings of Merton Hall, begun in 1374[2] or of Corpus Christi College,[3] which were finished about 1380. No chapel was included in the original plan at Corpus; the low quadrangle was closed on the fourth side. Here, however, the master's lodge built by John Kynne, master from 1379 to 1389, was rather more spacious than usual, with a solar over the parlour; none the less it would not have borne comparison with the abbot's lodging even of a small monastery. A description survives of the old hall of Trinity Hall, built about 1374;[4] it might serve for that of the hall of a large manor. The hall

'has three double windows on each side, one of wch. at ye upper end on ye W. side is a Bow window in which stands ye Beaufet, with ye desk for ye chapter in Latin while at Dinner and Supper. This Hall is divided from ye Butteries by a Passage, and from the last by a Screen of Wood with two doors in it, ye one fronting ye Pantry, ye other ye

[1] It was replaced by a new library in 1383, destroyed in 1624.
[2] John Meppushall, the Ely architect, was employed here. Harvey in *Journ. Brit. Arch. Ass.* vi (1941), 45.
[3] Willis and Clark, i. 242.　　　　[4] Ibid. i. 233.

Buttry and over it a Gallery. The whole is roofed with old Oak Beams, very black and dismal, from ye charcoal wch is burnt in ye middle·of ye Hall; and over it in ye middle of ye Roof was an old awkward kind of Cupolo to let out ye Smoak. The Fellows Table stands on an Eminence at ye upper or S. end of ye Hall, with a Door on ye E. side to go into ye Master's Lodge. The Back of ye table of ye Fellows had ye arms of ye College painted pretty high against ye Wall, and below hung a large peice of tapestry.'[1]

Any works of art that such colleges might own had not usually been made for them, but were secular pieces inherited from their founders or given by their fellows. Elizabeth de Burgh in 1355 left to her college of Clare Hall[2] a set of red vestments embroidered with figures, and another of white and gold to use in Lent, and a set of hangings for an Easter sepulchre. It was probably from her, too, that the college acquired the ivory carvings of the Annunciation and the Epiphany which used to stand upon the altar.[3]   Queen's College, Oxford, still cherishes the founder's horn; Corpus Christi College, Cambridge, the mazer given by John Northwode, admitted fellow in 1384.[4]

The next stage in the history of collegiate buildings is marked by William of Wykeham's twin foundations of Winchester College and New College, Oxford. For the first time such a school as was sometimes attached to a college of chantry priests was given a new importance by being linked with a college of scholars at a university, in which secular priests not only prayed for the soul of the founder, but also directed the studies of the scholars. Both were chantry foundations, but the educational aspect was beginning to be of greater importance than the soul-masses.

William of Wykeham was experienced in the planning and exe-cution of fine buildings. The son of a small freeholder of Wick-ham, he had been taken up by the lord of the manor,[5] given some education, and taken into the household, where he began to learn something of the practical architectural supervision which was part of the routine of a feudal estate. When William of Edington

---

[1] The hall described was rebuilt soon after 1742.
[2] Nichols, 31.   [3] *Second Rep. Hist. MSS. Commission* (1871), III.
[4] Hope in *Arch.* l (1887) 144.   [5] See Steel, 13; Moberly, 123.

became bishop of Winchester in 1346 he recommended the young man to the king. By 1356 he was clerk of the works at Windsor,[1] and by 1359 keeper and surveyor of the other royal castles. Four years later he was keeper of the Privy Seal and factotum to the king. In 1366, sixteen years after he had assumed the first tonsure, he was elected to the see of Winchester against the wishes of the pope; by 1367 the village boy, now a man of forty-three, had become chancellor of England. By 1369 he had embarked on his college projects; two years later he began the new work at Winchester cathedral. The seven years of his disgrace only gave him more time for his projects, and in 1378 his fortunes mended and his projects could be accomplished. In 1374, when a carter, ploughman, or shepherd earned 13s. 4d. a year, his income from the see of Winchester was about £3,000, with incalculable additions from feudal dues and the income of vacant benefices. There was nothing that such a man could not do.

At New College, the earlier of his two foundations, all the elements of a college are for the first time included in a whole that is of royal magnificence[2] (Fig. 13). The chapel, hall, library, treasury, warden's lodgings, and a range of chambers are all included in one quadrangle entered by a tower gateway. The chapel and hall are set back to back in a continuous range: the altar stands on one side of the wall, the high table on the other. The collegiate choir of the chapel (Pl. 89) is approached through a wider ante-chapel, intended for disputations. This backs on to a cloister-cemetery with a separate bell-tower (Pl. 88). The first charter had been obtained in 1379, but the new society 'with cross erect, and singing a solemn litany', only took possession of their new college in 1386. They were under an obligation to go to mass daily and to remember the founder in their prayers; the college was still a chantry foundation.

The college is remarkable for its originality of plan rather than

---

[1] He fitted up the Round Tower for royal habitation and reconstructed the upper ward. A drawing by J. M. Turner of part of the lodging of Edward III and the gatehouse called La Spicere shows the kind of work he supervised. W. St. John Hope, *Windsor*, i. 187.

[2] We do not know what the ensemble owes to the College of the Garter that Wykeham had supervised at Windsor.

for any novelty of style. It is conceived throughout in the fine official Perpendicular with which Wykeham's experience had made him familiar. If the antechapel, for example, be compared with such a contemporary church as Yeovil, it is evident in what degree the official style was more carefully planned and more elegantly finished than that which sufficed for a parish church. The chapel windows were glazed by one Thomas, an Oxford man,[1] with the Crucifixion and the Coronation of the Virgin, and the Adoration of Christ, accompanied by the apostles, the Orders of the Angels, a company of unusual saints such as Pelagius and Athanasius, together with such English saints as Alphege, Cuthbert, and William of York.[2] The antechapel had the Patriarchs and Precursors of Christ; large single figures, of beautiful colouring, under rather commonplace canopies. The inventory of 1396[3] shows that the chapel was well supplied with vestments, missals, and altar vessels, though the linen for the hall and pantry was very simple and even the fellows ate off pewter.

Wykeham's parallel foundation of Winchester College, that was to prepare boys for Oxford, dates from 1382.[4] The gateway is even finer than that at New College; it holds enshrined two beautiful and slightly archaic Virgins, one of the Annunciation and the other beaming upon the laughing Child Jesus. The plan is based on that of New College. The outer gate contains the bursary and leads to a base court, beyond which the middle gate leads to the the chamber court, nearly 115 feet square, which housed the college. The middle gate tower originally held the warden's bedroom, oratory, and hall, while the upper rooms of the three sides of the court held the rooms of the ten fellows, three chaplains, head and second masters, and the rooms occupied by the warden of New College when he made his visitations. The ground floor held the six chambers where the scholars of the college slept. The south side of the court held the chapel, muniment tower, and the plain but

---

[1] Possibly Thomas of Dadington, who was employed at St. Stephen's chapel in 1352 and afterwards at Windsor.
[2] See Winston, in *Arch. Journ.* ix (1851), 30.
[3] *Arch. Journ.* xxviii (1871) 233 and *Second Rep. Hist. MSS. Commission* (1871), 134.
[4] The buildings were occupied in 1394, the chapel consecrated in 1395.

noble hall. The chapel windows were glazed by the glazier who worked at New College; his kneeling portrait, inscribed *Thomas operator istius vitri*, appeared in the east window beneath the great tree of Jesse set up in 1393. The chapel was even richer than that of New College in its treasures; Cardinal Beaufort in 1412 gave it a silver-gilt seated Virgin, and a later inventory includes images of the Annunciation, St. Swithin, and other saints.[1]

The chantry character of the college was intensified by the addition after 1422 of the chantry chapel of John Fromond, set in the middle of the cloister. It is a two-storied building, with an upper room that served as a lodging for the chantry priest. The statues of the founders stand in niches over the door.

The more monumental scale of New College was soon reflected in other collegiate buildings at Oxford, though none tried to emulate so majestic a whole. The embattled tower at Merton, with its statues of Henry III and Walter de Merton, dates from 1416; the chapel tower, one of the noblest in Oxford (Pl. 87), was finished in 1450. The lost hall and library at Balliol seem to have been plainer. Lincoln College—called *Collegiolum theologorum* by its founder Bishop Richard Fleming in 1427—was well planned for all its small size; a quadrangle with one open side held hall, with buttery and kitchen, library and oratory, with a gateway tower that was a lesser version of that at New College.

Wykeham's first imitator on a grand scale was Archbishop Chichele, himself a graduate of New College. His first Oxford foundation of 1436, St. Bernard's College (now incorporated in St. John's College), was built on one comprehensive plan, ranged as at New College round a fully enclosed quadrangle with an entrance tower. The hall and chapel, however, were separated by a passage and there was no antechapel. His second and more characteristic foundation, All Souls, dates from the next year; it was specifically a chantry foundation, with the title of Collegium Omnium Animarum Fidelium Defunctorum. Its statutes declare it to be a

'College of poor and indigent scholars, who are constantly bounden not so much to ply therein the various sciences and faculties as with all

[1] *Arch. Journ.* x (1853), 235.

devotion to pray for the souls of glorious memory of Henry V lately King of England and France . . . the Lord Thomas, Duke of Clarence, and the other Lords and lieges of the realm of England whom . . . the havoc of that warfare so long prevailing between the said two realms have drenched with the bowl of bitter death.'[1]

All Souls was planned on the New College scheme with some rearrangement of the elements.[2] The hall, as there, touches the chapel, but is at right angles to it; the chapel has an antechapel (Pl. 90) for disputations, the cloister lies to the north of the chapel. The inside of the quadrangle is rather severe in style; the outer front with its entrance tower, its battlements, and oriels, has rather the air of a nobleman's town-house than of a chantry college. Over the gateway, however, was a carving representing the souls in Purgatory.

The chief architectural riches of the college are centred in the chapel which was the cause and reason of its being. The founder lived to dedicate it himself, in 1443, to the four Fathers of the Church. The high altar had an image of the Trinity, painted and gilt, standing upon it; above were two images plated with silver. The chapel had eight altars to permit of the saying of many soul-masses; two were adorned with images of the Virgin and Child, and the rest with others of St. Vincent, St. John the Baptist, St. James, St. Ursula, and two tabernacle reliquaries.[3] The windows were filled by John the glazier.

Meanwhile at Cambridge the process of development was slow. Peterhouse, for example, continued to inhabit already existing citizens' houses until it was rebuilt round a closed quadrangle in 1424;[4] the chambers then built had fire-places, though the hall had a central hearth. At Pembroke John Langton, master from 1428

---

[1] The fellows of the college still fulfil the intentions of the founder at a solemn service on All Souls' Day.

[2] On its building see E. F. Jacob. John Druell, later a fellow, supervised the work until 1441, when he was succeeded by Roger Keys, who had been a fellow since 1438 and became warden in 1442. John Clerk and John Medehill were clerks of the works, and John Massyngham the chief sculptor; all went on to work at Eton.

[3] Inventory of 1448, *Arch. Journ.* li (1894), 120.

[4] Willis and Clark, i. 8, iii. 253. Further chambers were built in brick in 1438, and building went on until 1467.

to 1447, built an elegant oratory for his own use, with a room for the poor scholars to eat in underneath.[1] Lawrence Booth, master from 1452 to 1480, built the library, glazed the chapel, and adorned it with a rood-loft and figures of the four Doctors of the Church. Queens' College, which was begun in 1448, was built largely of brick, with a tower in each angle of the court, which was planned with the hall, kitchen, and butteries on the west and the chapel and library in the northern range.

Henry VI was surrounded by men who were interested in the new colleges. Cardinal Beaufort, as bishop of Winchester, was Visitor of Winchester College and New College; his rival, Humphrey of Gloucester, was a benefactor of Oxford university. Henry Chichele, the archbishop of Canterbury, and Thomas Beckington, the king's secretary, had both been fellows of New College. By 1440 the king was planning Eton, and in 1441 he went to Winchester to see how the college was run. As early as 1447 a great double foundation had been planned; the king's will made in that year[2] mentions 'my two colleges Roiall, one called the College Roiall of our Ladie of Eton beside Windesor, the other called the College Roiall of our Ladie and St. Nicholas of Cambridge, the edifications of which Colleges now by me begoun, advised and appointed. . . .' The two were to be linked in the same fashion as Wykeham's two colleges. Eton was, however, originally planned as a congeries of chantry foundations at the gates of Windsor, round the nucleus of the parish church refounded as a college of secular priests. The foundation charter of 1440[3] provides for a provost, ten fellows, four clerks, six choristers, a schoolmaster, twenty-five poor and needy scholars, and twenty-five poor and infirm bedesmen: a foundation closely resembling Chichele's at Higham Ferrers. The almshouse, however, was suppressed in the founder's lifetime; the new cadre included ten clerks, ten chaplains, sixteen choristers, thirteen bedesmen, and seventy scholars.[4] A further element was added by the establishment of a pilgrimage

[1] Willis and Clark, i. 138.   [2] Nicholas, 291.
[3] Maxwell Lyte, 4.
[4] Eton, like All Souls, derived some of its endowments from the suppressed alien priories.

and fair at the Assumption, for which feast the collegiate church was granted special indulgences equal to those of St. Peter ad Vincula at Rome, if the pilgrims made an offering and prayed for the founder. For this reason the chapel was planned on a new and larger scale.[1] The existing choir was intended to be entered from a nave of equal length, as wide, and a bay longer, than the nave of Lincoln cathedral. The king's will of 1447[2] decrees that it is to be built 'in large forme, cleane and substantially, well replenished with goodly windowes and vaults, laying apart superfluities of too great curious workes of entaile and busy mouldinge'. The stalls and rood-loft were to be based upon those in St. Stephen's chapel at Westminster; statues of the Virgin and the king's patron saint St. Nicholas were to stand at the ends of the high altar, and an elaborate reredos with Christ and the apostles was to rise behind it. The windows were glazed by John Prudde,[3] who also made the windows for John Fromond's chantry at Winchester and the Beauchamp chapel at Warwick.

The quarters for the school were being built at the same time, with John Hampton and Roger Keys[4] as supervisors, William Lynde as clerk of the works, and William Veysey as brickmaker. The buildings were planned round two courtyards; the cloister, like that at New College, was planned as a place of meditation, with no chambers communicating with it. The contract signed in 1443[5] provides for the erection of seven towers and turrets, ten chambers, and the cloisters. The hall, finished in 1448, had three fire-places; these were supplemented by a central fire under the louvre at certain feasts. It was intended to have two gatehouses and a great tower; but building stopped after the deposition of Henry VI in 1461 and was only continued by his executor Waynflete after 1475.

The work at King's College was begun simultaneously with that at Eton, but progressed far more slowly. Little remains that falls

[1] Lyte, 47.

[2] Nichols, 295. The new chapel was sufficiently advanced by 13 Oct. 1443, for Bishop Beckington to celebrate therein his first Mass as bishop of Bath and Wells, with a tent to take the place of the roof.   [3] Le Couteur, 30.

[4] Maxwell Lyte, ii. 47, states that he had already worked at All Souls, but seems to be in error in stating that he had been a fellow.

[5] Ibid. ii. 34.

within our period but the gateway, with a room over; the gateway has an angel cresting and squares of tracery to the exterior. The *University Almanac* of 1822[1] gives a view of more of the same range that is now destroyed; a rich cornice, corner turrets, pointed windows with hood-moulds, and sculptured details suggest that though King's was originally planned on a smaller scale it was rather more elaborately built than Eton. The buildings were set round a closed quadrangle, with the library, the hall, and the provost's lodge to the west, the chapel to the north, and chambers to the east and south. A cloister and bell tower on the model of New College were planned but were never executed.

Henry VI intended the chapel at King's to be like that of Eton, with a long nave before it. The first stone was laid in 1446 and work begun under John Langton, who resigned in 1447 on his consecration as bishop of St. Davids. The deposition of Henry VI brought all work to an end, and though it was resumed for a time in 1477, the existing chapel is a monument of the succeeding century.

The erection of such colleges, of which the members were under obligation to pray for the soul of the founder, was paralleled by gifts to universities in return for the promise of soul-masses. The schools quadrangle at Cambridge had been begun in 1347, but the first floor was not reached until 1372 when there was a long pause for lack of funds.[2] Work was not resumed until 1398, when Sir William Thorpe left money to build a Divinity school with a chantry chapel attached where masses were to be said for the souls of him and his wife. The school was plain, except for pleasant traceried windows; it exactly attained, indeed, the architectural level of other chantry foundations.

At Oxford the first money for a Divinity school was collected in 1426.[3] Richard Winchcombe supervised the work between 1430 and 1439 and cut the great east window.[4] The early work seems to have been regarded as too rich, for the deed appointing his successor Thomas Elkyn states: 'Because many great people of the realm and other wise men do not approve but censure the too

[1] Willis and Clark, i. 317.   [2] Ibid. iii. 9.
[3] Rashdall, iii. 166.   [4] W. St. J. Hope in *Arch.* lxxi (1914), 217.

great curiosity of the said work, therefore the said University wills
that the said Thomas hold back in future, as he has begun to hold
back, such superfluous curiosity . . . as tabernacles of images . . .
casements and fillets and other frivolous curiosities. . . .' The
observer to-day may see that the tabernacles in the window jambs
do not continue quite to the east end and are omitted on the south
front, and that while the windows to the north have casements and
fillets, those on the south have only their outer members worked.

Fortunately Cardinal Beaufort left the university in 1448 a noble
bequest for the completion of the Divinity schools, and though his
executors were slow to pay it and the university slow to use it, the
roof that it paid for fitly completes the whole[1] (Pl. 91), and a grate-
ful university promised many masses for his soul.[2] In 1439
Chichele persuaded his friend Humphrey, duke of Gloucester to
give to the university his splendid collection of manuscripts. An
upper story was added to the Divinity school to house them, and
the university promised more masses, when it came into use in
1448. Those who have used Duke Humphrey's Library through
the ensuing centuries make a noble company of his bedesmen.

[1] The work was not begun until 1470, under the guidance of his executor, Thomas
Kempe, bishop of London, and was not completed until 1483. See Hope, loc. cit.,
240; Weever states (36) that the celestial globe was painted behind the chair of the
presiding doctor.

[2] Anstey, i. 326.

X

TOWNS AND VILLAGES

THE stormy centuries that began with the reign of Stephen encouraged the strengthening of the defences of the cities, especially since the development of the art of war made the taking of a town of greater importance than the capture of a castle. Such fortifications were increased and renewed in the ancient cities of the realm, and were the first and most important requisite of any new towns that were constructed. The town gate-houses were usually flanked by round towers at the outer angles, like those at Conway, Winchelsea, and the west gate at Canterbury.[1] A later example is the Southgate of King's Lynn, which dates from 1437;[2] the cubical gateway has octagonal turrets at the angles. Such gateways were only a part of a system of wall defences. Yarmouth, for example, was defended between 1284 and 1396 by three walls set at right angles, to cover every aspect of the city except the sea-front. They were strengthened by sixteen towers and twelve gates.[3] The town walls at Norwich, begun in 1294 and finished in 1342, enclosed the largest area in the kingdom in a roughly circular enceinte, broken by forty towers and twelve gates. At Hull Michael de la Pole, before 1387, had caused the erection of a great town wall, with thirteen towers, remarkable for their being constructed of locally baked brick. Similarly bridges and other points of special importance received their own defences; London bridge, for example, was defended by towers built at either end by the citizens of London in 1426 and 1436. Stow tells us[4] that the four foundation stones of the first were each inscribed IHESUS.

The prosperity of many English towns and villages dates from

[1] See A. Hamilton Thompson, *Mil. arch.* 296. The Canterbury gate dates from 1378, when invasion was possible.   [2] A. Harvey, 230.

[3] Considerable remains survive built into later constructions.

[4] *Survey*, i. 60.

the period that lies between the reigns of Edward II and Henry VI, yet that prosperity has since been too continuous for many urban houses of the period to have survived. Moreover, it must be remembered that they were nearly all built not of stone or brick, but of timber-framing filled with the local variant of wattle and daub.[1] In the fourteenth century, indeed, stone houses were rare enough in London to be mentioned as landmarks in official documents. Timber-framed houses are peculiarly subject to decay, to destruction by fire, and to successive modifications; few kinds of architecture—if indeed the word can be applied to them—are harder to use as historical evidence.

The level of city house-building was raised by the town-houses of great nobles and rich knights; not one of these survives. We have no idea what Coldharbour in Eastcheap was like, where Prince Henry was living in 1410.[2] We know little even of Ely House in Holborn, rebuilt by Bishop Arundel,[3] with a gatehouse and a separate chapel of St. Etheldreda raised over a vaulted undercroft. It had a great hall 72 feet long and 32 wide, with six traceried windows, screens, and a dais with the bishop's lodgings behind the dais and a little cloister for him to walk in round a garden. The measure of elegance of such houses can be guessed from such records as Blomefield's statement[4] that Sir John Fastolf's town-house at Norwich, in his time surviving as a baker's, had bow windows set with glass representing St. Margaret, St. John the Baptist, the Virgin, St. Blaise, St. Katherine, the Nine Worthies, and a fight between two knights.

The fourteenth century was the beginning of the great age of English trade, especially in cloth and wool. It is easy to forget how widespread the weaving industry was in England at this time. A deed of 1316[5] transfers the collection of aulnage, the royal duty on cloth, to John Pecok, on 'canvas, linen cloth, napery as well English as from elsewhere, wadmells, heydokes, mendeps, kerseys, says of Louth, worsted of Norwich, Ireland and Cawston, and all other says and scarlets and all kinds of cloth of Lincoln, Essex, Norfolk,

---

[1] On this system see S. O. Addy, *Evolution of the English House.*
[2] It stood where the Heralds' College now is.
[3] Bentham (Stevenson), 80.   [4] v. 1552.   [5] Riley, xliv.

Suffolk, Kent, Stamford, Beverley, St. Osyth, Devon and Corn-wall'. The Company of the Staple, that had the monopoly of the export of wool, tin, and hides to the Low Countries, was established in 1313 and in its prime by the middle of the century.[1] By 1353 the Staple of Wool was removed to England and established at York, Newcastle, Lincoln, Norwich, Westminster, Canterbury, Chichester, Winchester, Exeter, and Bristol; Boston was added to the list in 1369. It brought trade not only to these towns but also to Hull, which served as port to York, Yarmouth for Norwich, and Sandwich for Canterbury. By 1351 the city of London could make the king a loan of 20,000 marks in exchange for the farm of its own customs; by 1373 Bristol could contribute as many ships as London —twenty-two—to the French wars; by 1376 the common council of London was elected by the trades, and not by the wards of the city.

These commercial advances did not necessarily involve a comparable advance in the arts. The English industries of the middle ages were for the most part like mining and quarrying, occupied with raw materials, or else were simple manufactures such as tile-making, cloth weaving, and brewing. The tax assignment of the inhabitants of Colchester made in 1301[2] includes a great multiplicity of trades, but not one that manufactured anything decorative. Even in London the goldsmiths alone were of any importance in the time of Edward II; the cofferers and painters do not appear as an organized trade before 1328, the tapicers in 1331, the pewterers in 1348, and the glass-makers in 1364.[3] The finer sorts of weaving were nearly all in foreign hands, witness the Flemish weavers in London, officially recognized in 1364, and the French clothiers of Bristol: Walter, Gerard, and Evrard le Français, and a family of Tourtels.[4] The seal of one of the Tourtels on a deed of 1317 is the earliest known merchant's mark in England. The importance of such men is attested by the feelings of antagonism that they aroused. Restrictions against alien merchants were enacted in 1392, 1400, 1402, and 1456; in every case the ground of complaint was that they imported goods ready-made from abroad.

[1] Ward in *Eng. Hist. Rev.* xxxiii (1918), 298.
[2] Thorold Rogers, i. 103.   [3] Unwin, 87.   [4] Hudd, 7.

By the reign of Richard II, however, if London and the other great English cities had not produced a great generation of artificers, they had produced the first generation of English capitalists. Already they had begun to creep into the feudal class— 'soap-sellers and their sons for silver have been knights'—and already they had begun to imitate the town-houses of the nobility. The contract for the house built in the city of London for William de Haningtone, skinner, in 1308[1] shows that it contained a hall with an oriel behind the high table, and a parlour with a chimney, with a larder tucked away between them; a solar over the parlour and larder; two cellars beneath, a kitchen with a garret over and a stable outside. In a lease of Packman's Wharf, Thames Street, drawn up in 1354-5, the lessee, Richard Wyllesden, covenants to build warehouses towards the street, with a dwelling-house alongside containing a hall 40 feet by 24, a parlour, kitchen, and buttery, with cellars beneath.[2] We may guess at the general aspect of such houses from the surviving house that the great wool merchant, William Grevel, built at Chipping Campden in Gloucestershire towards the end of the fourteenth century (Pl. 92), with a magnificent two-storied oriel. The Angel inn at Grantham has a corbelled-out oriel over the entrance, as well as others at either side;[3] the old White Hart at Newark has a double row of tabernacle-canopies each holding a little image of a saint.

The Fish House at Meare remains as an example of a cottage of the period; it was built by Adam de Sodbury, abbot of Glastonbury from 1322 to 1335, as a house for his chief fisherman. The ground floor is entirely occupied by a storehouse; a separate door leads up to the two rooms, one large and one small, that formed the living-quarters.

The civic buildings of the fourteenth and fifteenth centuries in England were comparatively modest. We know little of the London Guildhall to which some of the city tolls were applied in 1419,[4] but we know that it in no wise rivalled the contemporary *hôtels de ville* of Flanders. There was an enormous number of

---

[1] Riley, 65.   [2] Turner, ii. 183.
[3] These were all fitted with sash windows in the eighteenth century.
[4] Riley, 674.

charitable foundations, but comparatively few were civic. Hospitals were all due to private benefaction, though in 1414 parliament took a hand in their supervision and reform, since owing to the diminution in the number of lepers some were doing no useful work. New ones, however, were still being established; in 1418, for example, a foundling of Sevenoaks who had risen to be lord mayor of London celebrated the year of his mayoralty by building a hospital for the poor and a free school in his native place.[1] The almshouses at Sherborne founded in 1438 by the bishop of Salisbury and four lay donors are another instance of disinterested charity; but it must be admitted that most of such foundations in our period were intended rather to assure soul-masses than to aid poor citizens.

The most important town churches, apart from cathedrals and Benedictine abbeys, were usually those of the Mendicant Orders. They had houses in most of the great towns of the Staple: at Bristol and Ipswich, for example, all the Orders of friars were represented.[2] Boston by the time of Edward II had churches of Austin Friars, Black or Dominican Friars, Grey or Franciscan Friars, who seem here to have been brought in by the Hanse, and White Friars or Carmelites. There were Grey Friars at Grimsby, Black, Grey, and White at Stamford, Yarmouth, and Northampton. Newcastle-on-Tyne had all three, with Friars of the Sack and Trinitarians as well.

The great Franciscan church of London[3] was begun in Newgate Street in 1306. It was 300 feet long, with slender piers and a long range of windows that provided a model for many town and city churches. Most of the English Franciscan churches[4] had flat east ends; Winchelsea alone had a three-sided apse. They were planned as two churches, one, sometimes aisled, that served as a nave for sermons, and one set beyond an intervening tower that served as a choir for the friars themselves. Of the sixty-one English houses, some thirteen remain in part, though comparatively few fall into

---

[1] Weever, 324.
[2] Some remains of the Dominican house at Ipswich remained into the nineteenth century.
[3] See Clapham and Godfrey, 250; plan, 251. [4] See Martin.

our period. The nave at Reading, with a fine west window of about 1310; the graceful octagonal towers of the friars' churches at Coventry and King's Lynn; and the remains of the cloisters at Walsingham and Yarmouth may suffice to give us some idea of what a fourteenth-century Franciscan house was like.[1] That they were richly adorned by the gifts of the faithful is suggested by a passage in *Pierce the Plowman's Crede*,[2] in which the Franciscan says to his penitent:

> Thou shouldest knely before Christ
> In compas of gold
> In the wide window westward
> Welnigh in the myddel
> And Saint Franceis hymselfe
> Shal folden the in his cope
> And presente the to the Trinite
> And praye for thy synnes.

The same poem[3] includes a description of a Dominican church, and depicts it, as was permitted by the statutes, as architecturally even richer than that of the Franciscans.

> Þanne y munte me forþ þe mynstre to knowen,
> And a-waytede a woon wonderlie y-beld,
> Wiþ arches on everiche half & belliche y-corven,
> Wiþ crochetes on corners wiþ knottes of golde,
> Wyde wyndowes y-wroȝt y-written full þikke
> Schynen wiþ schapen scheldes to schewen aboute,
> Wiþ merkes of marchauntes y-medled betwene . . .

The Dominicans were especially strong in the wealthy East Anglian towns; they were established at Thetford before 1345, and had a fine church at Yarmouth by 1380. Their earliest and most important East Anglian house was that at Norwich, founded in 1226, moved in 1309, the church built between 1345 and 1350, and burned and rebuilt between 1440 and 1470.[4] The buildings

---

[1] A wider cult of the saint is represented by a few crude wall-paintings in parish churches: St. Francis preaching to the birds at Wiston, Suffolk, and Little Kimble, Bucks., and St. Francis receiving the stigmata at Slapton, Northants., and Doddington, Kent. Little, *Francisc. Hist.* 7.   [2] l. 245; cf. *Piers Plowman*, B. iii. 47.

[3] l. 171.   [4] Burnt down 1525.

here were completed by a large preaching-yard, which probably
once contained such a preaching-cross as is described in *Pierce the
Plowman's Crede:*[1]

> *A curious cros craftily entayled*
> *With tabernacles y-tight to toten al abouten*
> *The pris of a plough-lond of penyes so round*
> *To aparaile that pyler were pure lytel.*

One of the Erpinghams was a friar of the house, and the family
contributed to the building and beautification of the church. It
had a rectangular nave in rather severe Perpendicular style[2] and
a long, narrow, square-ended choir clearly separated from it.
Dominican buildings, both for church and lodging, were by
tradition long and low;[3] the cemetery admitted the bodies of
tertiaries and benefactors to burial, and was usually very large.

'The old proverb, "as sure as God's at Gloucester"', Stukeley
tells us,[4] 'surely meant the vast number of churches and religious
foundations here; for you can scarce walk past ten doors but some-
what of that sort appears.' So it was in many of the great towns
of England, as in Bristol until the second world war, as in York to
this day. Bristol, besides its religious houses and its parish churches,
had in St. Mary Redcliffe a church that both served a parish and
was a place of pilgrimage. The rebuilding of the south aisle of the
nave was begun in the second quarter of the fourteenth century;[5]
the building of its porch was stopped by the Black Death. The
rest of the rebuilding began again about 1355; the Lady chapel was
nearly finished in 1385. Then in the middle of the fifteenth
century the clerestory windows were enlarged, the transepts
heightened, and the walls panelled, to give the whole a loftier
effect.

All Hallows at York[6] is a more typical town church. Contemporary wills show that it was being built between 1407 and
1450. Its tower and spire are fine, but its chief glory is its stained

---

[1] This survives as St. Andrew's Hall. See Harrod, 7 and 83.
[2] Ed. W. W. Skeat (1906), 7. An outside pulpit, a good deal restored, survives at
Hereford.   [3] Jarrett, 26.   [4] i. 67.
[5] On its dating see Brakspear in *Bristol and Gloucester Arch. Soc. Trans.* xliv (1922),
271.   [6] See P. J. Shaw, 19.

glass, notably the Prick of Conscience window that has already been mentioned[1] and that given by Nicholas Blackburn and his wife in 1440. This represents St. John the Baptist in one panel, and St. Anne teaching the Virgin to read in another: a group of rather sentimental charm. In the lower range the donors, with their son and his wife, kneel before a little panel of the Trinity.

Before the Great Fire the city of London was studded all over with little medieval churches, many of fourteenth- and fifteenth-century date. Some were the gift of a single citizen: Sir John Poultney, for example, four times lord mayor of London before his death in 1348, not only built a chapel for his burial in St. Paul's, the chantry college of St. Lawrence Poultney, and the Carmelites' church at Coventry, but also built the parish church called Little All Hallows in Thames Street.[2]

About the time of Edward II, however, Sir Alfred Clapham[3] has noted a cessation of the multiplication of little town churches in favour of the erection of a single great church, as at Winchelsea, Hull, Boston, and Newark.[4] These great churches have wide naves, divided from the aisles by slender piers, and long ranges of windows, all in the tradition of the lost Franciscan churches such as that in Newgate. The nave of Newark, begun about 1390, after the Black Death had stopped work on the south aisle, is a magnificent instance (Pl. 93). The tall pier arcades of Holy Trinity, Hull, built between 1390 and 1425 in their amazing lightness, height, and consistency of style are extremely fine; the lofty aisles, with immense windows of similar tracery, complete the new proportion of the whole. The chancel and transepts are notable for being built, like the contemporary town walls, of brick.[5] The Franciscan church at King's Lynn was likewise of brick, but the great church of St. Nicholas there, begun in 1399 at earliest and finished in 1419 at latest, is all of stone. Its splendid east window, in its rather formal rectilinear style, is typical of the

---

[1] p. 94.

[2] Weever, *St. Paul's*, 371.

[3] Clapham and Godfrey, 250.

[4] Hull and Winchelsea were 'new towns', and a single church was a common feature of the plan of *villes-neuves*.

[5] The fourteenth-century font is of exceptional beauty.

rich town churches of the end of the century. Such churches were often crowned by a splendid tower or spire; St. Michael's, Coventry, has the tallest parish spire in England,[1] and Boston Stump is legendary.[2] In such churches, doubtless because of their common model, there is a remarkable homogeneity. The nave of Spalding has rather squat quadrilobed piers, a widely spaced clerestory, and rather plain mouldings, yet it is demonstrably in the same tradition as the splendid achievement of St. Peter Mancroft, though its piers are loftier, its arches more heavily moulded, and its clerestory windows squarer and more closely set; and St. Peter Mancroft, Norwich, with its vast uniform aisle windows and its architecture dominated by oblong rectangles, sets the note for the late Perpendicular East Anglian churches that are to come.

The city churches were often enriched by bequests from the private chapels of wealthy citizens. William Bruges, for example, in his will of 1449[3] left much to the church of St. George at Stamford: money for the roof, glass, desks, rood-loft, pews, paving in 'broad Holand tyle'; 'a solemnite of array' for the feast of Corpus Christi, and figures of angels bearing Instruments of the Passion set round a casket for the Sacrament, with a jewelled pyx. Besides all this he left the church, out of his private chapel, images of the Virgin and St. George of painted stone, two great latten candlesticks, and a stone image of the Trinity with a triple candlestick before it, which he directed was to be set upon a stone bracket above the heads of the other images.

When we turn from the great cities to the lesser towns and villages, the scale may be less but the story is the same. Some were due to the benefaction of a single man: the church of Wymington in Bedfordshire, for example, was built by John Curteys, mayor of the Staple of Calais, who died in 1381. The east window is filled with good foliate tracery; the aisle windows are square-headed with reticulated fillings. The octagonal piers of the nave have moulded capitals; the chantry tomb of the builder stands beside the chancel. The altar once had a sculptured retable with heavy

---

[1] It dates from the last quarter of the fourteenth century and was finished in 1394.
[2] It was built about 1350, but the lantern octagon and the panelling of the surface date from about 1500.   [3] *Test. Vet.* i. 267.

tabernacles; there are rich sedilia and piscina. Both outside, in the bold battlements and good drip-stones, and inside, in every sculptured detail, we can see that John Curteys lacked neither taste nor money. The church of Bardwell in Suffolk, again, is due in the main to the generosity of Sir William Bardwell, who died in 1434; there is an excellent portrait of him in a window of the nave.[1] The church of East Harling in Norfolk was almost entirely built about 1449 by Sir John Chamberlain, who was buried in a small chapel of the Virgin where he had founded a chantry.[2]

Sometimes the rector of a church was himself wealthy enough to undertake its rebuilding. Remi of Hethersett, for example, rector of Hingham from 1319 to 1359, entirely rebuilt his church with the aid of his patron John le Marshall. Wramplingham church was rebuilt by John Cavel, a rector who died in 1448.[3] About the same time William de Longthorne, rector of Fen Stanton in Huntingdonshire, built himself a chancel that is an admirable example of pure architecture.[4] It depends hardly at all upon sculptured detail for its effect, but frames a magnificent east window that could challenge the gifts of an archbishop to his cathedral. At Snetterton, in Norfolk, the contemporary glazing was a work of co-operation. The rector glazed the chancel windows with representations of the Apocalypse and of the apostles, each holding a scroll with a sentence of the Creed; the nave windows were glazed by the parishioners, and those in the north aisle by the lord of the manor, with scenes of the Creation, Baptism of Christ, and St. Christopher, accompanied by little figures of angels holding his arms.[5] At Garboldisham the roof of the nave was painted about 1450 with the names of Jesus and Mary and with this inscription:

> *Betwex syn yas and ye Rode loft,*
> *Ye Yongling han payd yis cost. Yat Lord yat*
> *deyid for alle mankynde have mercy upon hem at*
> *her ende.*

---

[1] M. R. James, *Norfolk and Suffolk*, Fig. on p. 9.
[2] Blomefield, i. 220.   [3] Ibid. i. 712.
[4] *Royal Commission on Historical Monuments, Huntingdonshire*, 90.
[5] Blomefield, i. 284.

While the young people thus roofed the nave, the parishioners in
general covered the chancel, which was inscribed:

Alle, alle hevin holpe to yes good Deed
God send hyer Sowle helpe to hyer mede.[1]

On the other side of England the west country clothiers were no
less generous. The brass of Robert Page, woolman, who was
buried at Cirencester in 1440, states that he used his wealth in
repairing churches and roads, and a like claim was made for
Thomas Fortey at Northleach in 1447. His son, John Fortey,
whose brass of 1458 shows him with one foot upon a sheep and
one upon a woolpack, paid for the clerestory of the church; the
south chapel was given a little later by another woolman, William
Bicknell. The church almost exactly reproduces that earlier given
to Chipping Campden by William Grevel (Pl. 46 *b*); the same
master-mason must have built both.

This is not the place to make any detailed investigation of the
lesser parish churches of England. Their history is inextricably
bound up with that of their locality; their architecture forms a
part of the great stream of English building. They initiated nothing,
though in them certain local peculiarities of style can best be
studied: the ogee-headed arches of Northamptonshire,[2] the flint-
and-stone inlays and clerestory rose-windows[3] of East Anglia,[4]
and other minor variations of style that are hardly perceived
outside their own regions. The process of development is a continuous one that may be marked by the changing form of the pier.
A quadrilobed form, with four half-columns set against a square
pier,[5] is succeeded by one with the half-columns octagonal;[6] and
finally the quadrilobed form is exchanged for an octagonal pier[7]
with a simple moulded capital.

---

[1] Blomefield, i. 179.

[2] e.g. Harlestone, Northants.

[3] At Cley and Snettisham, Norfolk, they alternate with simple arched windows;
circular clerestory windows are also found at Terrington St. John in Norfolk and
Seaton in Rutland. Farther to the west similar windows will be found at Padbury and
Streatley, and Kingsland and Pembridge in Herefordshire.

[4] e.g. Tunstead, Norfolk.   [5] e.g. Cotton, Suffolk.

[6] e.g. Stoke Bruerne, Northants; Kingsland, Herefordshire.

[7] e.g. Wheathampstead, Herts.; Byfield and Castle Ashby, Northants.

The parish churches are not usually particularly rich in architectural sculpture, but there are many exceptions, such as the group of Decorated parish churches in Lincolnshire.[1] Bloxham church, again, near Stow-in-the-Wold, has a doorway sculptured with ball-flower growing on entwined stalks, with friezes of birds, and an elaborate hood-moulding carved with foliage, with a stepped cresting. On the top step Christ sits in judgement with angels bearing symbols of the Passion on either side and the apostles below.[2]

The parish churches were rich in every kind of furnishing: even now there are few ancient parish churches but contain some medieval work of art. Stained glass is perhaps the commonest, though often no more remains than a heraldic border or quarry, the top of a canopy, or a mosaic of shattered pieces from several windows.[3] Wall-paintings, once as common, are less well preserved and far less accomplished. Their subjects are the Life of the Virgin,[4] the Virgin and Child,[5] the Apostles and Saints,[6] the Temptation and Expulsion from Eden,[7] the Doom[8] and Passion scenes,[9] and St. Christopher.[10] At Trotton in Sussex[11] there are rough paintings of the Seven Deadly Sins and of the Tree of the Seven Acts of Mercy. None are of any artistic interest; their importance in the history of English medieval art is to show the gulf that yawned between the rustic dauber and the artist of such wall-paintings as those of St. Stephen's chapel.

The chief glory of the parish church is not uncommonly its rood-screen.[12] This was often the gift of a single wealthy parishioner.

[1] See above, p. 31.

[2] The Melcombe chapel adjoining the porch is ascribed to the master-mason Richard Winchcombe.

[3] A list may be compiled from Nelson, 51 et seqq.

[4] Wimborne, Chalgrove.   [5] Canfield.

[6] Cold Overton, Elsing, Chalfont St. Giles, Newington by Sittingbourne, and many other places.

[7] Colton.

[8] West Somerton, Chalgrove, Catherington.   [9] West Somerton.

[10] See Brindley in *Antiq. Journ.* iv (1924), 28. Aldermaston, West Somerton, Paston, Little Baddow, Seething, St. Albans, Castor, Croydon, Shorwell, and Witton.

[11] Borenius and Tristram, 37; it dates from soon after 1387.

[12] See Vallance.

At Burford the brass of John Spicer, who died in 1431, is inscribed:

> *I pray yow all for charite*
> *hertely that ye pray for me*
> *to oure lord that sytteth on hye*
> *fful of grace and of mercye.*
> *The wiche rode-soler in this chirche*
> *Upon my cost y dede do wirche*
> *Wt. a laumpe brenyng bright*
> *to worschip God both day and nyght . . .*
> *Now Ihū that dydyst on a tre*
> *On us have mercye and pite.   Amen.*

The rood-loft and screen at Woodbridge in Suffolk was given by John Albrede, twill-weaver, who died in 1444. It is now partly destroyed, but earlier descriptions[1] show that it was once painted with the Crucifixion, the Coronation of the Virgin, the archangels, with the apostles, saints, and martyrs, including Paul, Edward, Kenelm, Oswald, Cuthbert, Blaise, Quintin, Leger, Jerome, and eight virgin saints. Such painted screens were particularly favoured in Norfolk and Suffolk, and reached their full development in the second half of the fifteenth century.[2] Many have lost almost all their painted decoration, but are still beautiful by reason of their tracery; Wimbish, St. Nicholas, King's Lynn, Wallington near by, and Castle Hedingham may be cited in East Anglia, and Winchcombe in the west country. A few examples of stone rood-screens survive, for example at Hillmarton in Wiltshire, that resemble the stone screens of the chantry chapels; in a few instances these are extended to fill the chancel arch, window fashion.[3]

The construction of the wooden screens was paralleled by that of magnificent oaken roofs, adorned with figures of angels and other sculptures; these, again, found their full development in the

---

[1] Weever, 752; B.M. Add. MS. 8987.

[2] Southacre, Barton Turf, and possibly Southwold fall within the earlier period.

[3] Stebbing and Great Bardfield, Essex; Eastwell, Leics.; and Sandridge, Herts. See Vallance, Pls. 80 and 81.

second half of the century.[1] The fonts, too, were often the fruit of an individual benefaction: that at Kirton in Lincolnshire was inscribed: + *Orate pro anima alani burton qui fontem istum fieri fec. a.d.* MCCCCII.[2] The richer examples were adorned with panels of figure sculpture. That at Ware, of about 1380, has rather restless compositions of Saints Christopher, George, Katherine, James, John the Baptist, and Margaret, and the Annunciation; that at Orford in Suffolk, but little later, has coarse but showy sculptures of the Trinity, God the Father, the Crucifixion, and the Evangelistic symbols, above a cornice of angels; the base is carved with lions and selvage men.[3] Most parish churches have lost their carved reredoses of stone or alabaster; Mattersey in Nottinghamshire still has a little St. Martin and an Invention of the Cross,[4] and there are in the Victoria and Albert Museum[5] reredos panels of about 1400, perhaps from Northamptonshire, with the Orders of the Angels.

The medieval portable furnishings of the parish churches are now scanty; there are good fourteenth-century chests at Icklingham in Suffolk and at Huttoft in Lincolnshire; and a fine chalice-case of *cuir-bouilli* at Cawston in Norfolk.[6] The churchyard usually contained a preaching-cross; Stukeley[7] describes that at Coventry: 'a beautiful gothic work, sixty six foot high; in niches are the statues of the English kings'. Two good examples survive in Gloucestershire: one at Ampney Crucis, of the beginning of the fifteenth century, and one at Iron Acton, given by Sir Robert Poyntz, who died in 1439. That at Ampney Crucis has an octagonal shaft rising from three squared steps to a total height of some 13 feet. The head has on the eastern side carvings of the Virgin, the Crucifixion, and St. John, and on the west the Virgin and Child. On the north is a headless man with a collar of roses,

---

[1] Outwell, Norfolk, has a north chapel dated 1420 with an angel roof; the roof at Bardwell is dated 1421 and also had angels, now lost. The roofs at Wymondham, Norfolk; March, Cambs.; and Stonham Earl St. Mary, Suffolk, date from the years around 1450.   [2] Stukeley, i. 33.

[3] The font at Luton is remarkable for its enclosure.

[4] Prior and Gardner, Fig. 422.   [5] W 34–34c, 1912.

[6] It bears the arms of Hastings and other local families and is inscribed: + IHESVS NAZARENVS REX IVDEORVM.

[7] i. 49. Cf. the cathedral screens with statues of the kings, p. 86.

perhaps the donor, and on the south St. Lawrence, probably his patron. At Iron Acton (Pl. 95) the tall arcaded base is surmounted by a frieze of shields of arms, and of Instruments of the Passion; above this four niches for sculptured figures form a basis for the lost crucifix.

The importance of the parish church in town and village life lay not only in its communal masses but also in its serving as a focus for the life of brotherhoods or guilds. Their foundation seems to spring from the foundation of the feast of Corpus Christi on the Thursday after Trinity Sunday by Pope Urban IV about 1264.[1] The first known English guild of Corpus Christi was that of the chaplains of the collegiate church of St. Mary at Norwich, founded in 1278, but the movement soon spread among the laity, especially in East Anglia; six such guilds are known to have been founded in the first half of the fourteenth century.[2] They were followed by innumerable parish guilds, sometimes dedicated to the Body of Our Lord, sometimes to a saint. Men who had made a pilgrimage together might agree to form a confraternity, like the Palmers' guild at Ludlow or the guild at Burgh in Lincolnshire founded in 1365 by five men who had gone to Compostella and made a vow to build an altar to St. James when they were in peril of shipwreck on the way back.[3] The official cult of St. Anne after Richard II's marriage is reflected in a guild dedicated to her founded in the undercroft of St. Paul's in 1391;[4] and the cult of the Holy Name of Jesus instituted by Richard Rolle led to the formation of at least two guilds with that dedication.[5]

Such guilds might only exist to provide a candle or a lamp to burn before an altar, like the guild of Corpus Christi in the parish of St. Botolph's without Aldgate that provided thirteen lights about the sepulchre at Eastertide,[6] yet they often grew to include the provision of soul-masses for departed members. Their number

[1] Westlake, 49.
[2] Bury St. Edmunds, 1317; Louth, 1326; Coventry, 1343, and three more before 1349.
[3] Westlake, 33.   [4] Dugdale, *St. Paul's*, 76.
[5] Undercroft of St. Paul's, 1459, Dugdale, 76. Weever, 380; St. Peter Mancroft, Norwich, 1455.   [6] Heales, 272.

was very great; few parishes in Norfolk, for example, had not a guild; many had two or three; Wymondham as many as ten.[1] No less than 909 guilds are known to have existed in Norfolk.[2] Their existence was menaced for a time in 1388–9,[3] when parliament enacted that guilds and fraternities should be suppressed, except for those that maintained chantries, or were ecclesiastical foundations, or held a royal licence. In fact, all could claim a religious colour, and the measure effected nothing.

The English guilds were not such great patrons of the arts as were those of France, but none the less they filled a certain role as patrons. The guild of St. Edmund of Pontigny at Lincoln, for example, of which the statutes date from 1363, owned an image of him and carried it in an annual procession. The guild of Holy Trinity at Ingham in Norfolk, about 1370, made a yearly offering of a 'flower' or jewel. The guild of Corpus Christi at Holbeach in Lincolnshire seems in 1447 not only to have performed a Nativity play but also to have given sculptures to the church.[4] Sometimes, indeed, the guild seems to have grown out of a work of art. In 1358[5] one John de Rughton had a beautiful image of St. John painted for the parish church of Spalding. With some friends he provided a perpetual light to burn before it. In 1383 John Torarld and other friends provided funds for a chaplain to serve the altar beneath it. Similarly the guild of Holy Trinity in the same church sprang from the gift of a fully furnished altar which John de Toft made in 1370.

It was not long before the guilds were engaged in actual building. In 1343[6] John Enfield and other citizens of London founded a fraternity in the church of All Hallows', London Wall, primarily to restore the church, and secondly to keep a perpetual light burning in it. They rebuilt the steeple and re-roofed the church. All the members but Enfield died in the Black Death, but when it was over he refounded the guild. In 1338 Geffrey Wynchecombe and a friend added a chapel in honour of St. Katharine on the south side of St. Mary Colechurch, and founded

---

[1] Blomefield, i. 735.
[3] Steel, 169; Westlake, 36.
[5] Westlake, 29.

[2] Taylor, 75.
[4] Stukeley, i. 26.
[6] Ibid. 27.

a fraternity to provide lights and a chaplain. An aisle was added
to St. Giles', Cripplegate, in like fashion in 1399.[1] St. Nicholas'
chapel at Diss in Norfolk was built in the time of Henry V by
the brethren and sisters of the guilds of St. Nicholas and Corpus
Christi, then incorporated.[2]

Occasionally such work was extended to the building of bridges
and other pious work. The fraternity of Holy Cross, founded
about 1389 in the church of St. Helen, Abingdon, not only set up
a rood in the church but also helped to build the new bridge and,
a few years later, undertook the maintenance of the road from
Abingdon to Dorchester. In 1446 it founded a hospital for thirteen
poor men and women, and soon after the guild set up an octagonal
cross in the market-place with three rows of statues and carved and
painted coats of arms.[3] The guild of St. Mary at Stamford, that by
1392 had a chantry in the chapel of St. Mary of the Bridge,[4] had
likewise aided in its building. The admirable timbered building
of the grammar school of Stratford-on-Avon was erected about
1417 by the guild of Holy Cross that helped to maintain it; it
adjoins the tower of their chapel.

The parish guilds and the palmers' guilds were ultimately less
important than the guilds of craftsmen, tradesmen, and merchants.
The latter came to play a part in the development of trade and
commerce that has caused them to live on when parish guilds are
forgotten.

One of the earliest of the merchant guilds was the Puy of London,
founded in 1280 by Sir Henry le Waleys, lord mayor of London,
who in 1275 had been mayor of Bordeaux.[5] It was modelled on
the French *Puys* dedicated to Our Lady, of which that of Amiens
is perhaps the most famous, and combined piety and feasting. The
Liber costumarum declares it to be a brotherhood of the French and
English traders of London, united for charity and the cultivation
of music and poetry. There was a yearly feast, at which a prince
and his twelve companions were elected, and a crown was awarded
for the best song. In 1299 the brethren of the Puy made a gift

[1] Westlake, 20.
[2] Blomefield, i. 21.
[3] Cook, 20.
[4] Ibid. 44.
[5] Unwin, 98; Riley, 42.

towards the support of a chaplain saying mass in the new chapel
of Our Lady at the Guildhall, and in 1356 a chantry was endowed
there.[1]

Such trade guilds were soon in existence all over the country,
often on a very small scale. By 1328 the tailors of Lincoln were
bound together in a confraternity of Corpus Christi;[2] and even
a small place like Holbeach had its guild of tilers, dedicated to the
Assumption and burning a light before the image of the Virgin,[3]
and its Shepherds' guild, in honour of the Nativity, that did likewise.[4] By Chaucer's time

> An haberdasher, and a Carpenter,
> A Webbe, a Deyer and a Tapiser,
> Were alle yclothed in o livere
> Of a solempne and grete fraternite.

Such guilds not only regulated their trade, as the Goldsmiths'
Company of London still does, but also administered the trade
charities, as the London city companies still do, and served as
corporate chantry foundations. It was a natural thing for men of
one calling to be members of one guild, and the custom soon
spread. The fraternity of the mariners of Bristol was founded in
1445[5] for the maintenance of the hospital of St. Bartholomew for
a priest and twelve poor sailors who were required to pray for the
king, the mayor, and the commons of Bristol, and for all merchants
and mariners passing and labouring on the sea whether out or
home. The Shipmen's guild of Hull, founded as the guild of the
Holy Trinity in 1369 and confirmed by royal charter in 1473,
still survives and still bestows its charity upon sailors.

The particular art of the trade guilds was that of drama. By
1391 the guild of the parish clerks of London acted the plays of
the Passion of Our Lord and the Creation of the World at Skin-
nerwell after the feast of St. Bartholomew;[6] the *Towneley Mysteries*
were enacted in Yorkshire by guilds of tanners, glovers, and
fishermen. Their contribution to the visual arts was more acci-

---

[1] Curiously enough the Company of the Staple do not seem to have formed a
religious fraternity.
[2] Westlake, 49.   [3] Ibid. 23.   [4] Ibid. 33.
[5] Ibid. 88.   [6] Devon, 244.

dental; the London Puy, for example, did not, like that of Amiens, dedicate a picture annually to the Virgin. Rather exceptionally, when the church of St. Mary of Beverley was rebuilt in the reign of Henry VI, the guild of minstrels gave it a pillar and had a band of musicians carved round the capital.

The natural home of the purely religious confraternities was the parish church, though by the end of our period the Trinity Guild of St. Botolph's, Aldgate, already mentioned, owned a hall with a fine arched timber roof and a great window at the end.[1] The Dominican church at Bristol included the Guildhall of the bakers, and the Cirencester guilds used the rooms in the three-storied porch of their parish church as their halls. Soon, however, independent halls became a necessity for the great commercial organizations into which the London trade guilds developed.[2] The Merchant Taylors of London took over the town-house of Sir Oliver de Ingham on his death in 1331; and by 1364 the Goldsmiths had a Hall, with a hall, kitchen, pantry, buttery, and two bed-chambers, to which a new parlour and a cellar were added in 1380, and an oriel to the dais in 1454. It was, in fact, a fine town-house of a purely domestic character: a communal imitation of the city residence of a great nobleman. The same model seems to have been followed by the six other city companies' halls that were built during our period.[3]

Outside London the divers guilds of one place tended to be consolidated into one body possessing one fine building. At Coventry the guilds of St. Mary, St. John Baptist, St. Katharine, and the Trinity, founded between 1340 and 1364, were all united by 1369; they represented the cloth and wool trades, dyeing, iron-founding, and glazing. They had as members not only the men of Coventry engaged in these trades, but also the farmers and wool-men of Warwickshire, many from Lincolnshire, not a few from Norfolk and Wiltshire, and even William Grevel from Chipping Campden. On their rolls are to be found the names of an alabaster-mason from Tutbury, Richard Whittington from London, two

---

[1] Unwin, 124.   [2] Ibid. 176, 181.
[3] Saddlers' Hall, 1395; Brewers' Hall, before 1422; Carpenters' Hall, 1426; Fish-mongers' Hall, 1434; Vintners' Hall, c. 1446; Salters' Hall, 1454.

Italians, and a number of women. The political importance of the guild was such that esquires, knights, nobles, ecclesiastics, and great men were glad to be admitted; even Henry IV and the dukes of Bedford and of Gloucester appear upon its rolls.

St. Mary's Hall was begun for the consolidated guilds in 1394, and finished in 1414; it followed the usual plan, with screens and an oriel to the dais. The ceiling was panelled; most of the windows were filled with heraldic glass commemorating its most distinguished members, while other windows, together with the dais tapestry and the painting on the end wall, commemorated Henry VI's visit to the city in 1450. The great master's chair is of oak, carved with lions, elephants, seated figures, and the castle of Coventry. The Trinity guild, one of the constituent confraternities, in 1442 owned a dorsal of arras with hawking scenes, cushions with red and green elephants, wreaths and mottoes, and with 'ymages of men and damselles'. In their council chamber there was nothing but working furniture, but in their treasury, besides a cross for their altar, there was a fine collection of cups, ewers, spice-dishes, bowls, spoons, knives, and mazers for their feasts.[1]

The corporate guildhall at Norwich was begun in 1407 and finished in 1413;[2] little remains. King's Lynn, which had no less than seventy-five guilds in the course of the middle ages, was dominated by the merchants' guilds of the Holy Trinity and St. George the Martyr. St. George's Hall, built in 1420, is notable for its fine timber roof. The hall of the other guild (now the town hall) was burned down in 1421 and rebuilt at once. At York[3] the Guildhall (Pl. 96) was built in 1446 by the guilds of St. Christopher and St. George. Its great octagonal oaken columns, its open roof, and its fine Perpendicular windows remained until 1942 (when it was burned in an air-raid) to give us a fitting idea of the importance of the trade guilds of the fifteenth century.

[1] *Proc. Soc. Ants.* v (1870–3), 121.

[2] Blomefield, ii. 649.

[3] The Mercers' Hall there was built between 1357 and 1368; it is to undergo restoration shortly.

CONCLUSION

OUR story of the central period of English medieval art has reached its close, and that close finds it still purely medieval. The humanist Poggio might spend four years in England from 1418 to 1422, but his visit was not the beginning of an English Renaissance but rather served to turn his own interests for a time from humanism into the channels of purely patristic learning.[1] Pluto and Proserpina may appear in Chaucer's *Merchant's Tale*, but they play no part in contemporary art. Our period, the least austere and most intimate epoch of the middle ages, finds our country untouched by alien arts. Even the influence of France, that can never be accounted truly alien in Gothic art, is felt in detail and in decoration rather than in the architectural whole. Both the Decorated and the Perpendicular styles are peculiar to England, and are paralleled but not influenced by Rayonnant and Flamboyant French styles.

In our period we pass, as Stubbs phrases it,[2] from the age of heroism to the age of chivalry, and the process is continuous and uninterrupted. Not even the Black Death could break the chain of development. If we find the continuity difficult to establish, it is because of gaps that have been made by Time. The catastrophic demolitions of the Reformation were succeeded by destructions far more gradual yet hardly less disastrous.

In 1776 Stukeley wrote of Crowland abbey:[3]

'The roof, which was of Irish oak finely carved and gilt, fell down about twenty years ago: you see pieces of it in every house. The pavement is covered with shrubs for brass inscriptions, and people now at pleasure dig up the monumental stones, and divide the holy shipwreck for their private uses; so that, instead of one, most of the houses in the town are become religious. The painted glass was broke by the soldiers in the rebellion, for they made a garrison of the place. All the eastern part of the church is intirely razed to the foundation; and the ashes as well as the tombs of an infinite number of illustrious personages, kings, abbots,

---

[1] Weiss, 14.   [2] *Const. Hist.* ii. 317.   [3] i. 33.

lords, knights, there hoping for repose, are dispersed, to the irreparable damage of English history.'

Nearly two hundred years have passed, and to the tally of destruction has been added not only the inevitable damage of time, storm, and fire, but that of neglect, of rebuilding, of restoration, of tidying and conservation, and destruction by the bombardment of our enemies. Our great danger now is that we may forget how much once existed, and so falsify the proportions of our history of English art. The destruction of monastic and friars' churches, the rebuilding of palaces, castles, town-houses, and guildhalls, the continued use of parish churches and university colleges, have all blurred the outlines of the picture. Yet even now no Protestant country preserves so many of her medieval buildings and her medieval institutions as does England.

Our period, for all its continuity, contains some startling contrasts. Exeter cathedral and St. Augustine's, Bristol; Warkworth castle and Ockwells; the tomb of Crouchback and that of Richard, earl of Warwick; the parish churches of Heckington and Northleach, could not be more fundamentally different if they lay centuries apart. Yet these contrasts are but part of the counterchanged pattern of the whole.

Enough remains, at least, for us to have a clear idea of the general character of English art between the reigns of Edward II and Edward IV, though we may see it as a series of vignettes rather than as a continuous story. We can see the masons and imagers setting up the Eleanor crosses; the team of illuminators engaged upon the Tickhill Psalter; the abbot of Gloucester transforming his Norman choir into something modern; the Black Prince planning his funeral with the pageantry of a tournament; his son striving to bring fanciful beauty into his court. We can envisage the whole gamut of religious celebration, from the coronation of Richard II to the Shepherds' guild of Holbeach hearing their Christmas Mass and remembering the shepherds who came to Bethlehem. We see men like Wykeham and Chichele engaged in the eternal routine of educational administration, and the city companies establishing trade regulations that still in part survive, and charitable endowments that still do good. With a peculiar sympathy we can see men determining to carry on private and public life in spite of war, plague, and famine; and continuing, in spite of everything, their efforts to bring beauty and goodness into an imperfect world.

Like the English lyric, English medieval art owes something to accidental felicities; like the language of that lyric, it has the peculiar richness that comes from a double source in north and south. The most shining beauties of its architecture depend, as English beauties should, on fortuitous changes of light and shadow. English fourteenth-century buildings should be seen in the early morning or towards sunset, or at a time when passing clouds or driving rain give them the beauty that is no stronger than a flower. The charm of English decorative art of the same period lies in a minute and jewelled brightness, a courtly elaboration that none the less still holds an element of provincial simplicity. It has real originality, not merely in the basic themes of ogival arcade and cusped panel, but also in a hundred fancies; the little figure of Lady Percy holding the shield of her arms, the alphabet round the Studley Royal bowl, the babewyns of the psalters, the crowded initials of the Bibles and missals, and the birds and beasts that flutter and creep from the pattern books of the illuminators into every form of decoration. English art of our period can express grief better than tragedy; the Eleanor crosses are one of its characteristic creations, but there are no English entombment groups. It is less interested in individual portraiture than in the impersonal pageantry of heraldry. Its symbolism is rarely esoteric, though sometimes literary; its narrative is clear and moving, though not gifted in the exactitude of iconographical creation.

We must not allow our natural sympathy with the English middle ages, whose heirs we are, to blind us to the true proportions of its art. That art has the qualities of the art of a small country; it is more often decorative and pretty than monumental or noble. York Minster is not Bourges cathedral; the façade of Exeter is not that of Rheims. The alabaster carvers are not Morel or Sluter, nor are the East Anglian psalters the *Très Riches Heures*. There is no English castle with sculpture as rich as that at La Ferté-Milon, no English hall as fine as that in the castle of Poitiers, no city walls that can rival those of Avignon. France once had as many, and far richer, brasses, and as many, and more delicately sculptured, effigies, as we can boast. We may claim with reason that France has no sculptured canopies to compare with Aymer de Valence's, and no chantry chapels like Lady Idoine Percy's or Cardinal Beaufort's; but we have no enamelled tombs of English manufacture. If we excelled in our embroidery, France was our mistress in goldwork. Finally, we must admit that English medieval art lacks the quality of surprise. Neither York nor Exeter has the breathtaking quality of Bourges or Beauvais. English art does not seem supernatural; rather, its charm lies in its naturalness and in a touching kind of simplicity. Few Englishmen can have grown up without having some work of medieval art as a familiar part of their lives: school or college, church or cathedral, guildhall or almshouse, stained-glass window or pictured manuscript. They may never have studied them seriously, but they have unconsciously accepted them as part of their heritage. We may therefore of right claim such art as holding a special meaning and a peculiar beauty for us, whose forefathers created it; and show it to the rest of the civilized world without arrogance as without shame.

APPENDIX A

Christic of the Trades

Christ of the Trades

PROFESSOR BORENIUS and Professor Tristram[1] have claimed a series of wall-paintings in English churches, for the most part small country parish churches, as representing an iconographic scheme, 'Christ of the Trades', inspired, directly or indirectly, by the vision of *Piers Plowman*. They all represent the Christ of the Passion, crowned with thorns and covered with wounds, with a number of curious implements ranged round Him. One of the earlier and better paintings, that at Ampney St. Mary's in Gloucestershire that dates from about 1400, shows Our Lord with a kind of halo formed of the implements: hammer, mallet, knife, dish, axe, pincers, a ball of cord, and others more doubtfully identified as a wheel, comb, and saddle.

Dr. Charlotte d'Eveleyn in 1919[2] and Dr. Ruth Ryan in 1929[3] have contended that these implements are not there, as Professors Borenius and Tristram suggest, to identify the suffering Christ with the suffering artisan, but represent the Instruments of the Passion, the list of which was in the fifteenth century extended to almost fantastic length. There is something to be said for their view. Langland never specifically identifies Christ and artisan;[4] though it is true that he sees Piers Plowman in the person of a labourer working and suffering among his fellows, and in a later book half-identifies him with Christ. But when he sees Christ in modern guise, it is as an armed knight. Few manuscripts of *Piers Plowman* are illustrated[5] and the exceptions do not to my knowledge show any analogous scene.

Moreover, the study of such a manuscript as B.M. Royal MS. 17 A 27, fol. 72 b,[6] which illustrates each separate Instrument of the Passion, shows a remarkable analogy with the implements represented at Ampney St. Mary. The 'wheel' may be a representation of the reeds,

---

[1] *Eng. Med. Painting*, 29; Tristram in *Burl. Mag.* xxxi (1917), 135.

[2] In *Modern Language Notes* (Baltimore), xxxiv (1919), 247.

[3] *Art Bulletin*, xl (1929), 302.

[4] Though he comes near to it at the beginning of Passus 18 and 19, B. text, and in P. 19, 116 et seqq.

[5] An exception is B.M. MS. Egerton 1991.

[6] The illustrations are rather inadequately reproduced in E.E.T.S. xlvi, *Legends of the Holy Rood*, ed. R. Morris (1871), 172.

schematically shown in the manuscript; the 'comb' may in fact be the
ladder; and the 'saddle' is not unlike the unusually shaped forceps or
tongs shown in the manuscript. The certainly identified objects are all
among those that might appear among the Instruments of the Passion.[1]

Other representations of the 'Christ of the Trades' which fall within
our period are equally inconclusive. The painting at West Chiltington
is very indistinct; it seems to show a hatchet and a knife, a shuttle-
shaped object, a square, and a wheel. That at Oving is practically
indecipherable; that at Stedham in Sussex is now destroyed and the
evidence concerning it is unreliable.[2]

The Rev. Dr. Christopher Woodforde, in a publication which he has
most generously allowed me to see in manuscript, offers another and I
think more convincing explanation of the subject. He links it with a
window recorded at Walsham-le-Willows, Suffolk, which showed the
Body of Christ wounded and dismembered by those who swear by it
and its parts: a subject not uncommonly referred to in contemporary
literature, and here confirmed by inscriptions. The representation of
Christ was here surrounded by the implements of some thirty trades,
which symbolize—according to Dr. M. R. James[3] and Dr. Woodforde—
the injuries inflicted upon Christ by all manner of people. In several
paintings of the kind the tools and instruments not only surround but
touch, pierce, or cut the body of Christ; at Walsham-le-Willows the
cutting-edge of an axe touches Christ's left hand. In a wall-painting
of the same kind in the church of San Miniato at Florence there is an
inscription which says that the pains of Hell await the man who dis-
regards the sabbath. There can, I think, be little doubt that the paintings
were intended as warnings against profanity and sabbath-breaking
rather than as representations of 'The Christ of the Trades', though in
some instances there seems to have been a *contaminatio* from the parallel
representation of Christ with the Instruments of the Passion.

[1] Dr. Saxl takes this view in considering a manuscript at Rome, Bibl. Casanatense,
MS. 1404, fol. 40, 'Aller Tugenden und Laster Abbildung', *Festschrift für Julius
Schlosser* (1927), 104.

[2] I have not seen the wall-paintings at Hassett in Suffolk.

[3] *Suffolk and Norfolk*, 75. See also E. Breitenbach and Th. Hillmann, 'Das Gebot
der Feiertagsheilung, ein spät mittelalterliches Bildthema im Dienste volkstümlicher
Pfarrpraxis', *Anzeiger für Schweiz. Altertumskunde*, Zürich, xxxix (1937), 23.

APPENDIX B

THE traveller and the student will find a great quantity of work of the second order of the period here covered, all over England. It would take a volume to give a comprehensive list, but a few indications may be of use.

A fairly complete series of churches that can be more or less exactly dated affords an indication of the development of the styles.

1315	Badgworth, Glos.
c. 1320	Methwold, Norfolk.
c. 1325	Haconby and Heckington, Lincs.
1340–52	St. Mary the Less, Cambridge.
1341	Great Bookham, Surrey.
c. 1347	Elsing, Norfolk.
1348	Buckland, Herts.
1357	Donington, Lincs.
Before 1359	Hingham, Norfolk.
1369	Worstead, Norfolk.
c. 1370	Sleaford, Lincs. (Chancel 1403.)
1373	Arlingham, Glos.
After 1381 and before 1405. North Walsham, Norfolk.	
Temp. Ric. II	Cley, Norfolk.
1390–1400	Balsham, Cambs. (Chancel).
Soon after 1391	Sutton Ashfield, Notts.
1396	Colmworth, Beds.
c. 1400	Cirencester. (Trinity chapel c. 1430.)
c. 1400	Curry Rivel, Somerset.
1412	Catterick, Yorks.
1420–31	Ipswich, St. Laurence.
1423–5	Walpole St. Peter, Norfolk.
1424–33	Bury St. Edmunds, St. Mary's.
1430	Wells, St. Cuthbert's (Tower).
1442	Cromwell, Notts. (Tower).
c. 1400–45	Louth, Lincs. (The tower later.)
1442–73	Blythburgh, Suffolk.
1445	Landwade, Cambs.
1445–57	Brington, Northants.
1455	St. Peter Mancroft, Norwich.

A great decrease in their number occurs between 1450 and 1470, no doubt because of the Wars of the Roses.

Most counties will be found to contain some fine churches of the period. Suffolk is especially rich in Decorated churches; besides those enumerated in the text, Rickenhall, Redgrave, Boxhall, Great Livermere, Cotton, Hitcham, and Stowmarket may be mentioned. Norfolk is no less rich in Perpendicular churches, though many of these fall outside the limits of this book. Reticulated tracery may be studied at Wareham, Dorset; Great Baddow, Essex; Ware and Wheathampstead, Herts.; New Romney, Kent; Docking and Shipsham, Norfolk; at Higham Ferrers, Milton Malson and Stowmarket, Northants. A local type of reticulated tracery with a quatrefoil as its chief element is found, for instance, at Chartham, Kent, and Winchelsea, Sussex.

A list of parish churches with fourteenth-century glass sufficiently important to contain figures[1] would include:

Beds.	Cockayne Hatley, Edworth.
Berks.	Compton Beauchamp, East Hagbourne, Sparsholt.
Bucks.	Chetwode, Hitcham.
Cambs.	Trumpington, Wimpole.
Cheshire	Grappenhall.
Cornwall	Lancast.
Derbyshire	Cubley, Dronfield, Norbury.
Devon	Beer-Ferrers, Exeter cathedral, Haccombe.
Essex	Great Bardfield, Hornchurch, Lindsell, Newport, Sheering.
Glos.	Arlingham, Breedon, Deerhurst.
Hants	Mottisfont, Winchester (St. Cross).
Herefordshire	Brinsop.
Herts.	Paul's Walden.
Kent	Chartham, Kingsdown, Selling, Stowting, Willesborough.
Lancs.	Cartmel, Fell, Halsall.
Leics.	Coston, Lockington, Ratcliffe-on-Wreake.
Lincs.	Haydor, Lea, Wrangle.
Norfolk	Bawborough, Elsing, Mileham, Gooderstone, Pulham Saint Mary, Dunston.
Northants	Lowick, Stanford.
Notts.	Popplewick.

[1] See Nelson, 51 et seqq.

Oxon.	Beckley, Dorchester, Kidlington, Waterperry.
Rutland	North Luffenham.
Salop	Cound, Delbury, Kinlet, Morville, Munslow, Shrewsbury (St. Mary's), Worfield.
Somerset	Farleigh-Hungerford.
Staffs.	Checkley, Weston-under-Lizard.
Suffolk	Great Bricett, Icklingham All Saints, Dennington.
Surrey	Oxted, West Horsley, Worplesdon.
Sussex	Tortington.
Warwickshire	Mancetter, Merevale, Wolverton.
Wilts.	Oaksey.
Worcs.	Himbledon.
Yorks.	Hornby, Normanton; York: All Saints, St. John the Evangelist, St. Mary Castlegate, St. Michael's-le-Belfrey.

Fine alabaster tombs of the period are those of Lady Montacute in Oxford cathedral, c. 1350; William, Lord Lovel at Minster Lovel, Oxon.; John, Lord Ros, d. 1421, at Bottesford, Lincs.; Sir Ralph Grey, d. 1443, at Chillingham, Northumberland; Sir John Cassey, d. 1444, at Dodford, Northants; John Beaufort, duke of Somerset, d. 1444, and his wife in Wimborne Minster; Sir Richard Vernon, d. 1451, and his wife at Tong, Salop; and Sir John Verney, d. 1461, at Stogursey, Somerset.

The alabaster tombs of the FitzHerberts at Norbury in Derbyshire are notable for their many weepers. Other alabaster tombs with weepers will be found at Warkworth, Abergavenny, Warwick (Prior and Gardner, Fig. 514), Earl's Colne, Minster Lovel, Sparsholt, Berks., and Bartholmey in Cheshire. A Totternhoe stone tomb with weepers is at Clifton Reynes.

Angels carrying shields may be studied on the tombs of John, Lord Ros, d. 1421, Bottesford, Lincs.; a tomb at Strelley, Notts.; Sir John Cassey, 1444, Dodford, Northants.; a Cockayne tomb, 1447, at Ashbourne, Derbyshire; and the Warwick chapel at Tewkesbury, c. 1422.

The series of canopied wall-niches for tombs extends all over England.

A tomb-niche at Exeter exceptionally has its gable filled by a canopied niche to contain a statue; another at Tewkesbury (S. Gardner, 177) has no gable; the arch is ogival, the mouldings are filled with ball-flower, and the crockets and finials are of heavy foliage. Good foliage mouldings may also be seen on the wall-canopy of the tomb of Archbishop Peckham at Canterbury; it has a heavy rosette in the gable. Another good tomb-niche at Exeter is that of Sir John de Stapleton, *c.* 1320.

A tomb of about 1310 at Gosberton, Lincs., has angels in the spandrels (Prior and Gardner, Fig. 420). Another of about 1340 at Ducklington, Oxon., has the tree of Jesse rather inappropriately introduced in the cresting. One at Grantham, Lincs., has angels as cusps and angels holding the helm and shield in the spandrels.

Similar niches for Easter sepulchres are no less widespread in their distribution; good examples may be seen at St. Peter's, Dorchester, Dorset; Writtle, Essex; Tring, Herts.; Cheriton and Hythe, Kent; Ravenham, Norfolk; Stanton St. John, Oxon.; Gorleston, Suffolk; Bosham, Sussex; All Hallows, Barking, near London; Withybrook, Warwickshire; Holcombe, Devon; Gosberton, Lincs. Easter sepulchres of a rather more elaborate kind may be studied at Harlington, Middlesex; St. Helen's, Bishopsgate; Northwold, Norfolk; Horling, Lincs.; Sibthorpe and Arnold, Notts.; and Patrington, Yorks. An exceptional western example may be found at Bampton, Oxon.

Sepulchral brasses can be studied everywhere, though they are most numerous in the eastern half of England. A type which shows figures of saints on a bracket with the person commemorated kneeling below seems to have been popular between 1340 and 1457; nine of this type are of priests, seven of citizens and ladies, and only two of men in armour. Good instances are the brasses of John Snete, priest, d. 1405, Upper Hardres, Kent; Thomas Nelond, prior, d. 1433, Cowfold, Sussex; and others will be found at Boston, Castle Ashby, and Ringwood.

Good brasses of merchants will be found in the Almshouse chapel at Bristol, 1411; St. Lawrence, Norwich, 1425 and 1436; Cirencester, 1440 and 1442; Dunstable, 1450; and Holy Trinity, Hull, 1451. Good brasses of woolmen will be found at Northleach and Cirencester and Bristol in the west country; at St. Albans and Hitchin in Herts.; at Wimington, Ampthill, and Dunstable in Bedfordshire; and at Lynwood and Stamford in the east.

Lesser houses of the period which survive in whole or in part are Boringdon Hall, Plympton St. Mary, Devon; Morwell House, near Tavistock, Devon; Sutlanger, near Stoke Bruern, Northants.; Southwick, Northants; Woodborough, Notts.; Battle Hall, Kent; Hampton Court, Herefordshire. Parts of Ightham Mote date from the time of

Edward III. Fine barns may be seen at Glastonbury, Wells, and Pilton, Somerset; Abbotsbury, Dorset; Great Coxwell, Glos.; Bredon, Worcestershire; and Harmondsworth, near Uxbridge, which passed to Winchester College in 1391.

BIBLIOGRAPHY

THE subject of English art in the fourteenth and early fifteenth centuries needs to be studied in a great number of detached and disparate sources. Certain books, however, stand out as the main guides to its chief branches, and may be recommended as a preliminary to more detailed study.

The most useful books of reference for the architecture of the period are probably F. Bond's two works, with E. S. Prior's *History of Gothic Art in England* as a valuable book of a more general scope. S. Gardner's *Guide to English Gothic Architecture* continues to be the best introduction for anyone not already possessing a certain familiarity with the styles. Professor Geoffrey Webb's forthcoming book on English medieval architecture should prove invaluable. At present the study of parish churches is bound to involve recourse to many books, some of considerable antiquity. The volumes of the Royal Commission on Historical Monuments are essential, but only cover a small fraction of the country. The *Victoria County Histories* vary greatly in value, and the student will often have recourse to such old authorities as Blomefield, R. and J. A. Brandon, J. P. Neale, and J. le Keux.

Domestic architecture can best be studied in the early volumes of the 'Country Life' publication of *English Homes*, and the development of the English castle in the book of H. Braun and the articles of W. Douglas Simpson. A useful account of the organization of the building craft will be found in Knoop and Jones's *Mediaeval Mason*.

For sculpture the monumental volume of E. Prior and Arthur Gardner is a classic: its very full illustration has justified me in giving little room to sculpture among the plates of this book. It may be supplemented for the alabaster carvings by the articles of Sir William St. John Hope and W. L. Hildburgh; for tombs, by F. H. Crossley's *English Church Monuments*; and for woodwork by the richly illustrated volume by F. E. Howard and F. H. Crossley and by the detailed study of screens by Aymer Vallance. Arthur Gardner's book on the alabaster tombs should be mentioned, together with H. W. Macklin's on brasses and G. H. Cook's recent study of medieval chantries.

A useful general account of medieval English art will be found in Elfrida Saunders's text-book. A fuller treatment of the illuminated manuscripts of the period has been given in E. G. Millar's well-illustrated volume and in Canon F. Harrison's smaller work; these need supplementing by the more detailed studies by Sir Sydney Cockerell and Dr. M. R. James, and by Dr. Egbert's recent work on the Tickhill Psalter. The English ivories have been well studied by Margaret Longhurst, the stained glass by many writers, notably J. D. Le Couteur, J. A. Knowles, and C. Woodforde, while *opus anglicanum* can be studied in Mrs. Christie's splendid volume. The English painting of the period is best illustrated in Professor Borenius's and Professor Tristram's *English Medieval Painting*, though this needs supplementing by the more detailed articles on the subject.

There is no satisfactory *corpus* of the documents relating to English medieval art.

LIST OF BOOKS

A complete bibliography of the subject would need a volume to itself. The following list only gives works which have been profitably consulted in the preparation of this volume. Unless otherwise stated, the place of publication is London.

S. O. ADDY, *The Evolution of the English House*, ed. J. Summerson (1933).
—— and J. CROSTON, *An Account of Winfield Manor in Derbyshire*, Derby (1885).
S. N. H. ALDWELL, *Wingfield, its Church, Castle, and College*, n.d. [1925].
J. F. ALLAN, *The Great Church Towers of England* (1932).
H. E. ALLEN, *English Writings of Richard Rolle, Hermit of Hampole*, Oxford (1931).
M. D. ANDERSON, *The Mediaeval Carver*, Cambridge (1930).
J. L. ANDRÉ, 'The Perpendicular Style in East Anglia, chiefly illustrated by Examples in North Norfolk', *Arch. Journ.* xlvi (1889), 377.
ANON., 'The Guilds of Lynn Regis', *The Norfolk Antiquarian Miscellany*, i (1877), 153.
H. ANSTEY, *Munimenta Academica*, 2 vols. (1868).
J. ANSTIS, *The Register of the Most Noble Order of the Garter*, 2 vols. (1724).
A. A. ARNOLD, 'Cobham College', *Archaeologia Cantiana*, xxvii (1905), 64.
ASHMOLEAN MUSEUM, *Catalogue of a Loan Exhibition of Silver Plate belonging to the Colleges of the University of Oxford*, Oxford (1928).
H. J. DUKINFIELD ASTLEY, 'Northborough Church and Manor House in Connection with Cromwell and the Claypoles', *Journ. Brit. Arch. Ass.* (1899), 1.
T. D. ATKINSON, *Architectural History of the Benedictine Monastery of Saint Etheldreda at Ely*, Cambridge (1933).

T. D. ATKINSON, 'Medieval Figure Sculpture in Winchester Cathedral', *Archaeologia*, lxxxv (1936), 159.

J. AYLOFFE, *Ancient Monuments at Westminster* (1790).

W. PALEY BAILDON, 'A Wardrobe Account of 16–17 Richard II, 1393–4', *Archaeologia*, lxii (1911), 497.

J. BARNES, *The History of that most victorious Monarch Edward III*, Cambridge (1688).

H. BATSFORD and C. FRY, *The Greater English Church of the Middle Ages* [1940].

W. BAZELEY (ed.), *Records of Gloucester Cathedral* (1920).

A. BEARDWOOD, 'Alien Merchants and the English Crown', *Economic History Rev.* ii (1929–30), 229.

—— *Alien Merchants in England, 1350 to 1377; their Legal and Economic Position*, Cambridge, Mass. (1931).

R. P. BEDFORD, 'An English Set of the Twelve Apostles, in Alabaster', *Burl. Mag.* xlii (1923), 130.

H. S. BENNETT, *The Pastons and their England*, Cambridge (1922).

G. BENSON, 'The Ancient Painted Glass Windows in the Minster and Churches of the City of York', *Yorkshire Philosophical Soc., Annual Report, 1914*, York (1915).

J. BENTHAM, *The History and Antiquities of the Conventual and Cathedral Church of Ely, from the Foundation of the Monastery A.D. 673 to the year 1771*, Cambridge (1771); and Supplement by W. Stevenson, Norwich (1817).

M. H. BERNATH, 'An East Anglian Primitive in Germany', *Burl. Mag.* lii (1928), 159.

P. BIVER and F. E. HOWARD, 'Les "Chantry-chapels" anglais', *Bull. mon.* lxxii, Paris and Caen (1908), 314.

—— 'Tombs of the School of London at the Beginning of the 14th Century', *Arch. Journ.* lxvii (1916), 51.

H. E. BISHOP and E. K. PRIDEAUX, *The Building of the Cathedral Church of St. Peter in Exeter*, Exeter (1922).

T. M. BLAGG, *A Guide to the Antiquities of Newark, and the Churches of Holme, and Hawton*, privately printed, n.d. [1906].

F. BLOMEFIELD, *An Essay towards a Topographical History of the County of Norfolk*, 5 vols. (1739–75).

Z. BLORE, *The Monumental Remains of Noble and Eminent Persons* (1826).

J. H. BLUNT, *Tewkesbury Abbey and its Associations*, London and Tewkesbury (1875).

F. BLIGH BOND and B. CAMM, *Roodscreens and Roodlofts*, 2 vols. (1909).

T. BODKIN, *The Wilton Diptych* (Gallery Books, no. 16) [1947].

F. BOND, *Gothic Architecture in England* (1905).

—— *Wood Carvings in English Churches: Stalls and Tabernacle-work*, Oxford (1910).

F. BOND, *The Chancel of English Churches*, Oxford (1916).

—— *An Introduction to English Church Architecture*, 2 vols., Oxford (1913).

J. K. BONNELL, 'The Easter *Sepulchrum* in its Relation to the Architecture of the High Altar', *Publications of the Modern Language Association of America*, xxxi, Baltimore (1916), 667.

T. BORENIUS, *English Primitives*, British Academy, Hertz Lecture (1924).

—— and E. W. TRISTRAM, *English Medieval Painting*, Florence and Paris

C. BOUTELL, *Monumental Brasses and Slabs* (1847).   [(1927).

—— *The Monumental Brasses of England* (1849).

H. BRAKSPEAR, 'Malmesbury Abbey', *Archaeologia*, lxiv (1913), 399.

—— 'St. Mary Redcliffe, Bristol', *Bristol and Gloucester Arch. Soc. Trans.* xliv (1922), 271.

—— 'The Abbot's House at Battle', *Archaeologia*, lxxxiii (1933), 139.

R. and J. A. BRANDON, *Parish Churches*, 2 vols. (1851).

H. BRAUN, *The English Castle* (1936).

E. W. BRAYLEY and J. BRITTON, *The History of the Ancient Palace and Late Houses of Parliaments at Westminster* (1836).

—— and J. P. NEALE, *The History and Antiquities of the Abbey Church of St. Peter, Westminster*, 2 vols. (1818).

H. H. BRINDLEY, 'Notes on the Mural Paintings of St. Christopher in English Churches', *Antiq. Journ.* iv (1924), 227.

J. BRITTON, *An Historical and Architectural Essay relating to Redcliffe Church*, Bristol (1813).

—— *The Cathedral Antiquities*, 5 vols. (1836).

A. CLUTTON BROCK, *The Cathedral Church of York* (1899).

N. C. BROOKS, 'The Sepulchre of Christ in Art and Liturgy', *University of Illinois Studies in Language and Literature*, vii, Urbana, Illinois (1921), 139.

J. BROWNE, *The History of the Metropolitan Church of St. Peter, York*, 2 vols., London, Oxford, and York (1847).

BURLINGTON FINE ARTS CLUB, *Catalogue of an Exhibition of British Mediaeval Art* (1939).

Cambridge Medieval History. Vol. vii, *Decline of Empire and Papacy*, Cambridge (1932).

—— Vol. viii, *The Close of the Middle Ages*, Cambridge (1936).

C. J. P. CAVE, 'The Bosses on the Vault of the Quire of Winchester Cathedral', *Archaeologia*, lxxvi (1926), 161.

—— 'Roof Bosses in the Nave of Tewkesbury Abbey', *Archaeologia*, lxxix (1929), 73.

—— 'The Roof Bosses of Canterbury Cathedral', *Archaeologia*, lxxxiv (1934), 41.

—— *The Roof Bosses of Bristol Cathedral*, Bristol (1935).

—— *Roof Bosses in Medieval Churches*, Cambridge (1948).

D. CHADWICK, *Social Life in the Days of Piers Plowman*, Cambridge (1922).

M. CHAMOT, *English Mediaeval Enamels* (1930).

F. CHANCELLOR, *The Ancient Sepulchral Monuments of Essex* (1890).

P. B. CHATWIN, 'The Decoration of the Beauchamp Chapel, Warwick, with Special Reference to the Sculptures', *Archaeologia*, lxxvii (1928), 313.

H. CHITTY, 'Fromond's Chantry at Winchester College', *Archaeologia*, lxxv (1926), 139.

—— and S. PITCHER, *Medieval Sculptures at Winchester College*, Oxford (1932).

A. G. J. CHRISTIE, *English Mediaeval Embroidery*, Oxford (1938).

A. W. CLAPHAM, *The Augustinian Priory of Little Dunmow*, Colchester (1914).

—— 'The Architecture of the Premonstratensians, with Special Reference to their Buildings in England', *Archaeologia*, lxxiii (1924), 117.

—— and W. H. GODFREY. *Some Famous Buildings and their Story* (n.d.).

CLARENDON, LORD, and S. GALE, *The History and Antiquities of the Cathedral Church of Winchester* (1715).

M. V. CLARKE, *Fourteenth Century Studies*, Oxford (1937).

A. B. CLIFTON, *The Cathedral Church of Lichfield* (1898).

S. C. COCKERELL, *The Gorleston Psalter* (1907).

—— and M. R. JAMES, *Two East Anglian Psalters at the Bodleian Library, Oxford: The Ormesby Psalter . . . and the Bromholm Psalter*, Oxford (1926), Roxburghe Club.

W. G. CONSTABLE, *Royal Academy of Arts, Exhibition of British Primitive Paintings from the Twelfth to the Early Sixteenth Century*, Oxford (1924).

—— 'The Date and Nationality of the Wilton Diptych', *Burl. Mag.* lv (1929), 36.

M. CONWAY, 'English Mediaeval Painting', *Burl. Mag.* liii (1928), 30.

—— 'The Wilton Diptych', *Burl. Mag.* lv (1929), 209.

—— 'An English Alabaster Figure in Leningrad', *Burl. Mag.* xlvi (1925), 245.

G. H. COOK, *Mediaeval Chantries and Chantry Chapels* (1947).

I. M. COOPER, 'Westminster Hall', *Journ. Brit. Arch. Ass.*, 3rd series, i (1937), 168.

W. D. COOPER, *The History of Winchelsea*, London and Hastings (1850).

H. C. COOTE, *Ordinances of some Secular Guilds of London from 1345 to 1496* (1871).

G. G. COULTON, *Chaucer and his England* (1908).

—— *Art and the Reformation*, Oxford (1928).

J. C. COX, *Notes on the Churches of Derbyshire*, 4 vols., Chesterfield, London, and Derby (1877).

—— 'The College of Fotheringhay', *Arch. Journ.* lxi (1904), 241.

—— *English Church Fittings, Furniture, and Accessories*, n.d. [1923].

—— and A. HAMILTON THOMPSON, *Lincolnshire* (Little Guides), 2nd ed. (1924).

H. Craig. *The Coventry Corpus Christi Plays* (E.E.T.S., Extra Series, lxxxvii) (1902).

F. H. Crossley, 'On the Remains of Mediaeval Stallwork in Lancashire', *Trans. Historic Society of Lancashire and Cheshire*, lxx (1918), 1.

—— *English Church Monuments* A.D. *1150–1550: an Introduction to the Study of Tombs and Effigies of the Mediaeval Period* (1921).

—— 'On the Importance of Fourteenth-Century Planning in the Construction of the Churches of Cheshire', *Journ. Chester and North Wales Architectural, Archaeological and Historic Soc.* N.S. xxxiii (1937), 5.

W. Cunningham, *Alien Immigrants to England* (1897).

—— *The Growth of English Industry and Commerce during the Early and Middle Ages*, 5th ed., Cambridge (1915).

Curzon of Kedleston, Marquess, *Bodiam Castle, Sussex*, London, Boston, and New York (1925).

—— and H. Avray Tipping, *Tattershall Castle, Lincolnshire* (1929).

J. Dart, *Westmonasterium, or the History and Antiquities of the Abbey Church of St. Peter's, Westminster*, 2 vols. (1723).

—— *The History and Antiquities of the Cathedral Church of Canterbury* (1726).

H. W. C. Davis (ed.), *Mediaeval England*, Oxford (1924).

F. Devon, *Issue Roll of Thomas de Brantingham, Bishop of Exeter, Lord High Treasurer of England . . . 1360* (1835).

—— *Issues of the Exchequer . . . from King Henry III to King Henry VI . . .* (1837).

Viscount Dillon, 'Inventory of the Goods and Chattels belonging to Thomas Duke of Gloucester . . . 1397', *Arch. Journ.* liv (1897), 275.

M. Dimitresco, *Pierre de Gavaston*, Paris (1898).

W. Dugdale, *Monasticon Anglicanum*, ed. J. Caley, H. Ellis, and B. Bandinel, 5 vols. (1817).

—— *The History of St. Paul's Cathedral* (1658), ed. H. Ellis (1818).

Durham, *Historiae Dunelmensis Scriptores tres*, Surtees Society, ix.

P. Durrieu, 'Un Siècle de l'histoire de la miniature parisienne à partir du règne du roi Louis', *Journ. des savants*, N.S. vii (1909), 1.

R. E., 'A Mediaeval Painted Panel', *Burl. Mag.* xxvi (1914–15), 93.

D. D. Egbert, 'The Grey-FitzPayn Hours', *Art Bulletin*, xviii (1936), 527.

—— *The Tickhill Psalter and Related Manuscripts*, New York and Princeton (1940).

[F. S. Ellis], *Horae Pembrochianae* (1880).

W. A. D. Englefield, *The History of the Painter-Stainers Company of London* (1923).

Joan Evans, *Pattern: a Study of Ornament in Western Europe from 1180 to 1900*, 2 vols., Oxford (1931).

—— 'Chaucer and Decorative Art', *Rev. English Studies*, vi (1930), p. 403.

JOAN EVANS, 'A Prototype of the Eleanor Crosses', *Burl. Mag.* xci (1949), 96.
JOHN EVANS, *Notices of Edmund of Langley and his Tomb* (1880).

H. P. FEASEY, 'Salmeston Grange', *The Antiquary*, xxxix (1903), 264.
R. FLENLEY, 'London and Foreign Merchants in the Reign of Henry VI',
    English Historical Rev. xxv (1910), 644.
W. G. D. FLETCHER, 'Battlefield, Salop', *The Antiquary*, xxix (1903), 201.
J. KESTELL FLOYER, 'English Brick Buildings of the Fifteenth Century', *Arch.
    Journ.* lxx (1913), 126.
J. FOWLER, *Representations of the Tree of Jesse and of the Last Judgment,
    specially in reference to the Great East Window of the Abbey Church, Selby*,
    Selby (1890).
FOWLER, CANON, *Rites of Durham*, Durham (Surtees Society), London, and
    Edinburgh (1903).
F. F. FOX, 'The History of the Guilds of Bristol', *Bristol and Gloucester Arch.
    Soc. Trans.* iii (1878–9), 90.
G. E. FOX, 'Notes on Painted Screens and Roofs in Norfolk', *Arch. Journ.*
    xlvii (1890), 65.
—— 'Mediaeval Painting', *Victoria County History, Norfolk*, ii. 529.
W. G. FRETTON, 'Memorials of St. Mary's Hall, Coventry', *Birmingham and
    Midland Institute, Archaeological Section, Trans.* xvii (1891), 14.
F. FREYHAN, *Die Illustrationen zum Casseler Willeham Codex*, Marburg (1928).
R. FREYHAN, 'English Influences on Parisian Painting of about 1300', *Burl.
    Mag.* liv (1929), 320.
A. C. FRYER, 'Monumental Effigies made by Bristol Craftsmen', *Archaeologia*,
    lxxiv (1925), 1.

V. H. GALBRAITH, 'A New Life of Richard II', *History*, xxvi (March 1942),
    223.
J. GALLOWAY, *Eleanor of Castile, Queen of England, and the Monuments erected
    to her Memory* [1910].
A. GARDNER, 'Alabaster Tombs of the Gothic Period', *Arch. Journ.* lxxx
    (1923), 1.
—— *A Handbook of English Medieval Sculpture*, Cambridge (1935).
—— *Alabaster Tombs of the Pre-Reformation Period in England*, Cambridge
    (1940).
J. GARDNER, *The Paston Letters*, 3 vols. (1872).
S. GARDNER, *A Guide to English Gothic Architecture*, Cambridge (1922).
H. GILL, 'A Local Patron of Architecture in the Reign of Henry VI', *Trans.
    Thoroton Soc.* xix (1915), 105.
E. W. GODWIN, 'Bristol Cathedral', *Arch. Journ.* xx (1863), 38.
T. GOODWIN, *The History of the Reign of Henry the Fifth, King of England, &c.*
    (1704).
J. A. GOTCH, *Growth of the English House* (1909).

R. Gough, *Sepulchral Monuments of Great Britain*, 6 vols. (1786).

A. R. Green, 'Painted Lid of a Reliquary Chest or Altar Chest in Winchester Cathedral', *Papers and Proceedings of the Hampshire Field Club and Archaeological Soc.* x (1926–31), 220.

E. Green, 'The Identification of the Eighteen Worthies commemorated in the Heraldic Glass in the Hall Windows of Ockwells Manor House', *Archaeologia*, lvi, pt. 2 (1899), 323.

T. D. Grimké-Drayton, 'The East Window of Gloucester Cathedral', *Bristol and Gloucester Arch. Soc. Trans.* xxxviii (1915), 69.

W. H. Gunner, 'Inventories of Plate, given to the College of Winchester and to the College Chapel by William of Wykeham, the Founder, and Subsequent Benefactors', *Arch. Journ.* x (1853), 235.

H. Haines, *A Manual for the Study of Monumental Brasses*, Oxford (1848).

M. Dormer Harris and G. Templeman, *Records of the Guilds of the Holy Trinity, St. Mary, St. John the Baptist and St. Katharine of Coventry*, Publications of the Dugdale Society, xiii and xix (1935 and 1944).

F. Harrison, *The Painted Glass of York* (1921).

—— *Treasures of Illumination: English Manuscripts of the Fourteenth Century, c. 1250–1400*, London and New York (1937).

H. Harrod, 'Goods and Ornaments of Norwich Churches in the 14th Century', *Norfolk Archaeology*, v (1859), 89.

—— *Gleanings among the Castles and Convents of Norfolk*, Norwich (1867).

A. Hartshorne, *Portraiture in Recumbent Effigies and Ancient Schools of Monumental Sculpture in England*, Exeter (1899).

A. Harvey, *The Castles and Walled Towns of England* (1911).

J. H. Harvey, 'The Medieval Office of Works', *Journ. Brit. Arch. Ass.* vi (1941), 20.

—— 'St. Stephen's Chapel and the Origin of the Perpendicular Style', *Burl. Mag.* lxxxviii (1946), 192.

—— *Henry Yevele: the Life of an English Architect* (1944).

—— 'Some Details and Mouldings used by Yevele', *Antiq. Journ.* xxvi (1947), 51.

—— *Gothic England, a Survey of National Culture 1300–1550* (1947).

A. Heales, 'Easter Sepulchres, their Object, Nature and History', *Archaeologia*, xlii (1869), 263.

J. A. Herbert, *The Sherborne Missal*, Oxford (1920), Roxburghe Club.

W. L. Hildburgh, 'English Alabaster Tables', *Proc. Soc. Ants.*, 2nd series, xxxii (1919–20), 117.

—— 'Notes on some English Alabaster Carvings', *Antiq. Journ.* i (1921), 222.

—— 'A Group of Panels of English Alabaster', *Burl. Mag.* xlvi (1925), 307.

—— 'Some Unusual Medieval English Alabaster Carvings', *Antiq. Journ.* viii (1928), 54.

W. L. HILDBURGH, 'Mediaeval English Alabaster Figures of the Virgin and Child', *Burl. Mag.* lxxxviii (1946), 30 and 63.

R. COLT HOARE, *History of Modern Wiltshire* (ed. R. Benson and H. Hatcher), *Old and New Sarum or Salisbury* (1843).

J. F. HODGSON, 'On the Difference of Plan alleged to exist between Churches of Austin Canons and Those of Monks, and the Frequency with which such Churches were parochial', *Arch. Journ.* xli (1884), 374; xlii (1885), 96, 215, 331, 440; xlii (1886), 52, 290, 403.

H. H. HOLLIS, *The Monumental Effigies of Great Britain*, n.d. [1840].

G. HOME, *York Minster* (1936).

W. ST. JOHN HOPE, 'On the English Mediaeval Drinking Vessels called Mazers', *Archaeologia*, l (1887), 129.

—— 'Notes on the Benedictine Abbey of St. Peter at Gloucester', *Arch. Journ.* liv (1897), 77.

—— 'On the Funeral Effigies of the Kings and Queens of England', *Archaeologia*, lx (1897), 517.

—— 'On a Painted Table or Reredos of the Fourteenth Century in the Cathedral Church of Norwich', *Norfolk Archaeology*, xiii (1898), 295.

—— *The Stall Plates of the Knights of the Garter, 1348–1485* (1901).

—— *The Abbey of St. Mary in Furness, Kendall* (1902).

—— 'On the Early Working of Alabaster in England', *Arch. Journ.* lxi (1904), 221.

—— 'The Episcopal Ornaments of William of Wykeham and William of Waynflete sometime Bishops of Winchester, and of certain Bishops of St. Davids', *Archaeologia*, lx (1906), 465.

—— *Windsor Castle, an Architectural History*, 2 vols. (1913).

—— and S. PRIOR, *Illustrated Catalogue of the Exhibition of English Medieval Alabaster Work held in the Rooms of the Society of Antiquaries 26th May to 30th June 1910* (1913).

—— 'The Heraldry and Sculptures of the Vault of the Divinity School at Oxford', *Arch. Journ.* lxxi (1914), 217.

—— *The History of the London Charterhouse* (1925).

F. E. HOWARD and F. H. CROSSLEY, *English Church Woodwork*, London and New York, n.d. [1917].

J. J. HOWARD, 'Inventory of the Gild of Holy Trinity of Coventry in 1442', *Proc. Soc. Ants.*, 2nd series, v (1870–3), 121.

A. E. HUDD, 'Bristol Merchants' Marks', *Clifton Antiquarian Club*, vii (1912), 1.

J. HUNTER, 'On the Death of Eleanor of Castile, Consort of King Edward the First, and the Honours paid to her Memory', *Archaeologia*, xxix (1942), 167.

J. HUTCHINS, *The History and Antiquities of Dorset* (1861).

T. G. JACKSON, *Gothic Architecture in France, England, and Italy*, 2 vols., Cambridge (1915).

E. F. JACOB, 'The Building of All Souls College 1438–43', *Historical Essays in Honour of James Tait*, Manchester (1933), 121.

M. R. JAMES, 'On the Paintings formerly in the Choir at Peterborough', *Proc. Cambridge Antiq. Soc.* ix (1894–8), Cambridge (1899), 178.

—— *The Sculptures of the Lady Chapel at Ely* (1895).

—— *Catalogue of the Manuscripts and Early Printed Books . . . now forming Portion of the Library of J. Pierpont Morgan* (1906).

—— *The Sculptured Bosses in the Roof of the Bauchun Chapel of Our Lady of Pity in Norwich Cathedral*, Norwich (1908).

—— *The Illustrations of the Book of Genesis (B.M. Egerton MS. 1894)*, Oxford (1921), Roxburghe Club.

—— 'An English Medieval Sketch-book, No. 1916 in the Pepysian Library, Magdalene College, Cambridge', *Walpole Society*, xiii (1924–5), 1.

—— *Norfolk and Suffolk* (1930).

—— and E. G. MILLAR, *The Bohun Manuscripts: a Group of Five Manuscripts executed in England about 1370 for Members of the Bohun Family*, Oxford (1936), Roxburghe Club.

B. JARRETT, *The English Dominicans* (1921).

F. KENDON, *Mural Paintings in English Churches during the Middle Ages* (1923).

A. F. KENDRICK, *English Embroidery* (1905).

T. D. KENDRICK, 'Humphrey, Duke of Gloucester, and the Gardens of Adonis', *Antiq. Journ.* xxvi (1946), 118.

C. E. KEYSER, *A List of Buildings in Great Britain and Ireland having Mural and Other Painted Decoration* (1883).

—— 'Sculptured Cornices in Churches near Banbury and their Connexion with William of Wykeham', *Antiq. Journ.* iv (1924), 1.

C. L. KINGSFORD (ed.), *A Survey of London by John Stow, reprinted from the Text of 1603*, 2 vols., Oxford (1908).

D. KNOOP and G. P. JONES, 'Masons and Apprenticeship in Mediaeval England', *Economic History Rev.*, April (1932), 346.

—— *The Mediaeval Mason*, Manchester (1933).

E. H. KNOWLES, *The Castle of Kenilworth* (1872).

J. A. KNOWLES, 'John Thornton of Coventry and the Great East Window in York Minster', *Notes and Queries*, 12th series, vii (1920), 481.

—— 'Glass Painters of York', *Notes and Queries*, 12th series, viii (1921), 127.

—— 'Artistic Craftgilds of the Middle Ages', *R.I.B.A. Journ.*, 3rd series, xxxiv (1926–7), 263.

—— *The York Glass-Painters* (1927).

—— 'A History of the York School of Glass Painting', *Journal of the Brit. Soc. of Master Glass Painters*, iv and v (1932–3).

J. A. KNOWLES, 'Additional Notes on the St. William Window in York Minster,' *Proc. Yorkshire Architectural and York Archaeological Soc.* i (1934), 5.

K. KORNFELD, 'An English Alabaster Relief', *Burl. Mag.* lxi (1932), 126.

H. KRONBERGER-FRENTZEN, 'The Melk Chasuble, an Opus Anglicanum', *Burl. Mag.* lxi (1932), 68.

C. L. KUHN, 'Herman Scheerre and English Illumination of the Early 15th Century', *Art Bulletin*, xxii, New York (1940), 138.

R. DE LASTEYRIE, 'Observations sur l'architecture gothique en Angleterre', *Journ. des savants*, N.S. vi (1908), 57.

H. V. LE BAS, 'Mount Grace Priory', *The Yorkshire Archaeological Journ.* xviii, Leeds (1905), 241.

J. D. LE COUTEUR, *Ancient Glass in Winchester*, Winchester (1920).

—— *English Mediaeval Painted Glass* (1926).

J. WICKHAM LEGG, 'On an Inventory of the Vestry in Westminster Abbey, taken in 1388', *Archaeologia*, lii (1888), 295.

L. G. WICKHAM LEGG, 'Windsor Castle, New College, Oxford, and Winchester College: a Study in the Development of Planning by William of Wykham', *Journ. Brit. Arch. Ass.*, 3rd series, iii (1938), 83.

JOHN LELAND, *The Itinerary of John Leland*, ed. by Lucy Toulmin Smith, 5 vols. (1906–10).

W. R. LETHABY, 'London and Westminster Painters in the Middle Ages', *Walpole Society*, i (1911–12), 69.

—— 'A Fourteenth-Century English Triptych', *Burl. Mag.* xli (1922), 110.

—— *Westminster Abbey Re-examined* (1925).

—— 'Mediaeval Paintings at Westminster', *Proc. Brit. Academy* (1927), 123.

—— 'The Westminster Portrait of Richard II', *Burl. Mag.* lxv (1934), 220.

W. W. LILLIE, 'The Retable at Thornham Parva', *Proc. Suffolk Institute of Archaeology and Natural History*, xxi (1933), 153.

—— 'A Mediaeval Retable at Thornham Parva', *Burl. Mag.* lxiii (1933), 99.

A. G. LITTLE, *Franciscan History and Legend in English Mediaeval Art*, Manchester (1937). (Brit. Soc. of Franciscan Studies, xix (1935–6).)

E. LINDBLOM, 'The Cope of Skå', *Burl. Mag.* xxviii (1915), 178.

N. LLOYD, *A History of the English House* (1931).

E. T. LONG, 'Painted Roofs in East Anglian Churches', *Burl. Mag.* lv (1929), 74.

M. H. LONGHURST, *English Ivories* (1926).

W. LONGMAN, *The History of the Life and Times of Edward the Third*, 2 vols. (1869).

R. S. LOOMIS and L. H. LOOMIS, *Arthurian Legends in Medieval Art*, Oxford and New York (1938).

W. LOVELL, 'Queen Eleanor's Crosses', *Arch. Journ.* xlix (1892), 17.

H. C. Maxwell Lyte, *A History of Eton College, 1440–1910*, 4th ed. (1911).

H. W. Macklin, *The Brasses of England* (1907).

J. Maclean (ed.), *The Lives of the Berkeleys . . . by John Smyth of Nibley*, 3 vols., Gloucester (1883).

C. E. Mallet, *A History of the University of Oxford*. Vol. i, *The Mediaeval University* (1924).

A. R. Martin, *Franciscan Architecture in England*, Manchester (1937).

H. J. and J. Massé, *The Cathedral Church of Gloucester* (1898).

—— —— *The Abbey Church of Tewkesbury* (1900).

J. T. Micklethwaite, 'Notes on the Abbey Buildings of Westminster', *Arch. Journ.* xxxiii (1876), 15.

E. G. Millar, *English Illuminated Manuscripts of the XIVth and XVth Centuries*, Paris and Brussels (1928).

G. H. Moberly, *Life of William of Wykeham*, Winchester and London (1893).

J. B. Morrell, *York Monuments*, n.d. [1944].

M. Morris, 'The Pienza Cope', *Burl. Mag.* vii (1905), 54.

—— 'Opus Anglicanum at the Burlington Fine Arts Club', *Burl. Mag.* vii (1905), 54.

R. B. Mowat, *Henry V* (1919).

J. N. L. Myres, 'Butley Priory, Suffolk', *Arch. Journ.* xc (1934), 177.

J. P. Neale and J. Le Keux, *Views of the Most Interesting Collegiate and Parochial Churches in Great Britain*, 2 vols. (1824).

P. Nelson, *Ancient Painted Glass in England, 1170–1500*, n.d. [1913].

—— 'Some Further Examples of English Medieval Alabaster Tables', *Arch. Journ.* lxxiv (1917), 106.

—— 'A Doom Reredos', *Trans. Lancashire and Cheshire Historic Soc.* lxx (1918), 67.

A. Nesbitt, 'The Manor House, Meare, Somerset', *Arch. Journ.* x (1853), 130.

J. Nichols, *A Collection of all the Wills . . . of the Kings and Queens of England* (1780).

—— *Liber Quotidianus Contrarotulatoris Garderobae, anno regis Edwardi primi vicesimo octavo* (1787).

J. G. Nichols, *Description of the Church of St. Mary, Warwick, and of the Beauchamp Chapel . . . also of the Chantry chapel of Isabella, Countess of Warwick, in Tewkesbury Abbey*, n.d. [1838].

—— 'On Collars of the Royal Livery', *Gentleman's Magazine* (1842).

N. H. Nicolas, *Testamenta Vetusta*, 2 vols. (1826).

J. G. Noppen, 'Early Westminster and London Painting', *Burl. Mag.* liv (1929), 200.

—— 'The Westminster School and its Influence', *Burl. Mag.* lvii (1930), 72.

—— 'The Painter of Richard II', *Burl. Mag.* lx (1932), 82.

J. G. Noppen, 'The Westminster Apocalypse and its Source', *Burl. Mag.* lxi (1932), 141.

J. P. Norris, 'Architectural History of Bristol Cathedral', *Bristol and Gloucester Arch. Soc. Trans.* xv (1890–1), 55.

G. Oliver. *Monasticon Dioecesis Exoniensis . . .*, Exeter and London (1846).
—— *Lives of the Bishops of Exeter*, Exeter (1861).

O. Pächt, 'A Grotesque Episode in English Mediaeval Art', *Journ. Warburg and Courtauld Institutes*, vi (1943), 51.

F. Palgrave, *The Ancient Kalendars and Inventories of the Treasury of His Majesty's Exchequer*, iii (1836).

J. H. Parker, *Some Account of Domestic Architecture in England from Richard II to Henry VIII*, 2 vols., Oxford (1859).

N. M. Penzer, 'The King's Lynn Cup', *Connoisseur*, cxviii (1946), 12 and 79.
—— 'The Founder's Cup at Oriel College, Oxford', *Connoisseur*, cxvii (1946), 13.

J. T. Perry, 'The Influence of the Hanseatic League on the Architecture of Northern Europe', *Journ. R.I.B.A.*, 3rd series, i (1894), 473.

T. J. Pettigrew, 'Notes on the Vicars' Close at Wells', *Journ. Brit. Arch. Ass.* xiii (1857), 34.

N. Pevsner, *The Leaves of Southwell*, London and New York (1945).

E. Power, *Mediaeval English Nunneries*, Cambridge (1922).
—— and M. M. Postan (ed.), *Studies in English Trade in the Fifteenth Century* (1933).

R. Pretyman, *Testamentary Documents preserved in the Chapter Muniment Room at Lincoln Minster* (Tract), n.d.

E. K. Prideaux and G. R. Holt Shafto, *Bosses and Corbels of Exeter Cathedral*, Exeter and London (1910).

E. S. Prior, *A History of Gothic Art in England* (1900).
—— *The Cathedral Builders in England* (1905).
—— 'A Sketch of English Mediaeval Figure Sculpture', *Walpole Society*, i (1911–12), 55.
—— and A. Gardner, *An Account of Medieval Figure Sculpture in England*, Cambridge (1912).
—— *Eight Chapters on English Mediaeval Art*, Cambridge (1922).

R. B. Rackham, 'The Nave of Westminster', *Proc. Brit. Academy*, iv (1909–10), 35.
—— 'Building at Westminster Abbey from the Great Fire (1298) to the Great Plague (1348)', *Arch. Journ.* lxvii (1910), 259.

J. Raine, *Testamenta Eboracensia*, Surtees Society (1836).
—— *Fabric Rolls of York Minster*, Surtees Society, xxxv, Durham (1859).

J. H. Ramsay, *Genesis of Lancaster*, 2 vols.

H. Read, *English Stained Glass*, London and New York (1926).

E. Rickert, *Chaucer's World*, New York and London (1948).

M. Rickert, 'Herman the Illuminator', *Burl. Mag.* lxvi (1935), 39.

—— 'The Reconstruction of an English Carmelite Missal', *Speculum*, xvi (1941).

—— 'Reconstruction of an English Carmelite Missal', *Burl. Mag.* lxvii (1935), 99.

H. T. Riley, *Memorials of London and London Life in the 13th, 14th and 15th Centuries* (1868).

—— 'Inventory of Goods belonging to a Warden of New College, Oxford, 1396', *Arch. Journ.* xxviii (1871), 232.

J. Armitage Robinson, 'The Fourteenth-Century Glass at Wells', *Archaeologia*, lxxxi (1918), 85.

W. K. Hamilton Rogers, *The Ancient Sepulchral Effigies and Monumental and Memorial Sculpture in Devon*, Exeter (1877).

Royal Commission on Historical Monuments (England). *An Inventory of the Historical Monuments in Essex*, 4 vols. (1921).

—— *Hertfordshire* (1910).

—— *Herefordshire*, 4 vols. (1932).

—— *Buckinghamshire*, 2 vols. (1913).

—— *Huntingdonshire* (1926).

G. McN. Rushforth, 'The Glass in the Quire Clerestory of Tewkesbury Abbey', *Bristol and Gloucester Arch. Soc. Trans.* xlvi (1924), 289.

—— 'The Burials of Lancastrian Notables in Tewkesbury Abbey after the Battle, A.D. 1471', *Bristol and Gloucester Arch. Soc. Trans.* xlvii (1925), 131.

—— *Mediaeval Christian Imagery as illustrated by the Painted Windows of Great Malvern Priory Church, Worcestershire*, Oxford (1936).

L. F. Salzmann, *English Industries of the Middle Ages* (1913).

F. Sandford, *A Genealogical History of the Kings and Queens of England and Monarchs of Great Britain*, 2nd ed., ed. S. Stebbing (1707).

O. E. Saunders, *English Illumination*, 2 vols., Florence and Paris, n.d. [c. 1930].

—— *A History of English Art in the Middle Ages*, Oxford (1932).

G. Scharf, *Observations on the Westminster Abbey Portrait and other Representations of King Richard II* (1867).

G. Schiffner, 'On the Hospital of St. Mary in Chichester', *Sussex Archaeological Collections*, ii (1849), 1.

G. G. Scott, *Gleanings from Westminster Abbey* (1863).

G. S. Seligman, 'Unidentified English Embroideries in the Musée Cinquantenaire at Brussels', *Burl. Mag.* xli (1922), 75.

T. Sharp, *Illustrative Papers on the History and Antiquities of the City of Coventry* (1871).

R. R. SHARPE, *Calendar of Wills proved and enrolled in the Court of Hustings, London, 1258–1688*, 2 vols. (1889).

N. A. SHAW, 'The Early English School of Portraiture', *Burl. Mag.* lxv (1934), 171.

P. J. SHAW, *An Old York Church: All Hallows in York Street*, York (1908).

W. DOUGLAS SIMPSON, 'The Affinities of Lord Cromwell's Tower-house at Tattershall', *Journ. Brit. Arch. Ass.* N.S. xl (1935), 177.

—— 'Warkworth: a Castle of Livery and Maintenance', *Archaeologia Aeliana*, 4th series, xv (1938), 115.

—— 'The Castles of Dudley and Ashby de la Zouch', *Arch. Journ.* xcvi (1939), 142.

—— 'Belsay Castle and the Scottish Tower Houses, *Archaeologia Aeliana*, 4th series, xvii (1940), 75.

—— 'The Warkworth Donjon and its Architect', *Archaeologia Aeliana*, 4th series, xix (1941), 93.

—— 'Hurstmonceux Castle', *Arch. Journ.* xcix (1942), 110.

—— '"Bastard Feudalism" and the Later Castle', *Antiq. Journ.* xxvi (1946), 145.

W. SPARROW SIMPSON, 'Two Inventories of the Cathedral Church of St. Paul, London, dated respectively 1245 and 1402', *Archaeologia*, l (1887), 439.

H. CLIFFORD SMITH, Victoria and Albert Museum, Department of Woodwork, *Catalogue of English Furniture and Woodwork*, vol. i, *Gothic and Early Tudor*, n.d.

J. T. SMITH, *Antiquities of Westminster* (1807).

—— *Ancient Topography of London* (1810).

T. SMITH, *English Gilds* (E.E.T.S., Original Series, xl) (1870).

A. STEEL, *Richard II*, Cambridge (1941).

F. M. STENTON, *The Development of the Castle in England and Scotland* (1910).

D. J. STEWART, *On the Architectural History of Ely Cathedral* (1868).

C. A. STOTHARD, *The Monumental Effigies of Great Britain* (1817).

W. STUBBS, *The Constitutional History of England*, 3rd ed., Oxford (1883), vols. ii and iii.

W. STUKELEY, *Itinerarium Curiosum*, 2 vols. (1776).

R. P. STYLES, *The History and Antiquities of the Abbey Church of Pershore* (1838).

C. A. SWAINSON, 'The Hospital of St. Mary in Chichester', *Sussex Archaeological Collections*, xxiv (1872), 41.

T. TANNER, *Notitia Monastica, or an Account of all the Abbies, Priories and Houses of Friers, formerly in England and Wales*, ed. J. Nasmith, Cambridge (1787).

R. TAYLOR, *Index Monasticus, or the Abbeys and other Monasteries . . . in the Diocese of Norwich*, London and Norwich (1821).

A. HAMILTON THOMPSON, *Military Architecture in England during the Middle Ages*, Oxford (1912).

A. HAMILTON THOMPSON, 'Notes on Colleges of Secular Canons in England', *Arch. Journ.* lxxiv (1917), 139.
—— 'The Statutes of the College of St. Mary and All Saints, Fotheringhay', *Arch. Journ.* lxxv (1918), 241.
—— *English Monasteries*, Cambridge (1923).
—— *The Building of York Minster* (1927).
—— *York Minster: the Fourteenth Century* (1927).
—— *The Cathedral Churches of England* (1925).
—— 'English Colleges of Chantry Priests', *Ecclesiological Soc. Trans.* N.S. i (1943), 92.
E. M. THOMPSON, *Customary of the Benedictine Monasteries of St. Augustine, Canterbury and St. Peter, Westminster*, Henry Bradshaw Society, xxiii (1902).
—— 'The Gorleston Psalter', *Burl. Mag.* xiii (1908), 146.
H. AVRAY TIPPING, *English Homes*, Periods I and II, 2nd ed. (1937).
T. F. TOUT, *The Place of the Reign of Edward II in English History*, Manchester (1914).
—— *Chapters in Administrative History of Mediaeval England: the Wardrobe, the Chamber and the Small Seals*, 6 vols., Manchester (1920–30).
G. M. TREVELYAN, *England in the Age of Wycliffe* (1899).
E. W. TRISTRAM, 'Piers Plowman in English Wall Painting', *Burl. Mag.* xxxi (1917), 135.
E. TROLLOPE, *Sleaford and the Wapentakes of Flaxwell and Aswardhurst*, London and Sleaford (1872).
D. TURNER, 'Will of Sir John Fastolf, touching the Establishment of his College at Caister', *Norfolk Archaeology* (1849), 225.
T. HUDSON TURNER, *Some Account of Domestic Architecture in England from Edward I to Richard II*, 2 vols., Oxford and London (1853).
S. TYMMS, *Wills and Inventories of . . . Bury St. Edmunds* (1850). (Camden Society, xlix.)

G. UNWIN, *The Gilds and Companies of London* (1908).

A. VALLANCE, *English Church Screens* (1936).
J. VAN DEN GHEYN, *Le Psautier de Peterborough*, Haarlem, n.d.
E. VENABLES, 'The Shrine and Head of St. Hugh of Lincoln', *Arch. Journ.* l (1893), 37.
K. H. VICKERS, *Humphrey Duke of Gloucester* (1907).
—— *England in the Later Middle Ages*, n.d. [1923].
VICTORIA AND ALBERT MUSEUM. *Catalogue of an Exhibition of English Mediaeval Art* (1930).
G. G. VITZTHUM, *Die Pariser Miniaturmalerei von Valois und ihr Verhaltnis zur Malerei in Nordwesteuropa*, Leipzig (1907).

M. E. C. WALCOTT, 'The Benedictine Abbey of St. Mary, Pershore', *Journ. Brit. Arch. Ass.* xxxii (1876), 330.

—— *Church Work and Life in English Minsters* (1879).

J. C. WALL, *Shrines of British Saints* (1905).

—— *Mediaeval Wall-paintings* (1914).

J. G. and A. B. WALLER, *A Series of Monumental Bosses from the 13th to the 16th Century* (1864).

G. FAULKNER WARD, 'The Early History of the Merchant Staplers', *English Historical Rev.* xxxiii (1918), 297.

G. R. M. WARD, *The Statutes of All Souls College*, Oxford (1891).

G. WARNER, *Queen Mary's Psalter* (1912).

R. H. WARREN, 'St. Augustine's Abbey, Bristol', *Proceedings of the Clifton Antiquarian Club*, v, Exeter (1904), 162.

W. T. WARREN, *Illustrated Guide to St. Cross Hospital, near Winchester*, Winchester (1907).

M. G. WATKINS, 'The Church of St. Andrew, Heckington', E. Mansel Sympson, *Memorials of Old Lincolnshire* (1911), 114.

A. WAY, 'Indenture for making a Pastoral Staff', *Bury and West Suffolk Arch. Inst. Trans.* (1850), 1.

J. WEEVER, *Ancient Funerall Monuments* (1631).

R. WEISS, *Humanism in England in the 15th Century*, Oxford (1941).

H. F. WESTLAKE, *The Parish Gilds of Mediaeval England* (1919).

R. WESTMACOTT, 'On the Monument of Edward II and Mediaeval Sculpture', *Arch. Journ.* xvii (1860), 297.

H. C. WHAITE, *St. Christopher in English Mediaeval Wall-painting* (1929).

B. WHITE, *The Dance of Death* (1931) (E.E.T.S., Original Series, clxxxi).

J. F. WICKENDEN, '"Joyalx" of John of Gaunt, bequeathed to the Cathedral Church of Lincoln', *Arch. Journ.* xxxii (1875), 317.

E. CARLETON WILLIAMS, 'The Dance of Death in Painting and Sculpture in the Middle Ages', *Journ. Brit. Arch. Ass.*, 3rd series, i (1937), 229.

—— 'Mural Paintings of the Three Living and the Three Dead in England', *Journ. Brit. Arch. Ass.*, 3rd series, vii (1942), 31.

R. WILLIS, *The Architectural History of Canterbury Cathedral* (1845).

—— and J. W. CLARK, *The Architectural History of the University of Cambridge*, 3 vols., Cambridge (1886).

C. WINSTON, 'Painted Glass in New College Chapel and Hall, Oxford', *Arch. Journ.* ix (1851), 29 and 120.

—— and W. S. Walford, 'On a Heraldic Window in the North Aisle of the Nave of York Cathedral', *Arch. Journ.* xvii (1860), 22 and 132.

—— 'The East Window of Gloucester Cathedral', *Arch. Journ.* xx (1863), 239.

C. WOODFORDE, 'Schools of Glass Painting in Kings Lynn and Norwich in the Middle Ages', *Journ. Brit. Soc. of Master Glass Painters*, v (1933), 3.

C. WOODFORDE, 'A Group of Fourteenth-Century Windows showing the Tree of Jesse', *Journ. Brit. Soc. of Master Glass Painters*, vi (1935), 184.
—— 'The Medieval Stained Glass of Long Melford Church, Suffolk', *Journ. Brit. Arch. Ass.*, 3rd series, iii (1938), 1.
—— *Stained Glass in Somerset*, Oxford (1947).
K. L. WOOD-LEGH, 'Some Aspects of the History of Chantries in the Later Middle Ages', *Trans. R. Hist. Soc.* xxviii (1946), 47.
W. WOOLNOTH and E. W. BRAYLEY, *Ancient Castles of England and Wales*, 2 vols. (1825).
F. WORMALD, 'The FitzWarin Psalter and its Allies', *Journal of the Warburg and Courtauld Institutes*, vi (1943), 71.
T. WRIGHT, *A History of Domestic Manners and Sentiments in England during the Middle Ages* (1862).
H. WYLIE, *The Reign of Henry V*, 2 vols., Cambridge (1914).

K. YOUNG, *The Drama of the Medieval Church*, 2 vols., Oxford (1933).

INDEX

References in black type are to plates

Edward II, king, 15 n. 4, 20–1, 23, 40, 44, 49, 56, 67–8, 86 n. 4, 114 n. 3, 119, 134–5, 153, 159, 164–5, 177, 190 n. 3, 209; **69, 73.**
— III, king, 44–6, 49, 53–4, 57, 60, 62, 76, 81–4, 88, 90, 102–3, 118, 139, 145, 152–4, 158–9, 164, 183, 192.
— IV, king, 36 n. 2, 65, 116.
— of Caernarvon, 56.
— of Maley, 165.
— of Woodstock, *see* Black Prince.
— of York, 164, 186.
Edworth, Beds., 228.
EFFIGIES, FUNERAL, 103 n. 2, 139–60.
Egbert, Dr., 11, 13.
Egfrid of Northumbria, 106 n. 1.
Eglesfield, Robert de, 190 n. 2.
Ela Shardelowe, 106 n. 2.
Eleanor of Castille, 1–5, 46 n. 3, 152, 175.
Eleanor crosses, 1–5, 31, 59, 159; **1–2.**
Elephants, 220.
Elford, Staffs., 156 n. 5, 160.
Elkyn, Thomas, 199.
Eloi, St., 41.
Elsing, Norfolk, 140, 212 n. 6, 227–8.
Elsing, William, 188.
Eltham, Middlesex, 57.
Eltham, John of, 114 n. 3, 153, 159, 163, 164.
Ely, Cambs., cathedral, 7, 22, 32–4, 43 n. 2, 46, 52, 105–6, 115 n. 5, 161, 163, 191 n. 2; **16, 18.**
Ely, bishops of, 18, 113.
Emayn, William, 178.
Embattled mouldings, 168.
EMBROIDERY, 8–9, 16–17, 19, 56, 58–9, 62, 64, 89, 99 n. 3, 104 n. 4, 138, 170, 192; **8a.**
ENAMEL, 58, 62.
Enfield, John, 216.
English inscriptions, 88–90, 142, 150, 174–5.
Enguerrand de Marigny, 168 n. 1.
Entombment groups, 172.
Erkenwald, St., 161.
Erpingham, family, 207.
— Thomas, 88.
Erpingham, gate, Norwich, 112.
Essex, Humphrey, earl of, *see* Bohun.
— John, 157.
Estone, John de, 76 n. 4.
Estouteville triptych, 48 n. 6.

Estria, prior d', 30.
Etheldreda, St., 34, 106, 146, 161, 202.
Eton College, Windsor, 54, 79, 111, 197 & n. 2, 199.
Eu, France, 163 n. 3.
Evesham, Worcs., 28, 51 n. 3.
Evrard le Français, 203.
Evre, Thomas de, 146.
Ewelme, Oxon., 189.
Ewerby, Lincs., 32 n. 3, 154 n. 3.
Exeter, Devon, cathedral, 7, 20, 22, 24, 27–8, 34, 36, 46, 49–50, 52, 54–6, 69, 83, 87, 90 n. 6, 111, 114 n. 1, 161 n. 5, 164, 166, 167 & n. 4, 228–30; **11, 13, 30a;** Law library, 62.
Falaise, siege of, 138.
FAN-VAULTS, 69–73.
Fanhope, lord, 177.
Farleigh-Hungerford, Som., 228.
Farleigh, Richard of, 28–9.
Fastolf, John, 126, 128, 138, 185 n. 3, 202.
Faudkent, Peter, 54.
Faulkborne, Essex, 128.
Fell, Lancs., 229.
Fen Stanton, Hunts., 210.
Fetterlock badge, 63.
Fiennes, Roger, 128–9.
Firearms, use of, 119.
Fitton, Alice, 8 n. 4.
Fitzalan, baron, 159.
— Thomas, earl of Arundel, 186.
FitzHerbert family, 229; **72.**
FitzPayn, Joan, 14.
Fitzurse, Francis, 35 n. 1.
FitzWarin Psalter, 96.
Flavecourt, Guillaume de, archbp., 166
Flawford, Notts., 107–8; **53.** [n. 2.
Fleming, Alan, 144.
— Richard, bishop, 158, 190 n. 4, 195.
Flemish influence, 97, 101 n. 3, 110, 139, 144, 146, 154.
— merchants, 45.
— weavers, guild of, 92.
Fleury, France, 81.
Florence, 82, 165; Museo Nazionale, 105; S. Miniato, 226.
Flowers, 55, *and see* Foliage sculpture.
FOLIAGE SCULPTURE, 3–5, 9, 12, 14, 30, 33, 55–6, 66, 212, 229–30.
Foliot, Jordan, 11.
Foljambe family, 109.
FONTS, 209 n. 5, 214.

I. THE ELEANOR CROSS, GEDDINGTON, NORTHANTS., 1294

2. THE ELEANOR CROSS, HARDINGSTONE, NORTHAMPTON, 1291

3. MONUMENT OF EDMUND CROUCHBACK, EARL OF LANCASTER, *d*. 1296.
WESTMINSTER ABBEY

4. IVORY DIPTYCH, *c.* 1300

5. PAGE FROM THE PSALTER OF ROBERT DE LISLE, *c.* 1295. THE RESURRECTION; THE
MARIES AT THE TOMB; *NOLI ME TANGERE*; AND THE SUPPER AT EMMAEUS

in confilio impiorum: & in uia pec
catorum non stetit: & in cathedra pe
stilentie non sedit.
Sed in lege domini uolumtas eius:
& in lege eius meditabit die ac nocte.
Et erit tanquam lignum qd plan
tatum est secus decursus aquaru:

6. DETAIL OF THE WINDMILL PSALTER, c. 1300

7. PAGE FROM THE TICKHILL PSALTER, *c.* 1300

8. *a.* PANEL OF *OPUS ANGLICANUM*, *c.* 1310
   b. BORDER FROM QUEEN MARY'S PSALTER, *c.* 1308

9. *a*. PERSHORE ABBEY. THE CHOIR VAULT, BEGUN SOON
AFTER 1288
b. MALMESBURY ABBEY. THE NAVE VAULT

10. WELLS CHAPTER HOUSE. THE CENTRAL PILLAR, BEGUN *c.* 1290

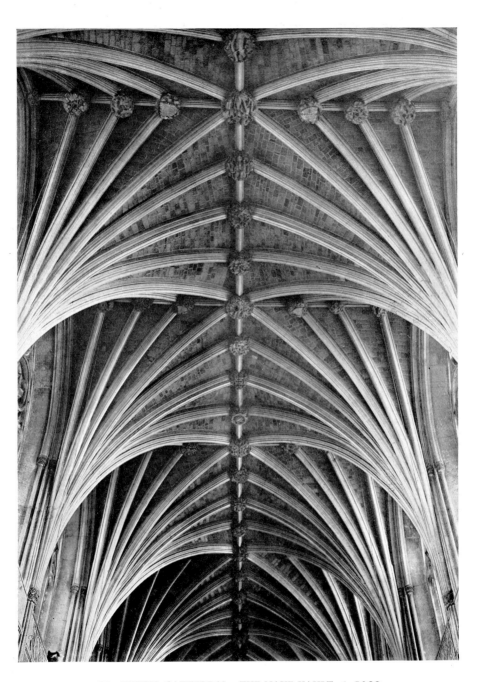

11. EXETER CATHEDRAL. THE NAVE VAULT, *c.* 1300

12. WELLS CATHEDRAL. THE LADY CHAPEL, 1300-5

13. EXETER CATHEDRAL. THE BISHOP'S THRONE, 1312

14. WINCHESTER CATHEDRAL. BEHIND THE CHOIR ENCLOSURE

15. NORWICH CATHEDRAL. THE PRIOR'S DOOR, 1297

16. ELY CATHEDRAL. DETAIL OF THE LADY CHAPEL, BEGUN 1321

17. LINCOLN MINSTER. THE CENTRAL TOWER

18. ELY CATHEDRAL. THE LANTERN, BEGUN *c.* 1323

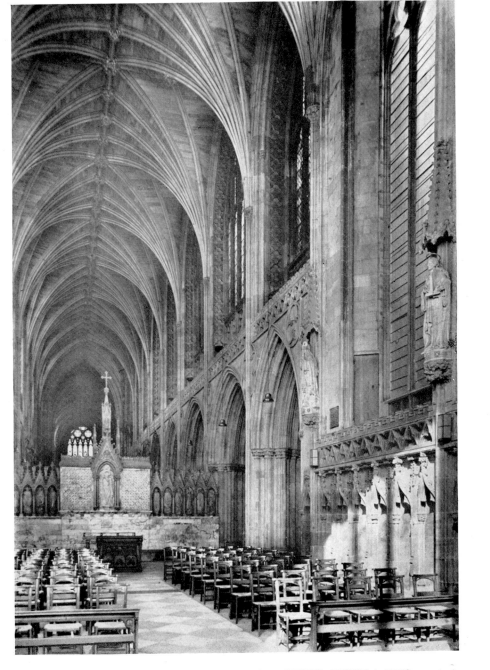

19. LICHFIELD CATHEDRAL. THE LADY CHAPEL, BEGUN *c.* 1310

20. YORK MINSTER. THE WEST END, BEGUN 1291, THE WINDOW GLAZED 1338

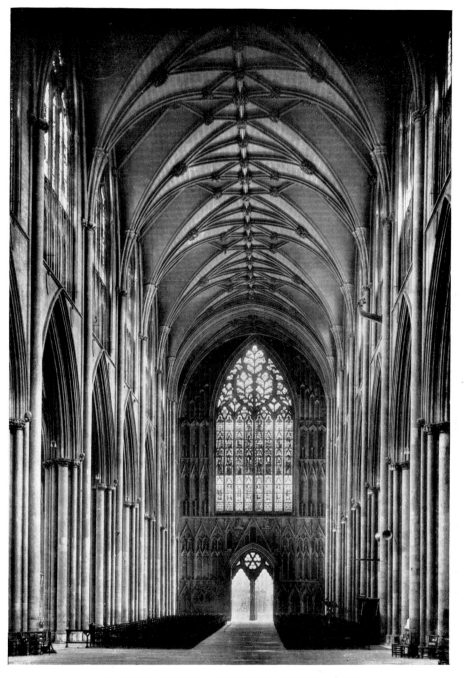

21. YORK MINSTER. THE NAVE, LOOKING WEST

22. ST. BOTOLPH'S CHURCH, BOSTON, LINCS. THE PORCH, *c.* 1370

23. TOTNES, DEVON. THE SCREEN, 1459

mois oepascet eos.

Rigans montes oe supio

truristi omnes sepes eius: posu

24. *a–b*. DETAILS FROM THE GORLESTON PSALTER, *c.* 1305
c. THE MONKEY WAGGONER. LUTTRELL PSALTER, *c.* 1340

25. *a*. DORCHESTER ABBEY, OXON. CORBEL, *c.* 1320
b–c. WELLS CATHEDRAL. MISERICORDS, *c.* 1300

26. *a.* THE LYNN CUP, *c.* 1340
b. DETAIL OF THE SAINT OMER PSALTER, *c.* 1325

27. ST. STEPHEN'S CHAPEL, WESTMINSTER. DETAIL OF WALL
PAINTINGS, 1350–63

28. THORNHAM PARVA CHURCH, SUFFOLK. THE RETABLE, c. 1320

29. DETAIL OF AN ALTAR-PICTURE. THE EDUCATION OF THE VIRGIN, *c.* 1325

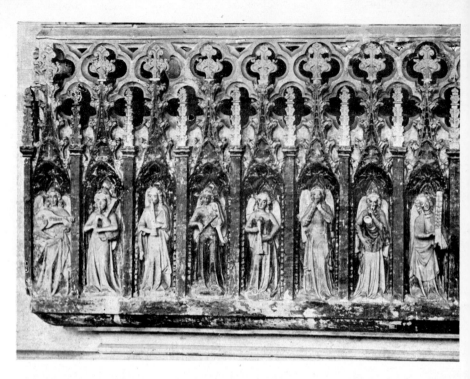

30. *a.* EXETER CATHEDRAL. MINSTRELS' GALLERY, 1340
b. LINCOLN MINSTER. FIGURES OVER THE MAIN DOOR, *c.* 1360

31. IVORY TRIPTYCH, ONCE BELONGING TO JOHN GRANDISSON, BISHOP OF
EXETER, c. 1340

32. FRAGMENT OF A STATUE OF THE VIRGIN AND CHILD, *c.* 1340.
WINCHESTER CATHEDRAL

33. DETAIL OF THE PERCY TOMB, BEVERLEY MINSTER

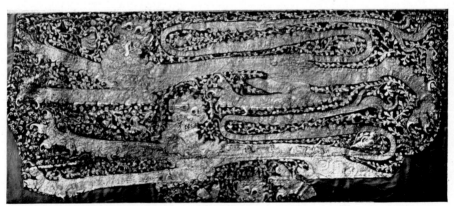

34. *a.* SILVER–GILT CENSER, *c.* 1380
    b. HORSE–TRAPPING OF RED VELVET EMBROIDERED IN GOLD, *c.* 1337

35. *a.* ST. AUGUSTINE'S, BRISTOL. EAST END OF THE LADY CHAPEL
b. BUTLEY PRIORY, SUFFOLK. DETAIL FROM GATEHOUSE, *c.* 1326

36. *a*. CARVED OAK COFFER, *c*. 1350
    b. SIR GEOFFREY LUTTRELL ARMING. LUTTRELL PSALTER, *c*. 1340

37. GLOUCESTER CATHEDRAL. ANGEL FROM THE CHOIR VAULT, 1337–50

38. *a*. ST. AUGUSTINE'S, BRISTOL, *c*. 1320

39. GLOUCESTER CATHEDRAL. THE CHOIR VAULT, 1337–50

40. TEWKESBURY ABBEY. THE CHOIR VAULT, *c.* 1350

41. GLOUCESTER CATHEDRAL. THE CLOISTER, 1351–1407

42. EDINGTON CHURCH, WILTS., 1352–61

a. GENERAL VIEW.　*b*. WEST END

43. WINCHESTER CATHEDRAL. THE NAVE, TRANSFORMED 1394

44. CANTERBURY CATHEDRAL. THE NAVE, 1377–91

45. CHIPPING CAMPDEN, GLOS. THE NAVE, SHORTLY BEFORE 1401

46. CANTERBURY CATHEDRAL. THE CHOIR SCREEN, *c.* 1400.
EDWARD II AND EDWARD III

47. PAGE FROM A PSALTER WRITTEN FOR A MEMBER OF THE BOHUN
FAMILY, c. 1370

48. a. INITIAL S FROM THE MISSAL OF THE LONDON CARMELITES, c. 1390–1410

49. THREE PANELS FROM THE NORWICH RETABLE, c. 1381

50. THE WILTON DIPTYCH, LEFT WING. ST. EDMUND THE KING, ST. EDWARD THE
CONFESSOR, RICHARD II, ST. JOHN THE BAPTIST

51. THE WILTON DIPTYCH, RIGHT WING. THE VIRGIN AND CHILD WITH ANGELS

52. THE ADORATION OF THE MAGI. HALF OF A DIPTYCH, *c.* 1390

53. ALABASTER VIRGIN FROM FLAWFORD, NOTTS., *c.* 1400

54. ALABASTER GROUP OF THE TRINITY, *c.* 1410

55. ALABASTER PANEL FROM A PASSION RETABLE. THE DEPOSITION

56. BURY ST. EDMUNDS, SUFFOLK. THE ABBEY GATEWAY, *c.* 1327

57. THORNTON ABBEY, LINCS. THE GATEWAY, 1382

58. LUMLEY CASTLE, CO. DURHAM. THE GATE HOUSE, 1389–92

59. THORNTON ABBEY, LINCS. THE GATEWAY, 1382

60. *a*. HURSTMONCEUX CASTLE, SUSSEX, 1440
b. BODIAM CASTLE, SUSSEX, 1386

61. TATTERSHALL CASTLE, LINCS., 1434–43

62. *a*. MARKENFIELD HALL, YORKS., 1310
b. WOODLANDS MANOR, MERE, WILTS., *c.* 1380

63. SOUTH WINGFIELD MANOR, DERBYSHIRE, *c.* 1440. THE ORIEL OF THE DAIS

64. OCKWELLS, BRAY, BERKS., c. 1460

65. THE BARN, PLACE HOUSE, TISBURY, WILTS. EARLY 15TH CENTURY

66. TATTERSHALL CASTLE, LINCS. CARVED STONE CHIMNEY-PIECES

67. OCKWELLS, BRAY, BERKS. THE SCREENS, *c.* 1460

68. TOMB OF SIR ROGER DE KERDESTON, *d.* 1337. REEPHAM CHURCH, NORFOLK

69. HEAD OF THE EFFIGY OF EDWARD II, *c.* 1331. GLOUCESTER CATHEDRAL

70. EFFIGY OF THE BLACK PRINCE, *d.* 1376. CANTERBURY CATHEDRAL

71. EFFIGY OF HENRY IV, 1405. CANTERBURY CATHEDRAL

72. *a.* TOMB OF SIR NICHOLAS FITZHERBERT, *d.* 1463. NORBURY CHURCH, DERBYSHIRE
b. TOMB OF BISHOP BECKINGTON, *d.* 1465. WELLS CATHEDRAL

73. TOMB OF EDWARD II, 1329–34. GLOUCESTER CATHEDRAL

74. TOMB OF THE BLACK PRINCE, 1376. CANTERBURY CATHEDRAL

75. TOMB OF WILLIAM, LORD GRAUNSON, *d.* 1335. HEREFORD CATHEDRAL

76. TOMB OF THOMAS, LORD BERKELEY, *d.* 1461. ST. MARK'S CHURCH, BRISTOL

77. *a*. TOMB OF A LADY, *c*. 1360. LEDBURY CHURCH, HEREFORDSHIRE
b. TOMB OF SIR GEOFFREY LUTTRELL, *d*. 1345, AND EASTER SEPULCHRE.
IRNHAM, LINCS.

78. THE EASTER SEPULCHRE, *c.* 1330. HAWTON CHURCH, NOTTS.

79. THE PERCY TOMB, MIDDLE OF THE 14TH CENTURY. BEVERLEY MINSTER

80. WINCHESTER CATHEDRAL.   THE CHANTRY CHAPEL OF
WILLIAM OF WYKEHAM, *c.* 1404.

81. WINCHESTER CATHEDRAL. THE BEAUFORT CHANTRY, *c.* 1447

82. ST. MARY'S, WARWICK. CHAPEL OF RICHARD BEAUCHAMP, EARL OF WARWICK, 1442–65. DETAIL OF THE EAST WINDOW

83. ST. MARY'S, WARWICK. CHAPEL OF RICHARD BEAUCHAMP, EARL OF WARWICK, 1442–65. WEEPER AND ANGELS FROM THE TOMB

84. TEWKESBURY ABBEY. THE WARWICK CHANTRY, 1422

85. *a.* THE CHAIN GATE, THE VICAR'S CLOSE, WELLS *c.* 1450
b. THE CLOISTERS, CHETHAM'S HOSPITAL, MANCHESTER

86. HIGHAM FERRERS, NORTHANTS., 1422

a. THE BEDEHOUSE. *b.* THE CHANTRY CHAPEL

87. MERTON COLLEGE, OXFORD. THE CHAPEL TOWER, 1450

88. NEW COLLEGE, OXFORD. THE ANTECHAPEL, 1383, CLOISTER AND
BELL-TOWER, 1400

89. NEW COLLEGE, OXFORD. THE CHAPEL, 1383

90. ALL SOULS COLLEGE, OXFORD. THE ANTECHAPEL, CONSECRATED 1442

91. THE DIVINITY SCHOOLS, OXFORD, 1430–83

92. WILLIAM GREVEL'S HOUSE, CHIPPING CAMPDEN. BEFORE 1401

93. NEWARK, NOTTS. THE NAVE, BEGUN C. 1390

94. CHIPPING CAMPDEN, GLOS. THE TOWER, *c.* 1400

95. IRON ACTON, GLOS. THE CROSS, BEFORE 1439

96. THE GUILDHALL, YORK, 1446, BEFORE ITS DESTRUCTION BY
A GERMAN BOMB, 1942